THE FORCE OF ART

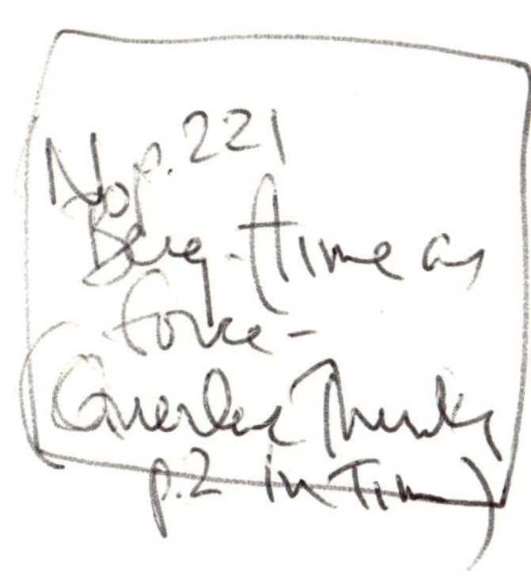

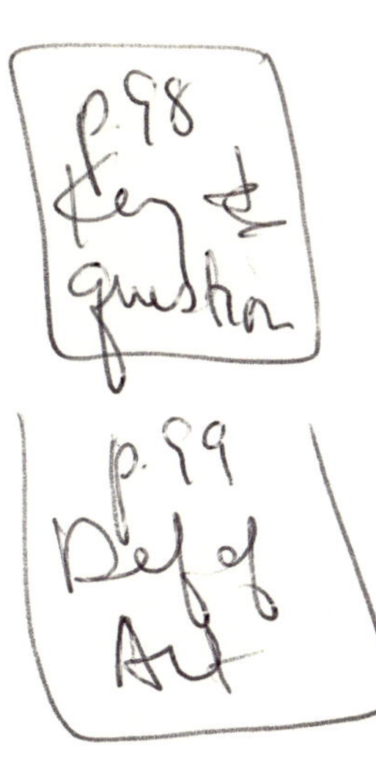

Cultural Memory
in
the
Present

Mieke Bal and Hent de Vries, Editors

THE FORCE OF ART

Krzysztof Ziarek

STANFORD UNIVERSITY PRESS
STANFORD, CALIFORNIA
2004

Ziarek, Krzysztof
The force of art / Krzysztof Ziarek.
p. cm. — (Cultural memory in the present)
Includes bibliographical references and index.
ISBN 0-8047-5010-6(cloth : alk. paper) —
ISBN 0-8047-5011-4 (pbk. : alk. paper)
1. Avant-garde (Aesthetics). 2. Art and society. I. Title. II. Series.
BH301.A94Z53 2004
111'.85—dc22 2004013180

Printed in the United States of America

Original Printing 2004
Last figure below indicates year of this printing:
13 12 11 10 09 08 07 06 05 04

Typeset at Stanford University Press in 11/13.5 Adobe Garamond

Contents

Acknowledgments

I am happy to acknowledge here the support that this book received from individuals as well as institutions. The initial impetus for this project came from an invitation by Erich Hertz to present a paper at a conference titled "Rethinking the Avant-Garde: Between Politics and Aesthetics," which he co-organized with Jim Hansen at the University of Notre Dame. I am happy that this idea developed into a book, and I would like to mention that part of the research and writing for *The Force of Art* was conducted during a research leave supported by the University of Notre Dame.

I would like to thank Stephen Barker, Gerald Bruns, Marjorie Perloff, Jean-Michel Rabaté, and Hent de Vries for their support and advice. Ewa Płonowska Ziarek read with great care the introduction and chapter 3. I am grateful for her suggestions and overall support.

For permission to quote material from Amiri Baraka, *Funk Lore*, ed. Paul Vangelisti (Los Angeles: Littoral Books, 1996), I am grateful to the publisher, Littoral Books.

Earlier versions of two sections of this book have already appeared in print. Part of the introduction was published in 2002 in *New Literary History* (vol. 33, no. 1) under the title "The Turn of Art: Avant-Garde and Power"; I gratefully acknowledge the editor's permission to use that material here. Sections of chapter 1 appeared in 2002 in *Existentia* (vol. 11). Portions of the introduction and of chapter 1 were also presented at two conferences: "Rethinking the Avant-Garde," at the University of Notre Dame, and the Modernist Studies Association meeting, at Rice University, in a session kindly organized by Dan Blanton.

THE FORCE OF ART

Introduction: The Turn of the Avant-Garde

> Talk of machines, technologies, capabilities, costs, markets, infrastructures, offers no guidance and is inadequate and irrelevant to the development of our inner lives. This is why art today, traditionally the articulation and expression of the "why" side of life, is now so important and so vital, even though it remains confused and inconsistent in its response to the new demands and responsibilities placed on it in this time of transition.
>
> —Bill Viola, "Between How and Why"

At the turn of the new millennium, almost a hundred years after the Modernist explosion and the great promise of the avant-garde, art appears to have lost whatever meager vestiges of force and importance it still might have held in the increasingly technological and commodified culture of the twentieth century. This crisis in aesthetics, which began in the nineteenth century, has been exacerbated by the rapid growth of mass culture with its corollaries, the entertainment industry, commercialization, and information technologies. In the process, art has become increasingly marginalized, as contemporary reality has come to be determined by technoscience and various technologies of power, while the aesthetic plays at best a secondary role, as it is most often reduced to a tool in cultural, ideological, and identity wars. What underlies this sense of the powerlessness, even irrelevance, of contemporary art is the determination, firmly embedded in the fabric of modern society, that reality is elsewhere, as one might say, and that its centers of power are digital technology, economic globalization, and increasing commodification. With the speedy advances in information technologies, the Internet, and new modes of advertising, even cultural and aesthetic innovations seem to lie more in the domains of the virtual and the commercial than in the artistic. Thus what was experienced at the beginning of the last century as the crisis of aesthetics has apparently resolved itself into the problematic contained within technologies of power, which have incorporated the advances of modernist aesthetics, transformed them, and often in the process dulled and popularized these new techniques for the sake of profit.

With the annexation of modernist aesthetics by advertising and popular culture, aesthetic issues have come to be disclosed, as the commercial collages of Web pages make amply evident, as essentially technological issues, that is, as a matter of advancing information technologies, which, far from coming into conflict with capitalist modes of production, increase their ability to translate reality and experience into data, codes, and programs in the service of globalization and the accumulation of capital. The problem at the turn of the millennium is therefore less that the radical aesthetics of the avant-garde has become popularized than that the aesthetic itself has become exposed as intrinsically technological—a situation that, ironically, may be taken to represent precisely the fulfillment of some avant-garde dreams, especially those of F. T. Marinetti and Francis Picabia. Andy Warhol's remark "I want to be a machine" and the rise of material technology in the sculpture of Donald Judd or David Smith further illustrate this increasing sense of the aesthetic as technological. In such works, the essence of the aesthetic appears to be fundamentally consonant with technicity, and thus to constitute the matter of the same manipulation, reducibility to information, and reprogramming that we see rapidly advanced in the realms of digital technology or genetic engineering. With those intensifying social and cultural changes in view, it seems almost inevitable that art would continue to lose its social and cultural status and find itself even further marginalized in relation to the technoscientific, consumer-oriented, entertainment-driven society. It is therefore not surprising that aesthetics at the beginning of the new millennium is once again dominated by visions of the end and of exhaustion, and that, as a reaction, many critics—for instance, Richard Shusterman[1]—turn toward areas marginal to traditional aesthetics (popular music, film, or mass media) in search of vitality and significance.

In response to this impasse and pessimism concerning art's social function, my approach aims to recover and redefine art's transformative force. I claim that we have not yet recognized how radically avant-garde art redefines the problematic of power and freedom, and how this redefinition makes it possible to rethink art's force beyond the boundaries of aesthetics. The single most important problem raised in this book concerns art's relation to power, and it hinges on how one reads the current—de facto correct and widespread—diagnosis of the powerlessness of art in contemporary society: does one take it to mean that art is without force, barely important, and thus hardly worth the effort in the global culture of the twenty-first century, or that perhaps a significant and unexamined "truth" addresses itself to us in the idea of art's powerlessness? To phrase it differently, how to understand the relation between powerlessness and power in the context of art? how to read the all-important yet often unthought suffix "-less"? Unexamined, this suffix is almost always taken for granted as signifying absence of power, and so the word "powerlessness," in the context of art, suggests that artworks, when compared with social, political, or even physical forces, lack any effectiveness in changing reality. Art, determined by power, is without a critical force of its own; and, in the world defined by exponentially increasing technopower on the macroglobal and microgenetic scales, this means that art is progressively drained of significance. In particular in the context of capital accumulation and consumption, the suffix "-less" will always be construed as privation, loss, or lack of "profit"—will be construed, that is, as Theodor Adorno was quick to note, exclusively in negative terms. Yet when we take the notion of the powerlessness of art not as an all too obvious product of contemporary technocratic society but as a question posed to us and our culture, the possibility of a different understanding opens up: a different understanding not only of art but also, and perhaps more important, of power and its relation to art. Insofar as art discloses an alternative to the paradigms of production, mobilization, and technical manipulation at the core of contemporary operations of power, art's work is never exclusively negative but constitutes as well a "positive," albeit paradoxical, articulation of the possibility of freedom. The "-less" in the adjective "powerless," when attached to art, does not necessarily mean lack of power but instead indicates an alternative economy of forces, which changes the very makeup of power. In this view, the powerlessness of art is not a negative judgment rendered on artworks but a provocative indication that art functions otherwise than through dominant articulations of power. Though art, like everything else, is produced and regulated within the power-driven economy of modern being, art can become disencumbered of the governing configuration of power and open an alternative modality of relations. This ability to let go of power, to transform relations and enable their alternative configurations, constitutes the paradoxical force of contemporary art.

It would be hard to deny that modern reality is increasingly characterized by the intensifying play of power. Recent developments in globalization, as well as in genetic and information technologies, testify to the unprecedented reach of power on both the macro- and microscopic scales. Already in the late 1930's, Martin Heidegger described modernity as a constant drive toward the intensification of power, whose sole aim is to spread its domain and increase its magnitude. Power thus became the defining momentum of modern reality, a fluid complex of operations and relations whose increasingly technological character allowed it both a continuously expanding reach and greater flexibility. Later Michel Foucault, through his readings of Friedrich Nietzsche's "will to power" and Heidegger's lectures on Nietzsche, confirmed this diagnosis and extended the scope of modern power: technological power became biopower, reaching from individual bodies to the life of the population. At present, we have moved even beyond Foucault's horizon as power operates simultaneously on both the molecular and the global level. Power is understood here not only in terms of domination and violence but also as creation and production. These various aspects of power are two sides of the same coin, which has an increasing purchase on modern reality, determining its value in terms of the ability to make and manipulate. Power thus refers to the various flexible operations of producing, managing, and (re)programming, in which entities and relations come to be constituted into the modern world, whose standards of "reality" and "importance" are determined with a view toward a greater penetrative and formative reach of power. Such power, though often described in terms of efficiency, calculability, and normalization, certainly among the most important parameters of power today, is much too fluid and productive to be thought of simply under these rubrics. Its "domination" is more subtle, often blurring the distinction between creation, on one side, and manipulation or normalization, on the other. Modern genetics is one of the fields where contemporary operations of biopower efface the boundary between invention and manipulation, fluidity and calculability, crossing paths with technological calculus on the level of molecular codes, that is, with unprecedented efficiency and penetrative reach. It is such programming that appears to be the effective measure of what it means "to be" in contemporary culture.

Since contemporary forms of power are increasingly infotechnical in their modes of operation, the force of art, as I formulate it in this book, bears upon the modern technicity of power, interrogating its forms and flows, calling into question its increasing flexibility and reach. As Bill Viola suggests, contemporary art finds itself in a transitional stage, no longer capable or willing to play the old aesthetic and cultural roles assigned to it and yet uncertain, even confused, about its place in the technoworld of the twenty-first century. Technology, machines, and tools, as Viola remarks, function always as engines of "how" rather than "why" or "what for," and the centrality of technology in modern life and art evidences a shift not only in the manner of art's production but, more important, in the very direction of the aesthetic. This displacement at the heart of the aesthetic goes far beyond the occlusion of the aura, which Walter Benjamin diagnosed at the beginning of the twentieth century, as it now marks a much more fundamental and wide-reaching emergence of technicity as the "essence" of the aesthetic. In the face of what looks like a gradual disclosure of art's basically technological constitution, of the "how" replacing and altering the "why," Viola reawakens the dilemma of art's continuing (or disappearing) difference from the technological. The disorientation to which Viola points indeed signals the central dilemma facing art today: is art part and parcel of the continuing technological acceleration of modern culture, an aesthetic branch of technopower, as it were, or does it mark the possibility of a critical turn, even transformation, in the play of power? The impasse in contemporary discussions of art, our discomfort with the very term "aesthetics," stems in many ways from the evasion of this crucial question about the force of art in today's reality.

In order to move beyond this impasse and read the suffix "-less" in "powerless" as a paradoxical possibility of transformation, we need both a different understanding of power and a different conception of the artwork. For me, the transition from traditional cultural roles to new future(s) for art, which Viola mentions, is more than an indication of a period of instability and change in aesthetic practices, precisely because it draws attention to the transformative character of art. Current approaches to art tend to underestimate this transformative force and give up the attempt to articulate a notion of the artwork that would reflect this potential. Taking an overall view, contemporary approaches to art can be roughly divided into five categories: (1) post-Hegelian scenarios of art's death and exhaustion, (2) attempts to revive the old terms of the beautiful and the sublime in order to define the essence of art, (3) conceptions that put art on the "back burner" and concentrate on instances of subversiveness and aesthetic import in popular culture and mass forms of entertainment, (4) the apparently progressive fusion of art with technology, as in electronic or transgenic art forms, and (5) isolated but interesting attempts to think of art beyond or after aesthetics.[2] Perhaps with the exception of the last category, these often quite different views—whether attempts to refurbish "classical" aesthetic terminology, shift aesthetic concerns and critical legitimacy to popular culture, or explore the increasing proximity between artworks and technology in the age of informational and genetic revolution—all but confirm the "end of art," confessing the apparent absence of critical force in contemporary art. However, such judgments either overlook or abdicate the project of a radical critique of aesthetics, opened up by such twentieth-century thinkers and artists as Adorno, Heidegger, Benjamin, Luce Irigaray, Marcel Duchamp, and Gertrude Stein, to name a few.

Even though Heidegger and Adorno are often regarded as antithetical and incompatible thinkers—a perspective that leads to unfortunate retrenchment and self-enclosure of both Adornian and Heideggerian approaches—I argue that some of the most interesting possibilities for considering art "after aesthetics" emerge from the space between their work. In reflecting on the paradoxical force of modern art, I have found both Adorno's negativity and Heidegger's radical revision of the idea of poiēsis particularly useful for rearticulating art's transformative potential with regard to technological forms of power. Taking Heidegger's and Adorno's insights as the point of departure, I argue that art discloses the possibility of thinking not only beyond the currently existing forms of power but also, as I will explain later, beyond the very idea of being as power. Heidegger's and Adorno's engagement with art, in the context of the intensification of technologization and its modern forms of power, mandate a thorough reworking of aesthetic categories, which continue to dominate discussions of art. Until such a revision takes place—a revision only intimated and not carried through by these thinkers—art's relation to power will continue to be misunderstood and will remain constrained by aesthetic categorizations of the artwork. Yet in explaining the force of art in contemporary culture in a postaesthetic manner, as a redisposition of force relations and a transformation of the operations of power, my approach goes beyond the limitations of both Adorno's and Heidegger's thought.[3] It is meant to change the aesthetic optics that still determines much discussion of art, and to offer a new way of understanding art's intimate yet critical relation to the very modalities and operations of power in today's society.

To indicate the scope and the implications of this turn or transformation in power that characterizes the artwork, I approach art as a force field, where forces drawn from historical and social reality come be to formed into an alternative relationality.[4] I call this transformative event "forcework" and understand it as a specifically artistic redisposition of forces, in which relations are freed from power structures and the unrelenting, intensifying manipulative drive characteristic of modernity. Force has a double valence in my argument. On the one hand, the term refers to Foucault's and Gilles Deleuze's approaches to force, which understand force on the level of nonformalized functions and flows of energy, that is, in terms of the elemental constituents of "being" prior to their actualization into substances, objects, or bodies. On the other hand, force is seen in the Heideggerian perspective as rupture, change, transformation, that is, as the very dynamic of being and unfolding. In short, it is the force of the event. Thus the term "forcework" refers to the manner in which artworks redispose relations on the microlevel of forces—underneath the sedimented relations, so to speak, between objects, bodies, substances, and the operations of power forming them. Such transformation cannot be described in traditional aesthetic terms, because it is not a matter of form and content, of images and statements, of the seen and the said, or of the sensible and the intelligible. The rupture and transformation that art's forcework occasions describes the specific artistic force with which art "acts" in historical and cultural context. And the "occasion" of such a change constitutes art's event. The notion of contemporary art as forcework highlights the dynamic, transformative momentum of art's work over and against the notion of artworks as objects and/or commodities. It also revises art's relation to the "outside" world as well as its effect on the audience. What the artistic forcework occasions in the world around it and in its viewers cannot be explained either in traditional aesthetic terms of affect, perception, and judgment or through the sociocultural categories of production, manipulation, and critique. Rather, the *work* that takes place in art—"work" understood here not as a produced object but in the active, transformative sense—needs to be approached on the level of force relations. To develop such an understanding of art's transformative forcework, I consider a wide range of twentieth- and twenty-first-century artistic practices: from those of the Italian Futurists Marinetti and Boccioni to those of the Russian avant-garde artists Velimir Khlebnikov, Liubov Popova, and Dziga Vertov to the practices of Dadaism, Duchamp, and Stein to those of such contemporary artists as Bill Viola, Krzysztof Wodiczko, Amiri Baraka, Seiko Mikami, and Eduardo Kac. As such, my approach responds to and even further radicalizes Fredric Jameson's call for a nonreified, nonobjectified conception of the artwork.[5] Such a "postaesthetic" approach accounts for the *force* with which art redisposes relations and alters their mode of being in the world, releasing them from flexible and penetrative flows of technopower. This new way of thinking would suggest a radical and transformative significance of art vis-à-vis the predominance of power-oriented relations, not only in the realms of commerce, politics, and technology but also in the everyday practices of living. Yet this power-free relationality, to the extent that it occurs in art, can be called artistic.

As forcework, art can no longer be conceived as an object but instead should be understood as an event, that is, as a dynamic, "force-ful" redisposition of relations inscribed in it through the sociocultural determination of artistic production. The emphasis placed here on the "event" of art does not cancel the inevitable, and necessary, materiality and objectification of artworks but points to their double character as both "act" and shaped product. It is the "fact" of the physicality of artworks, their necessary existence as objects with their apparent constancy, that in fact highlights the "inconstant," volatile, and transformative event at the core of art. In Viola's installations, the juxtaposition of such objects as chairs, tables, jugs, television monitors, projection panels, and so on, with virtual, electronically generated or processed images gives these works their particular force in terms of the exploration and questioning of the boundary between the aesthetic and the technological. This interplay (to evoke Heidegger's terminology) between the thing-character and the work-character of works of art, their necessary interrelation and mutual determination and differentiation, foregrounds the fact that art's force is not at all abstracted from its material existence. On the contrary, materiality performs an active role in art's "work" precisely to the extent that the overt immutability of the thing-aspect of the work (the work as object) puts into play its active, verb features.[6] The "fact" of the work's existence as a thing both shelters and reinforces the "act" of its *working*, the event of transformation, the dynamic forcework of art. Thus the notion of "artwork" comes to play a double role here, not just an art *object* but also an art *work*: its "labor," performance, act, in a word, its force. Revealed in its full complexity, the artwork is the reciprocal animation of the nominal and the verbal sense of "work," the event of the actualization of art's status as an object into the performance of its work.

Perhaps the most significant, and yet most difficult, aspect of rethinking the work of art as forcework is the radical critique of the logic of production and the modalities of power that together regulate modern social praxis. The idea of production implicit in the aesthetic notion of art as "formed content" remains inadequate for the type of performative displacement involved in art. The creation of an artwork, while it inscribes both the forces and the relations of production that regulate its social context, not only exceeds but also revises the very modality of transactions and relations between forces that obtain within the paradigm of production.[7] Production and action inscribe violence in their very mode of operation in this specific sense: that, as modalities of making or effecting, they shape and recast material that is regarded as passive. Artworks encode in their forcework the possibility of a different, nonviolent mode of relation, which does not saturate force relations with either creative or restrictive manipulation. It is true that many modern and contemporary works rely heavily on the aesthetics of shock, but the violence and power in art, as Adorno is right to contend, happen for the sake of nonviolence, even if this is ultimately unintentional and even counter to the artist's aims or interests. Even in works explicitly relying on the shock produced by power and violence, there is, I would argue, another dimension, in which the artwork has a force that is no longer violent, that is, not dominating through production or reconfiguration but rather releasing forces into reciprocal shaping and becoming.

For example, Amiri Baraka's recent poetry can be seen as an instance of work involving such a paradoxical role of violence and power in contemporary art. On the one hand, Baraka must be understood as quintessentially invested in power, as seeking alternative modes of power or strategies of resistance and counterpower, which are forcefully brought into the foreground both in the themes and in the rhetoric of his poetry, plays, and essays, all sharply critical of the modern technocapital. On the other hand, Baraka's remapping of art in poems like "Art Against Art Not" hearkens back to the idea of poiēsis and transformation at the heart of African art, as discussed by Léopold Senghor in his work on Negritude. The funky rhythm Baraka infuses into his poetry becomes not simply an alternative mode of power but, more radically, an alternative *to* power, a story of being ("'is' story") whose language is not technological, not the lingo of capital and power, but a transformative reweaving of relations. Let me be clear here: the force of art does not exclude the shock effects associated with power games and violence in modern art; on the contrary, it often incorporates such power games as part of what nevertheless works, overall, as a transformative and power-free redisposition of relations, for the force that I associate with art has a paradoxical effect of dissipating, annulling, or desisting from power. What art's forcework does is to open, inside relations of power, an inverse of power: not powerlessness but desistance from power, not to be misunderstood as indifference or passivity but to be seen instead as a transformation of the very nature of what it means to work and to act. We can describe this transformation as a shift from the active to the middle voice.

Heidegger's critique of the metaphysics of production underlying modern technicity captures this nonviolent modality of being in the middle voice, in its suggestive distinction between making/producing (*machen*) and letting/releasing (*lassen*) as two fundamentally different ways of disposing relations. Intrinsic to *machen* is the formation, production, and manipulation of relations and objects (*Machenschaft*) into the terms of an ever-intensifying power (*Macht*) whose operations become increasingly flexible and fluid. Traditionally, making is any form of praxis with a view to the realization of well-defined goals, or a telos. As such, it includes a modality of self-realization, which of course can be blocked, postponed, or derailed by opposing forces. Even in the postmodern fluid or fragmentary conception of power, the idea of making, as genetic manipulation suggests, is a type of relation in which a dominant active force shapes, produces, or subjugates either a passive material or a weaker force. By contrast, *lassen* refers to an active release from power, to a transformation in the very mode of relating, which becomes articulated through a reciprocal interaction of forces. Insofar as *lassen* is a departure from the binary articulation of domination and submission, from active form and passive matter, it enables a becoming, in which forces unfold through each other in a continuously reactivated field of reciprocal shaping, because in this type of articulation all forces are both affected and affecting: they unfold in the middle voice, eschewing the passive/active opposition. And it is precisely this modality of relation in the middle voice, predicated on a reciprocal enabling, that I refer to as power-free. *Lassen* signifies, therefore, an event in which forces are reactivated into an alternative modality of mutual enabling and becoming.

It is important to underscore here that this event in no way means leaving things as they are, because as they are, things are always already incorporated into the various layers and flows of power. Still, this sense of letting go and release indicates neither a forcible reshaping of forces within the nexus of power(s) nor a conferring of external identities upon them. Rather, letting go operates in the middle voice, neither active nor passive, neither forcible nor ineffective. This middle-voice tonality, as I show in chapter 1, does not refer to the ways in which power can change, produce, or reshape relations from both within and without—always inevitably into a new form of power—but rather to a new mode of relating, which emerges from the interaction and reciprocal shaping of forces. This alternative relationality is not some illusory beyond to power but instead indicates a critical inflection in the tonality of power, a change of momentum whereby forces become released from the circuits of power and are given a free space of occurrence. In this context, the artistic forcework can be seen as an enabling, transformative work, which radically changes the very momentum of relations. Artworks seek what Deleuze, commenting on Foucault, calls "a 'power of truth' which would no longer be the truth of power, a truth that would release transversal lines of resistance and not integral lines of power."[8] This power or, better, force of truth, which is no longer a truth of power, signifies, in my reading, a distinctive field of relationality, an event that grants forces, against the pervasive formative operations of power, a space for reciprocal shaping and becoming. This capacity, transversing the workings of power without either becoming a party to power or being rendered powerless by power's domination, constitutes the "event" of art.

To further explain this characteristic capacity of art to exceed aesthetic parameters, I adapt the Greek notion of aphesis for the purposes of my argument. My use of the term "aphesis," which denotes a releasing, a letting be or a letting go, and even liberty, is an attempt to describe in positive terms this alternative mode of disposing the relations at work in art. The register of meanings brought into play by aphesis begins to outline the forcework through which art, while borrowing from social relations of power, acquires its capacity to desist. The aphetic character of forcework indicates that relations become disencumbered from both disciplining and generative power, which means that art frees forces into a becoming, which is apart from the habitual relations of representation, action, and knowledge that form and regulate social praxis. Gertrude Stein's writing is often aphetic in this sense: in her linguistic freedom and inventiveness, Stein does not negate grammar or the power of signification but rather releases words and meanings from their investment in the various forms of power existing on syntactical, semantic, or cultural levels. Stein's language is written "merrily" and for pleasure, beyond the intention "to spell or spend," beyond articulation and profit (of meaning and the power that accrues with it). Avoiding the well-known idiom of power (grammar, meaning, name, image, narrative, and so on), Stein finds a new way of writing—using such devices as the continuous present, composition as explanation, naming without names, to mention just a few—that remains within power and yet does not comply with it. Stein's work shows how the customary practices that shape forces into the operational nexus of power come undone, and how a possibility of a new occurrence is opened up. The term "aphesis," with its connotations of releasing and liberation, indicates here how art's force is not an alternative power but an alternative *to* power, which releases forces into the element of reciprocal free play and becoming.

It is in terms of this tension between *machen* and *lassen*, between power and aphesis, that I explain art's forcework as the space where power-oriented dispositions of forces into the practices of calculation and production become transformed into an alternative modality of relation, in which forces enable each other's becoming. The difficulty that such an explanation entails is the impossibility of a positive translation or representation of art's forcework. Yet this "impossibility" is not at all negative; instead, it constitutes art's paradoxical capacity, its truly idiomatic force. Since art's forcework marks a critical inflection in power, it cannot be articulated in positive terms, for it would then enter the field of representation and become inscribed within the very flows of power that it reorients. But this (in)ability should not be misconstrued as a lack in art, as a moment of art's powerlessness or of negation of its power. Rather, it is a paradoxical capacity that art has to *not be* positive, or posited, and thus also to remain beyond the scope of negation. To be neither power-ful nor powerless is the enigmatic force of art. What Adorno calls "enigma" I redefine as a "third," in-between modality, which transverses the very essence of power. When social and cultural relations enter the "field" of art, art's "work" transforms their character, releasing them from the formative (either productive or restrictive) hold of power. Artworks instantiate an interface between the "external," social world and the "internal," artistic space, an interface that allows art both to be embedded in social praxis and yet to remain autonomous. It is this double character that endows art with critical and performative force. Art's forcework lets be by rupturing and displacing the patterns of power governing social praxis. As such, forcework defines the transformative dimension of art, which lies beyond the complicities with and/or resistances to regimes of power and ideologies that mark both the content and the formal aspects of artworks, and which also, so to speak, lies beyond power's ability to exercise and reproduce itself.

Whenever one claims a transformative potential for art, the question inevitably arises about the relationship between artistic transformation and radical political change. In response to such a question, I would like to make two claims. First, contra Adorno, I argue that the event of transformation is not a mere potentiality or semblance but that it occurs and has effects in the world. Second, I suggest that for this work of transformation to reach beyond the realm of art and not be subsumed into the matrix of power, it has to be continued by social and political transformation. This is how I propose to radicalize what Heidegger calls "preservation," understood as a continuous reactivation of the transformative work. And it is clear that such an ongoing reactivation of transformation requires radical democratic politics. Yet my task in this book is to articulate the specific role that art can play in regard to this political process, and this is why I do not theorize the process itself.[9] To that effect, the conclusion of this book presents, through a discussion of Khlebnikov, Vertov, Baraka, and Wodiczko, a conception of revolt in art, one that sees art's import not in its political engagement or its subversion of aesthetic forms but in the radical nature of its forcework. In this context, the task is not simply to "preserve" the work of art but also to continuously reactivate its transformative force in political life. This is also how I inflect Benjamin's call for the politicization of aesthetics, the process that ultimately necessitates the move beyond aesthetics.

Adorno, in terms different from Heidegger's but in a similar spirit, claims that art, deploying the forms of domination constitutive of modern society, turns this domination against itself and, beyond the confines and ideological stakes of any politics, opens the possibility of freedom. Thus what is at stake in art's forcework is not simply freedom from specific political, cultural, or technological forms of domination but release from the more fundamental "domination," or mobilization, of forces in service of the overall "politics" of the continuous intensification of power. What art recognizes is that the very inscription of force relations into the operations of power, with this inscription's corollary endorsement of power as the characteristically and inescapably modern way of life, is the political gesture par excellence, a gesture that "politicizes" being beyond any ideology or political statement. Since forces, in the artwork, are no longer "in the service of power"—whether for positive or negative purposes—but instead become realigned, as it were, for the sake of freedom, art is an event of a different "political" praxis. This praxis radicalizes politics by undoing what I have described here as being's primary politicization in service to power. In this specific sense, art can be said to instantiate not only an alternative politics but an alternative *to* politics. Art can do so because it instantiates the event as free from the most fundamental and pervasive kind of domination: the originary mobilization and shaping of force relations for the sake of power. This critical distinction between mobilization/production and transformative forcework constitutes the pivot of my analysis, in chapter 2, of art's relation to modern technology and forms of power, from the twentieth-century avant-garde, especially Italian Futurism, to contemporary Web-based and genetic art.

Art's transformation of the notion of production is particularly important to consider in the context of commodification, since it illustrates the way in which the redisposition of forces performed by art offers an alternative to the global commodifying effects of the productionist logic of modern power. As an aesthetic object, art is of course part of the production paradigm—that is, it is obviously formed and produced and thus already predisposed for commodification—but as forcework, it opens the different modality of an event, irreducible to a product. This event desists from power and constitutes an eminently political instantiation of transformative force. Performing a critique of the commodity culture, the event character of art, the forcework "at work" in it, is not reducible to the parameters of exchange. While the artwork's features as an object easily become inscribed into commodity exchange, art's dimension of forcework, its transformative "act," exceeds it. Thus, as I argue in chapter 3, art, in its forcework, escapes the logic of commodity, both its paradigm of exchange and its corollary tendency toward fetishization. Though it is increasingly important to nuance our understanding of how art comes to function as a commodity, and thus as an element in the global economy of power, it is even more vital to flesh out the way in which art calls this dominant practice into question and opens the possibility of a nonproductionist (in the widest possible sense) way of being.

Since the logic of power/production is inextricably linked to the subject-object dialectic, the notion of forcework displaces this model and its various heuristic roles in formalist, materialist, and cultural analyses. It delimits the scope of these approaches by pointing out that what makes art art—that is, its forcework—remains outside the scope of aesthetic and cultural critique. With such questioning of the subject, such corollary notions as pleasure, desire, aesthetic experience, judgment, the beautiful, and the sublime, though appropriate for aesthetic appreciation and critique of art, lose their binding relevance for the concept of art as forcework. Instead, the postaesthetic understanding of art approaches art as a certain type of transformation, engaging it on the level of the formation and redisposition of forces. In chapter 3, I discuss how this idea of art's forcework allows us, in the context of the work of Irigaray, Paul Gilroy, and Frantz Fanon, to rethink the notion of the subject after aesthetics. As Gilroy (in his analysis of race), Irigaray (in her thought on sexual difference), and Fanon (in his idea of "actional man") point out, the notions of production and labor cannot serve the emancipatory function in relation to raced and/or sexed subjects, because the subject- and power-oriented paradigm of production is itself responsible for patterns of racial and sexual inequality and oppression. In very different ways, they point to poiēsis rather than to labor as a source of liberation.

It is in relation to the operations of modern capital and its practices of production that we need to examine the problem of revolt in art. As Adorno would say, such a possibility of revolt is not a question of political subversiveness or radical ideas but, instead, of a certain redesigning of the modes of relation, one that happens in art on the level of force.[10] In Wodiczko's projections and performative instruments there is a dimension of "revolt" underneath social and political critique, a revolt in the aphetic mode, whose radical nature lies precisely in desisting from power and enabling a different modality of relations: a modality that is poietic and transformative precisely by virtue of being nonproductionist and power-free. Thus where art "re-volts" or "turns" against the logic of power is not, as I argue in this book's conclusion, in its explicit proclamations or formal innovations and subversions but in the very event of transforming relations, which disallows the fluid grip of power on experience while letting forces issue into configurations free from power.

This approach questions the position of critics who, like Raymond Williams, offer a rather dismissive evaluation of what Williams calls the "once liberating Modernism" and reduce its radical art to a phenomenon of merely historical importance without much relevance for contemporary life. My view, by contrast, is that we have not yet sufficiently addressed the problematic of freedom and power as it has been redefined in avant-garde artworks. Consequently, we need to consider how the avant-garde—and I employ the term to refer both to the early-twentieth-century avant-gardes and to the continuing avant-garde radicalism in contemporary art and poetry—contests power and redefines freedom. To put it simply, the avant-garde does not simply endorse, by attacking the absence of freedom in bourgeois society, the liberal notion of individual freedom; rather, it tries to change, amidst the galvanizing technological developments of twentieth-century culture, the very notion of what it means to be free in the face of growing technologization. Disagreeing with those who see art as exhausted or finished, I contend that art has never been more significant than it is now. I see art's "marginalization" in our technological society not as a judgment on art's importance but, conversely, as a disquieting confirmation of our narrowing and uncritical understanding of experience. A good example of this inverse relation is the video installations of Bill Viola—for instance, *The Crossing*, *The Greeting*, and *Migrations*[11]—which use the latest computer and video technology to show that experience cannot be reduced to a technoscientific calculus or, broadly speaking, to information. The force of radical art is, in my approach, its ability to call into question this restricted, technicist view of being, experience, and action.

The present volume, pointing to this revolt in art in relation to modern forms of technopower, constitutes a decisive departure from the current climate of discussions about avant-garde art. Against claims about the exhaustion and irrelevance of contemporary art, I postulate the growing importance of radical aesthetics in the face of the rapidly intensifying technologization of life, both in its global proportions and at the most basic level of genetic codes. The crucial point here is not just that art, in its most recent forms of electronic or transgenic artworks, and whether in critical or celebratory fashion, continues to be preoccupied with the most recent and culturally formative developments in science and technology and thus keeps pace with the "real" world. Rather, the point is also that art in its characteristic mode of existence, here called "forcework," remains centrally and critically engaged with the "nervous system" of contemporary forms of relationality: technicity and its evolving modalities of power. Elsewhere, I have underscored the continuing relevance of the modernist and postmodern avant-garde to our understanding of modern experience.[12] In *The Force of Art*, I offer a new conception of radical art as a transformative force in the midst of the globalizing work of power.

1

Art as Forcework

Every work is a force field.
—Theodor W. Adorno, *Aesthetic Theory*

Beyond the Object: Art as a Force Field

At the turn of the twenty-first century, we find ourselves in need of a redefinition of art, of a different way of conceiving its work beyond the aesthetic optics, in order to understand art's social significance in the contemporary world, a world increasingly regulated by technoinformational modalities of power. To develop such a "postaesthetic" approach, I envisage the artwork as a force field, a region where social forces and the historical moment inscribed in art through the process of its creation become reoriented and transformed, given a new momentum, as it were, beyond what appears possible within the historical parameters of the existing society. The work of art, understood as a force field, immediately reveals a different internal momentum and a new set of relationships to society. For one thing, the tensions and constellations of forces render the artwork dynamic, disclosing it as an event, a temporalizing occurrence and a transformative rupture, whose features become unrecognizable in the notion of an aesthetic object. The idea of art as an object, constitutive of aesthetic reflection and pivotal to the logic of commodification, distorts the most significant aspect of artworks, concealing the very force that makes art artistically and socially significant. As a field of forces, the artwork remains irreducible to its socially dictated functions—discrete object of aesthetic experience, and commodity—no matter how strenuously these roles are enforced by cultural commerce. At the same time, art's relation to society acquires a transformative force: art does not just reflect and represent society, bearing the power inscriptions of the existing order of things, or at best try to resist and subvert social forms of power. Rather, the artwork has to be thought of as a force whose "artistic" momentum is performative in just this sense: that it redisposes the social relations beyond the power impetus constitutive of them.

The idea that the artwork is primarily a force field and not an object allows us to call into question the two interrelated logics that weave their conceptual webs around art: the logic of objectification and the logic of commodification. To say that an artwork is *primarily* a force field does not disqualify the reality of art's constant relegation to the status of an aesthetic object and a commodity. However, it makes clear that those two conceptual apparatuses, even as they aptly diagnose and describe art's historically determined social functions, fail to address art's transformative force; worse, they often serve to cover it over and disqualify it a priori by enclosing art within a constrictive conceptuality that reflects the power formation of being into definable, measurable, exchangeable objects. I will address art's relation to commodification in more detail in chapter 3; here, let me just suggest that what intrinsically links aesthetics and commodification is a productionist understanding of forces and relations, which tends to objectify and calculate being with a view to the increased reach and flexibility of power. As I indicated in the introduction, to the extent that art calls into question the productionist and power-oriented constellations of forces, it disrupts and revises the very operations that *produce* being as objects and commodities. Therefore, to uncover art's significance, it becomes necessary to rethink the artwork beyond the notions of aesthetic object and cultural commodity, to approach it as a reworking or a transformation of forces at once intrinsic to the social makeup and yet forceful enough to alter it beyond the optics of power constitutive of the contemporary world.

Conceived as a force field, the work of art becomes a dynamic occurrence, a shifting and movable field of tensors and forces capable of repeatedly and differently rupturing the social conditions of production and reception. Heidegger's famous essay "The Origin of the Work of Art"—still the most radical critique of the idea of the work of art as an object—describes such a rupture created by an artwork precisely in terms of a displacement, a "multiple thrusting" of forces, and a redisposition of the socially constructed relations that determine everyday life: "But this multiple thrusting is nothing violent, for the more purely the work is itself transported into the openness of beings—an openness opened by itself—the more simply does it transport us into this openness and thus at the same time transport us out of the realm of the ordinary. To submit to this displacement means to transform our accustomed ties to world and earth and henceforth to restrain all usual doing and prizing, knowing and looking, in order to stay within the truth that is happening in the work."[1] "Practical" relations of evaluation and acting as well as the "theoretical" comportments, such as knowledge and representation, become radically transformed in the work of art. The ordinary forms of power relations that define each historical moment are thrust open, and a different set of vectors from those that determine the valence of social praxis—of how we act, know, value, and perceive—comes into play. Action, representation, and knowledge, as Heidegger suggests, are all altered, given a different momentum, a momentum that no longer realizes grasping and controlling forms of action and knowledge. He is also quick to remark that the reconstellation of forces initiated by the artwork, the thrusting and striving continuously at work in art, though reflective of differences and conflicts, is nothing violent, a point echoed by Adorno's claim in *Aesthetic Theory* that artworks stand for nonviolence. What is thus reinforced here is the notion that the field, the open region, as Heidegger calls it elsewhere in the essay, both undoes the momentum of the power that forms social relations and reopens social relations as a nonviolent modality of relation.

The redefinition of the artwork as a field takes the spotlight away from the formal aspects, the thematic and ideational questions, as well as the sociohistorical context of art while highlighting the (re)constitutive play of forces within the work. This play, however, is not to be misconstrued as somehow "internal" to art or separated from art's sociohistorical situatedness. In fact, it weaves together not only formal and thematic features but also the social, contextual relations, displacing the forms habitually imprinted on them. The forces at work in art tend to cut across formal and thematic issues, defying the limits of such a binary optics, as can be seen, for instance, in Heidegger's analysis of the strife and rifting intrinsic to what he calls art's figure (*Gestalt*), conceived as an alternative to the understanding of art in terms of the form/content doublet. Similarly, these forces also traverse the difference between the artwork and its "external" context, exerting their force beyond the moment of the work's existence in reception. In short, the transformative work performed by art redraws precisely the boundaries and delimitations constitutive of the aesthetic conceptualization of art: subject/object, form/content, internal/external. As a force field, art is seen in terms of how it "recirculates" the social forces inscribed in it through the artwork's thematic, formal, and social layers and links while radically reforming those relations and their socially produced and reinforced momentum—their "cryptogram of domination," in Adorno's words.

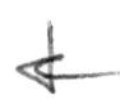

As a force field, the work of art is first and foremost a spatial-temporal and *nonviolent* play of forces, a play that remains in excess of and, as such, critical of art's function as an aesthetic commodity, the function that brings art in line with the general social economy of power and production. I describe this nonviolent disposition of forces with the Greek term "aphesis," which denotes a releasing, a letting be or a letting go, deliverance, and even liberty. Aphesis carries the legal sense of "release" from office, marriage, obligation, and so on, and also from debt or punishment. The primary English use of the term is in linguistics and rhetoric. *The American Heritage Dictionary of the English Language* defines aphesis as "the loss of an initial, usually unstressed vowel," gives the example of "cute" from "acute," and traces the term's etymology from Greek *aphenai, aphe-*, "to let go" (*apo-, apo-* + *henai,* "to send"). The *Oxford English Dictionary* traces the term's etymology from Greek *afesij,* "a letting go," and from *afienai* (af', "off, away" + *ienai*, "to send, let go"), noting the latter entry as a suggestion made by the dictionary's editor in 1880, and defines the term as "the gradual and unintentional loss of a short unaccented vowel at the beginning of a word," giving the examples of "squire" for "esquire" and "down" for "adown," among others, and including the use of the term in astrology, where it refers to a technique used by the second-century astrologer Vettius Valens to find the important times in an individual's life for matters regarding what astrologers call "the parts of fortune and spirit." In translations of the Bible and in biblical scholarship, "aphesis" usually means a release (from bondage or imprisonment), forgiveness and pardon (of sin), or remission (of a penalty). The primary senses of "aphesis" as release and letting go come into play in my argument as I describe an event of unfastening and disengagement from power, a moment of release that stays the formative influence of power on the various modalities of relation—social, cultural, political, personal—in modernity. In the context of my rethinking of force relations and power, the term "aphesis" is defined as a mode of redisposing forces that transforms their momentum away from power, discipline, or domination and enables an alternative, violence-free force field. In short, "aphesis" denotes a reorienting of forces that frees them from their confinement within the operations of power. It is a mode of unfastening and disengaging from power, a disposition that unbinds relations from power, a modality of relating that is constituted as liberty or remission from power.

When conceived as aphesis, art's force can be understood beyond the dialectic of power, that is, as a field of nonpower, where forces are no longer tethered by the logic of production or formed by the momentum toward increase of power. In my approach, what defines art is this opening up of a nonviolent, power-free disposition of forces—free not in the sense of freedom from domination or repression but rather in the sense of having been released, disencumbered, from the disciplining impact of power, power that saturates forces, determining their valence and momentum and channeling them into forms of relation that instantiate and produce more power. Imbued with power, forces participate, even through conflict and resistance, in the overall economy of power's intensification, increasing its flow and expanding its circulation by endowing experiences and relations with the valence of power. To speak about freedom in this context means that art's force field excepts itself from shaping forms of representation, knowledge, and action into the overall intensifying momentum of power. In other words, art transforms the "accustomed ties," the habitual relations of representation, action, and knowledge, that constitute social praxis. In the contemporary technoinformation civilization, forces come increasingly to be shaped and mastered as an all-purpose intensification of power, which keeps increasing its reach to microscopic "info" levels and global proportions. An artistic force field would then be an instance of revising and rechanneling this momentum of technopower. This ability, this *force* par excellence of art, reflects art's autonomous status within the social sphere and outlines its growing significance. Later I will explain this transformation in the momentum of power, which happens in the work of art in terms of the difference between making/producing (*machen*) and letting/releasing (*lassen*). Exempting itself from the formative impetus of power, this transformation has the character of aphesis, that is, of letting go and release (from the manipulative and productive flows of power). I will thus redefine Adorno's notion of art's autonomy, moving it away from the idea of the negative and, in terms of transformation in the momentum of force, from technic to poietic, from mobilization to aphesis, from power to nonpower. Briefly here, the technic momentum produces forces and their relations as intrinsically calculable and manipulable. By contrast, the change to a poietic momentum releases forces from the overmastering impetus toward power and lets them unfold in their spatial-temporal singularity, incalculable as such and irreducible to informational content or code.

As a force field, the work of art is never reducible to, even if it often becomes crudely confined to, the status of an isolated object, separable from social concerns and, by the same token, just as easily turned into an article of exchange, characterized by the commodification of aesthetic separation. The idea that the work of art is an active interchange, a switchboard of forces, where one of the critical links always in play on the level of force relations, even if formally and thematically indistinct, is the connection to history and society, provides a counterargument to the notions of commodity and aesthetic object. Gertrude Stein's "experimental" writings are never an idealized space of representational "nonsense," a disengaged modernist artistic edifice; on the contrary, they enact a radical dislocation and revision of social forces sedimented in the very interstices of language, in its semantic plays and syntactic layers. Stein's idea of "writing" the thing in itself, that is, in the singularity of its occurrence, is a way of literally rewriting the social practices of disciplining forces—"intensities" of being, in her words—into the "grammar" of power.[2] What Stein discloses and reforms are the power-oriented forms of being—reflected in definitions, labels, object naming, and so on—that have saturated and become sedimented in the practices of representation and objectification underwriting both ordinary language and the specialized idioms of literature and science. The intrinsically fluctuating semantic and syntactic spaces of Stein's work constitute the field of infinitesimal forces beyond the "experienced" and represented world, an open region where forces, like the "regrammared" language, are released into the intensity of their signification without the constraining and determining momentum of power: the power of meaning, definition, coherence, logic, but also, by the same token, the power of molding into objects, forms, and relations that are by definition, that is, through the very investiture of power, constituted as inherently calculable, (re)producible, and manipulable—in other words, constituted as predetermined elements in the "power grammar" of being. For Stein, the thing in itself is not a name or a label, just as it is not an object and thus not a site of the aesthetic and/or commodifying investment of power. Staging her language as a playful revolt against investments of power in the social and linguistic constitution of things and experiences as objects reducible to "nouns," that is, definitional labels, Stein releases in her work the "elemental" relations between forces, unencumbered, unregulated, and un(de)formed by the impetus of power.

Another articulation of the problem of force comes in Liubov Popova's 1921 series of space-force constructions, many of which were executed on pieces of plywood, with unpainted space showing the texture of the background and adding depth to the two-dimensional surface. These paintings come from the last phase of Popova's work, before she switched to utilitarian art, possibly under pressure from the official aesthetic line that mandated the abandonment of bourgeois art forms and the creation of productivist art, since at that time Russian Constructivism was entering a new, functionalist stage, in which production art "was to become the absolute and only viable artistic activity."[3] The word "construction," used in nearly all the titles of Popova's works from that time, indicates that they could be extended into three dimensions, even though she never produced such spatial equivalents. More important for our considerations, Popova's paintings offer us artistic constructions of force fields, a literal and abstract presentation of force relations, which organize the space of experience below the threshold of representability. In science, technology, or economics, forces are represented as intrinsically quantifiable and calculable, and the efficiency of such discourses is predicated on the technic, normative constitution of force, which makes the world into a field of measurable and organized forces, into the modern form of technicity. Popova's space-force constructions, which represent her most advanced form of experimentation with the pictorial medium, can also be seen as an artistic rethinking of how forces become formed into a dynamic, spatial-temporal construction that determines the order of representation.

Using very limited color schemes and linear configurations, with occasional circular patterns, Popova produces criss-crossing force lines whose intersections open the flat surface of the painting onto the third dimension, an effect further enhanced by the use of shadows and unpainted spaces that reveal the rough plywood texture. All of these compositions produce the impression of being merely small sections of large configurations that extend beyond the edges of the paintings into three-dimensional space-time. These paintings appear to endorse the functionalist idea of art at the same time that they clearly, almost emphatically, demonstrate their uselessness in the utilitarian scheme of things. It is as though, on the verge of being consumed by utilitarian purposes, Popova's constructions signal an autonomous, poietic "function" of art. And that function has to do specifically with an artistic redisposition of forces, with the construction of a poietic force field. The abstract lines of force, their intersections and tensions, represent a move beyond representational optics in an attempt to figure the spaces of relating, the mode of relationality, enhanced and catching the eye at the points of crossing, accentuated by thickening shadows. These lines, circles, and patches of shadow provide an aesthetic counterpart to the mathematical forms of abstraction, which constitute the technic, calculative grid of modern reality. But if technicity produces the historical force field as, in principle, an orderable and totalizable resource of forces, Popova's space-force constructions remain intrinsically open as their edges project and extend the painted surface into what lies beyond it. In Popova's hands, the abstract technicity of Constructivism on the verge of utilitarian aesthetics gets inverted into a nonviolent poiēsis of forces. As a kind of aesthetic parallel to the mathematical abstraction of experience into numbers and information bytes, technē shows here its double face, the possibility of enacting a different, artistic force field in the midst of the intensifying technicization.

What delimits the scope and the valence of the field of art's work, that is, the signification of the reworking of forces that is occurring in art, is the nonviolent disposition given to the relations refigured there. This is how I read what Heidegger calls "the truth that is happening in the work," that is, the truth of a nonviolent thrusting, of a power-free strife between forces that opens up a new modality of relation. What is necessary in encountering art is a critical and yet open attitude that would allow the work to unfold as a work, that is, as a transformation in the praxis of doing, seeing, and evaluating. Heidegger calls such an approach "preserving" (*bewahren*): "This letting the work be a work, we call preserving a work."[4] The German term indicates a comportment that takes care to allow the work to happen and thus lets the work remain true (*wahr*) to its transformative force. What Heidegger does not elaborate is that the nonviolent, power-free momentum of the displacement occurring in the artwork is carried over into praxis: in order to remain within the power-free disposition of forces, "to stay within the truth happening in the work," one needs "henceforth," that is, from the moment of the release initiated as the work *of* art, to keep the transformative momentum going. One needs, in other words, to stay within the different, power-free mode of acting, perceiving, and knowing, in order to maintain the nonviolent praxis. Thus staying "true" to the work of art is not limited to the event of the work itself but extends beyond it into the practice that "preserves" the power-free disposition of relations in the social sphere. As Krzysztof Wodiczko's projections and performative instruments suggest,[5] this is the instance in which the force field opened up by the artwork belies the artificial separation of the artistic and social domains as the artwork extends or radiates into the social context, reenacting the artistic release into the nonviolent "strife" of daily differences and conflict, into a power-free relationality. Such altered relationality reverberates through the forms of power relations, changing the forces' momentum by letting them unfold without being formed and constrained by the conduits of power. Rethought in this way, "preservation" is not an idyllic flight from reality or a utopian ideal but a reperformance of the alteration in the momentum of force relations, of the "truth" of nonviolence.

The Event of Transformation

The definition of the artwork as a force field focuses the discussion of art on its transformative work, that is, on the event by which the world opened up by an artwork alters social praxis. The event is a decisive and radical interruption of the way things have been before, an alteration in the historical force field, which frees up the force of the possible. Art thus marks a rupture, a displacement within the sociocultural world, an event whereby art originates by transforming the usual ways of perceiving, knowing, and acting that constitute this world. To say that art's force field should be thought of as an event places the emphasis on the temporal dynamics of art's occurrence, not just on the spatial "extension" of art's field. More important, characterizing art's force field as an event underscores the rupturing force of the transformation, the fact that such force exceeds and becomes uncontainable within the economy of presence and its linear temporality. To that extent, the event is, as Adorno would say, both "more" and "less" than praxis, for its transformative effect overflows the boundaries of practical rationality and, as such, "fails" to be fully articulable in a schema of social practice. Since art *works* in the specific sense of being an act, an event of transformation, it should be thought of in a verbal fashion, that is, as a happening, reactivated each time differently in its reception, rather than being seen as an object of the aesthetic and cognitive gaze, intrinsically subject to the manipulation and effects of outside forces. Beyond beauty and sublimity, beyond its status as a sociocultural object of production and consumption, with all their attending ideologies, art sometimes *work*s as art, transforming relations in an almost subterranean fashion, beyond the threshold of perception and representation. It is this transformative event that constitutes the force of art.

Art can have such a transformative effect only in a specific kind of reception, when the artwork is encountered as a work, that is, nonaesthetically, which means that, beyond its aesthetic/cognitive/commodity form, art is allowed *to work*. Thus the transformative work is itself a relation, an encounter with an artwork in which this work, in a rupture of displacement, transforms the web of social, political, and cultural relations within which both the work and its reception take place. Art's transformation works not on the level of objects, people, or things but in terms of the modality of relating, which, in the forms of perception, knowledge, acting, or valuing, determines the connective tissue of what we experience as reality. Understood as work, art draws attention to how the forms of the force relations that constitute a world depend on the mode of relating itself, on how relatedness—the connective tissue of beings—unfolds. One could say that this relatedness is itself a form of work: not a fixed structure or a scaffolding that props up and regulates the world but an event of temporalization that remains relative to the historical context of reception. This relational character should be distinguished from aesthetic relativism, which makes art dependent on subjective experience or relativizes its meaning vis-à-vis the particularity of each historical moment so that each age can claim a right to its own specific perspective on, say, *Hamlet*. Rather, the adjective "relational" refers here to a specific kind of interdependence between art and the historical circumstances of its reception, which suggests that a work can "occur" only within a particular context, one that, precisely, allows it to work, that is, to transform the very relations that bring about the encounter with art in the first place. It is not the case that a particular artwork has a different message for each epoch, context, or aesthetic subject—beyond such a multiplicity of interpretations, art performs the "same" work of transformation, even though this work remains relational in the sense that the historical relations it alters vary with the circumstances that, in each case differently, allow for the work's reception.

This complex relational character of the artwork is, strictly speaking, neither sensible nor intelligible, and therefore it does not fall under the rubric of either *aisthesis* or cognition. It eschews, then, the ancient quarrel between philosophy and poetry, remaining beyond the strictures of the rationality of cognition and the apparent nonrationality of aesthetic experience, for such work is a matter of reopening the world in a fashion that transforms the vectors of relations, which make up the blueprint for both sensibility and intellection. Thus this specific transformative event does not fall under the jurisdiction of judgment, whether aesthetic or cognitive, because such judgment becomes possible only when the event and its force field have been rendered neutral, foreclosed within the idea of the aesthetic object. In its transformative work, art reworks the very parameters within which we make judgments, the optics within which judgments become possible and make sense in the first place. To put it differently, the aesthetic relation to art does not experience its event and overlooks its transformative effects as it confines art within the conceptual boundaries of aesthetic experience, objectivity, and judgment, no matter whether this experience is limited to sensible intuitions or, as in Kant's case, includes the cognitive import of aesthetic ideas. The aesthetic strictures placed on art, themselves caught up in the aporias of feeling and cognition, of the subjective and the universally valid, make the work performed by art virtually inaccessible, hidden behind a tightly woven curtain of aesthetic sensibility and cultural clichés.

Forcework

Since the transformative work of art occurs on the level of force relations, I propose the term "forcework" to describe both what makes artworks distinctive from other objects and what allows art to intervene into social practice. In the introduction I characterized forcework in a preliminary fashion: as a release or a redisposition of forces into a constellation alternative to the sociopolitical conditions of art production. The work of art is a field, a multidimensional space-time event, where forces come to be transformed through the "force" of poiēsis, that which "makes" art: it is a kind of force or bearing specific to art. This poietic force remains, as Adorno and Heidegger each in his own way explain, an enigma, ungraspable and illegible within the discourses, whether aesthetic, scientific, or cultural, that this artistic force itself transforms in the process of inscribing them in the work. When worldly and social forces enter the "space" of art, they come under the bearing of poiēsis, which reconfigures and redisposes them. An artwork, as such a force field, becomes an interface between the "external" world and the artistic dimension of the work, repeatedly staging the very transformative event, the synapse between art and "reality," which allows art to remain autonomous precisely for the sake of critiquing and revising the real. Such forcework can be thought of as an alternative disposition of forces, which, breaking open the radical historicity of experience, ruptures and displaces the relations of power that regulate social commerce. As such, forcework defines the transformative dimension of art that lies beyond the complicities and/or resistances to regimes of power and ideologies that mark both the content and the formal aspects of artworks. In other words, the transformative thrust of forcework cannot be either limited to or satisfactorily explained in terms of the radical nature of formal experimentation or as a thematized resistance to dominant power formations or ideologies. Rather, this thrust has to be considered in terms of the unfolding of force relations, which—like the invisible infinitesimal forces in physics,[6] as Adorno suggests—operate as a second world of relations underneath not only social and political but also aesthetic phenomena.

The coined term "forcework" is meant to reinforce the distance between the kind of work I see modern art perform and the idea that art is primarily a cultural or an aesthetic object. It also underscores the flexible and active character of the unfolding of relations in a work of art—its valence as an event of a world-in-transformation, as a phenomenon irreducible to aesthetic experience, pleasure, judgment, and so on. Certainly all these aspects come into play in art reception, but what *works* in art, if only rarely, does not have a properly aesthetic status, whether aesthetics is conceived in cultural, philosophical, or "purely" aestheticist terms. I have already explained, in various ways, one of the elements of this compound word, "work," as signifying both the work of redisposing forces (work that is figured into the artwork) and the labor involved in the work's reception (a labor necessary in order to give art space to perform its work without being reduced to the parameters of aesthetic experience). This second meaning of "work" reflects the critique of the idea of a passive reception or contemplation of art, for it emphasizes the labor needed to let the work bring about the rupture and displacement within the usual doing, knowing, and valuing that are constitutive of social relations. This notion of the double work involved in art, linking the performative and the receptive/reperformative, indicates that forcework is never just a matter of the "objective" (art as object) or the "subjective" (art from the perspective of the reader/interpreter) brought together in an aesthetic experience of pleasure and judgment; rather, it concerns the historicotemporal workings of art's force field, whose event exceeds the scope and the power of judgment.

The first component of forcework, *force*, is more complex and difficult to define. I follow here the line of thinking that extends from Nietzsche to Heidegger, Adorno, Foucault, and Deleuze and see force(s) in terms of spatial-temporal play, that is, in relation to the momentum of unfolding or coming into being. On the one hand, force comes to be associated with Heidegger's redefinition of the term "being": in its spatial-temporal unfolding, being functions as a certain "force" that brings beings into existence. On the other hand, forces in the multiple signify, as in Foucault and Deleuze, instances of unformed matter and nonformalized functions, which enter various unstable, virtual, and shifting complexes of relations—in other words, relations between forces prior to, or on the level "below," the articulation of being into substances, objects, or bodies. The first sense of the term "force" is primarily ontological and remains indebted to Heidegger's redefinition of *physis* as the surge of happening, as the rupturing emergence of what comes to be. Heidegger's reading breaks with the traditional understanding of *physis* as nature (*natura*), for, as the actuation of being, *physis* remains beyond the oppositions nature/culture and nature/history. It refers to the unfolding of "natural" things as much as it describes the temporal existence of cultural products and historical phenomena. It certainly is not to be confused with the idea of the natural immediacy of experience, because *physis,* in Heidegger's approach, is always tantamount to a differential unfolding that is language-bound—both on its way to words and indissociable from its discursive articulations. In such a differential event, beings come to be what they are through and by virtue of a sheaf of relations that decide/constitute their "being." In other words, being here is inherently differential and mediatory: it instantiates not simply *what is* but also the very *relatedness* through which everything comes to be constituted as what it is. Kazimir Malevich's famous painting *White Square on White* can be seen as unfolding such an "abstract" relatedness, where the nearly invisible and constantly receding contours of what emerges—a white square profiled by a different shade of whiteness—underscore the nonperceptual status of the relation that is just arising into being. The painting focuses our perception not so much on what is related but on the link, on the occurrence or actuation of relating. The fact that these playfully withdrawing contours stay hardly visible underscores the limits of visibility and indicates that the relating figured by the painting, its forcework, remains beyond the threshold of representation, slipping away from the parameters of discursivity.

Force here is neither static, unchanging being nor its opposite, change or becoming. Contrasted with the notions of stasis and *essentia*, the term "force," in the post-Nietzschean sense, denotes the very temporality of happening, in which occurrence has the structure of an event extended into the coming future and therefore irreducible to any particular instant of the now. Temporality itself acts as a force of differentiation, which renders experience inherently differential, noncoincident with any fixed or definable content that can be assumed to represent an instance of being, a "now" fully existing within the closure of its own self-presence. In an event of unfolding or revealing, force does not have an identity or a presence of its own, for its "being" consists in merely *bringing into being.* Thought of in this way, force constitutes the material event of all relationality. But this materiality, as the field or the spanning where all relations become inscribed—that is, as the site from which the lines of force unfold—has its own protolanguage, one that works prior to and beyond the order of signification. It is a "language" in the specific sense of scripting the spatial-temporal play of forces, which fashions the blueprint for all relations. As such, this language bespeaks the ways in which forces materialize, the modalities according to which relations come to constitute history and become articulated in social formations. This is what Heidegger thinks in his late works, under the rubric of "being," whose actuation into a web of differences and relations forms a "saying" (*Sage*) that exceeds the order of signification—at least until he begins to cross out "being" and inscribes it into the notion of the event (*das Ereignis*), to avoid the familiar misinterpretations of being as a metaphysical notion. The actuation of such an event forms a wordless or preverbal language, like the one that Stein attempts to bring into play in her texts, a language or grammar that imprints all relations. It is in terms of such a "grammar" that the very bifurcation of the event into the material and the immaterial is effectuated in every moment. This notion of force as rupture or emergence underwrites the various social, political, economic, aesthetic, and so on, forms that forces assume in daily life as well as the types and models of relations into which they enter in accordance with the prevailing economies of power. Heidegger's and Foucault's interpretations of Nietzsche call into question vitalistic and biologistic misreadings of the Nietzschean force as a *vis,* or force of life, misreadings that run the risk of anthropologizing the force of happening, whose ontological status is not reducible to an anthropocentric or biological framework. What I have in mind, then, is the notion of a force that, though often dissembled, misshaped, or arrested, courses through the social formation of forces and into practices of production, representation, and exchange. In Malevich's painting, this force is marked as the drawing out of the relation between the two shades of whiteness, which delineates the visual field of the work. One could describe this invisible force field, its "whiteness on white," in terms of a literal drawing out of the site, of the underwriting relationality constitutive of the material, spiritual, social, and so on, aspects of experience.

Nevertheless, forces are also understood, in a Deleuzean perspective, as unformed matter, nonformalized functions, and flows of energy. Forces in the sense of unformed matter mark the possibilities of being affected by other forces, or of receptivity, in Deleuze's interpretation of Foucault, while forces' designation as nonformalized functions bespeaks the various manner of affecting other forces, which Deleuze terms "spontaneity."[7] These forces do not exist on their own but occur always already in relations with other forces, relations that flow through and shape substances, bodies, and objects.[8] For Foucault, these forces constitute the outside of the forms of power and knowledge, and thus they function both as the

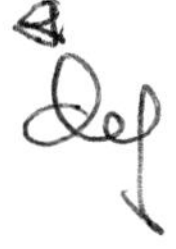

source of power and knowledge and, crucially, as the possibility of resistance to the manner in which power relations come to be actualized, modified, and redisposed into the forms of visibility and saying. Yet in their very status as the outside, forces as unformed matter and nonformalized functions traversing the entire field of forces—the field of the real, so to speak, beyond the actualization into knowledge—are always already being disposed (and redisposed) in a certain manner into their multiple, shifting, unstable, or virtual relations. It is this changing disposition (*Stimmung*) itself that, in Heidegger's thought, indicates the historically changing modalities of being. Being, understood itself as "force," thus describes the manner in which forces become disposed and composed into a shifting, molecular, and always only potential array of relations. This double sense of force is reflected in the double terminology that I adopt: on the one hand, I see the work taking place in art as forcework, that is, as a redisposition and recomposition of relations between forces; on the other, the term "forcework" designates the disposition, the momentum it imparts to the force relations it gathers into its field, and this specifically poietic momentum of force relations opened up by the artwork is what I call the force of art. In short, the force of art is the poietic momentum into which the artwork transforms the force relations it has brought into its field.

The term "forcework" brings the notions of force and work together to focus attention on the act or the event of redisposing forces, which constitutes the "critical" dimension of modern art. Forcework might also be called art's nonaesthetic dimension, a field that operates beyond the aesthetic features or the social and subjective inscriptions of artistic objects. Both segments of the term "forcework" are intended to reinforce the sense of flexibility, transformation, and reworking, that is, of the specific labor of force figured in the artwork and reactuated repeatedly in its reception. They call into question the still prevalent perception of artworks as static, inactive objects, perception overdetermined by the solid, unchangeable materiality of art and reinforced by the modern idea of art as constituted, first and foremost, as the *object* of production and consumption. But to think about art as an object is not only to locate it within the metaphysical economy of subject-object relations but also to render it, a priori, passive, a pawn in the hands of the larger, more "real" forces of the modern world: market, technology, labor. In comparison with the magnitude and influence of these other forces, art seems to have no power of its own, and whatever negligible force it has seems either to function as an extension of social forces, which means that art possesses no autonomy, or to contribute to the aestheticization of experience. In this approach, art lives on borrowed or reflected forces, at best faithfully representing them, and at worst dissimulating reality as an aesthetic construct. This enervation of art's work lets us easily compartmentalize art as one sector of cultural activity among others, and it makes possible the classifying of artworks as objects of analysis that require or allow no other terms than those used in describing other cultural products. If art appears to be something else, resistant to such sociocultural classifications, it confirms the suspicion that art has lost touch with "reality," and that it should be reprimanded, even denounced, for its apparent complicity with the constellations of power organizing everyday experience.

Adorno captures this dynamic well in his descriptions of the commodification of art: "The humiliating difference between art and the life people lead . . . must be made to disappear: This is the subjective basis for classifying art among the consumer goods under the control of *vested interests.* If despite all this, art does not become simply consumable, then at least the relation to it can be modeled on the relation to actual commodity goods. . . . Nothing remains of the autonomy of art—that artworks should be considered better than they consider themselves to be arouses indignation in culture customers—other than the fetish character of the commodity, regression to the archaic fetishism in the origin of art."[9] Such an approach, though, conceals art's forcework and limits its analysis to the forces "behind" art, searching in them for the sources and conditions of art's "politics," for the determinants of art's complicity with or resistance to the existing regimes of power. Adorno calls this foreclosure "de-arting" (*Entkunstung*) because it (re)makes art into an object like other objects or reduces it to the subjective experience of the viewer: "The poles of the artwork's de-arting are that it is made as much a thing among things as a psychological vehicle of the spectator."[10] Both market forces and cultural/political ideologies seem only too happy to de-art artworks in these ways, to deny that art could have any force beyond those that produce it or become projected into it. What such interpretations routinely neglect is the way in which artworks redistribute not the already actualized forms of power, that is, social forces and institutions, but forces that operate prior to such articulations, on the level of unformed matter and nonformalized functions: "The transformation occurs not on the historical, stratified, or archeological composition but to the composing forces, when the latter enter into a relation with other forces which have come from outside (strategies)."[11] Understanding the conditions in which art breaks out of the shell of being an object of ideological, commercial, or "aesthetic" manipulation makes it possible to discern the transformative impulse in art, to focus attention on art's forcework and the level on which it changes the momentum of force relations, that is, on the second level of "infinitesimal forces," which, as Adorno specifies in *Aesthetic Theory*, operates underneath images and statements. Thus the notion of forcework lets us reappraise the problem of art's autonomy in terms of such a refiguring of forces into a figure that transforms the very dynamic of the forces and relations of production. If art is autonomous, such autonomy does not signify its independence or separation from socioeconomic or technological forces but indicates its capacity to inflect or rework the very relationality of forces that underlies and stratifies social manifestations of power.

Aphesis, or the Poietic Momentum of Force

To flesh out the different momentum that art gives to force, I introduce a distinction between the poietic and the technical impetus of force relations. I draw this difference out of two rather distinct sources: Heidegger's contrast between the power-works (*Kraftwerk*) and artwork (*Kunstwerk*) in "The Question Concerning Technology," and Marinetti's often conflicting and even confusing remarks on Futurist art and technology (Marinetti's comments on technology will be discussed in chapter 2). In the subsequent sections, I redraw this difference through two related distinctions: first, the differentiation between enhancement and increase of force, which Heidegger traces in his reading of Nietzsche, and then the contrast between the productionist idea of making (*machen*), which underwrites the modern economy of technopower and the artistic "labor" of release (*lassen*) understood as transformation (*Verwandlung*) in the power momentum of force relations. These supplementary sets of distinctions serve to concretize the operation of forcework and explain its effects on power and society. Furthermore, as I explain in chapter 2, they point toward a fault in the notion of technicity and toward a possible turn within the technological forms of power that art dramatizes in its forcework. Finally, by proposing an alternative, nonproductionist understanding of the "work" that happens in art, they make possible a new critique of commodification and subjectivity, which I develop in chapter 3.

These kinds of convergences and distinctions between power and art, technicity and poiēsis, are intimated though not developed in Heidegger's famous juxtaposition between a hydroelectric plant on the Rhine and the artwork in "The Question Concerning Technology." Heidegger suggests that the power plant "set into the current of the Rhine" does more than control the flow of the river and use its energy to produce electricity. In fact, it alters what the river is: "What the river is now, namely, a water-power supplier, derives from the essence of the power station."[12] There is something more fundamental at work in the power plant than the actual transformation of water energy into electrical power, and that something more is a reworking of *physis* as force into a technologically disposed relations of power. The work that a power plant performs becomes possible and is a result of an already accomplished revealing of the world, as a *Bestand,* a standing reserve, which, in this context, can perhaps be thought of in terms of a power supply or reserve. To make the idea of a power plant possible in the first place, what is necessary is the prior disclosure of "nature" or "reality" as a global resource, that is, the revealing and establishment of the actual in terms of power, a formation that Heidegger terms *Technik,* or technics. In other words, the world has to be constituted in terms of a certain *technics*—that is, as resource, production, and power—and conceived as exploitable and usable matter and energy, before technology, in the narrow sense of technologically advanced modern production, can become possible at all. Being has to be revealed as a world that is technical in essence *before* science and technology can become effective ways of grasping and manipulating it. It is in this sense that Heidegger uses the term *Technik* to designate the modality of being that is characteristic of modernity: not essence, substance, or objectivity but the global *technicity* of being as a standing reserve of resources (*Bestand*). In effect, *physis* as a web of forces no longer works as emergence that lets be but organizes forces technologically for the benefit of power. I do not mean here just the literal production of electric power but the determination of relating itself, in terms of power: in other words, to relate means to *power relate*, to produce what is both *through power relations* and *into power formations*, to invoke Foucault's terminology.

Heidegger's discussion of the Rhine power plant as an example of the technological unfolding of forces culminates in the comparison between the plant's work and that of art, in "the contrast that is spoken by the two titles: 'The Rhine,' as dammed up into the *power* works [Kraft-*werk*], and 'The Rhine,' as uttered by the *art*-work [Kunst-*werk*], in Hölderlin's hymn by that name."[13] The juxtaposition seems quite surprising, and yet it sets up the points of proximity and tension that underlie Heidegger's entire reflection on art and technology. What both art and technology do is explained as work, which shows the closeness between the artistic and the technological, reflected in Heidegger's discussion of the two related meanings of technē as craft/art and as technics or technology. *Kraftwerk* denotes a power plant or station, but, composed of the German equivalents of English "force" (*Kraft*) and "work" (*werk*), it literally means *forcework.* One could indeed say that a power plant is, in its own way, a certain transformative forcework, in which natural forces become harnessed, maximized, and turned into technological forces. Reworking nature into culture, this technological "work" of a power plant marks a thin and problematic boundary between nature and artifice, between *physis* and technology. The play between forcework and *Kraftwerk* is important to the extent that it indicates the proximity between art's forcework and the technological forcework exemplified by the power plant. It also introduces the question of a possible difference between the two kinds of work, between the work that is properly art's work and the technic work that results literally in the production of power. After all, *Kraft* in German can also mean strength or power, and the English equivalents of *Kraftwerk*, "power plant" or "power station," leave no doubt about the direction of the technological forcework: power.

Art and technology are both described as modalities of revealing, as technic and poietic unfolding, respectively. The distinction between them is underscored in Heidegger's text through the difference between *Kraft* (power) and *Kunst* (art), between the work that I understand as a technological disciplining of forces and the work as it reflects the poietic, nonviolent forcework. When, near the end of the essay, Heidegger remarks that reflection on the essence of modern technology can take place in art, he once again emphasizes both the essential proximity and the irreducible difference between them: "Because the essence of technology is nothing technological, essential reflection upon technology and decisive confrontation with it must happen in a realm that is, on the one hand, akin to the essence of technology and, on the other, fundamentally different from it."[14] The "decisive confrontation" does not mean rejection or "destruction" of technology; it refers to bringing into thought the very space in which the modality of relations becomes decided, to what I would see as the rift in technē between the poietic and the technical momentum of forces. The statement "the essence of technology is nothing technological" reflects the distinction I mentioned earlier between the narrow understanding of technology as technological production or organization, as the development of technological innovations or technoscientific progress, on the one hand, and the "essence" of technology, on the other, which has to be explained in terms of the power-oriented revealing of the world as technic in its very constitution as a global resource. The "essence" of technology denotes a manner in which being unfolds, a historically modern mode, which has allowed for the development of science and of what is commonly understood as technology in its narrow sense. Instead of *technology*, the term used to translate Heidegger's *Technik*, we should talk about *technicity*, which I understand not as an abstract, overgeneralized concept to describe the modern understanding of being but rather as a concrete vector of relations among forces, relations that always already have formed themselves into flows of power. What such technicity has in common with art is its work of unfolding, and where it differs from the artwork is with respect to how this unfolding takes place: technicity aims toward power, while art attempts to let be.

But *Technik* and art are even closer than Heidegger lets it be known in his essay. They are both a type of *Kraftwerk,* or forcework, in the sense that what is at stake in them is the manner in which the forces of the world's unfolding work and become disposed. The contrast between *Kraft* and *Kunst* makes power the decisive issue but also implicitly signals the thin and fragile line that separates (and links) force and power in modernity, the narrow line between art's forcework and power/domination, over which Adorno constantly worries in *Aesthetic Theory.* Describing art as forcework, I want to reexamine this ambiguity, which continues to play itself out in modern art as a kind of self-doubt in art as to whether art can figure force otherwise than technologically. Such an approach requires that we conceive force in modernity as capable of having two generalized types of momentum: technic and poietic. Furthermore, I would argue that it is art that brings out and preserves this double capacity of force, which may make art able to open up spaces of transformation that remain impossible within the social organization of force. I would also claim that avant-garde art, at its best and most radical—for example, Futurism or Dadaism—instantiates precisely such transformative forcework.

Thinking about reality in a kind of Nietzschean-Foucauldian fashion, as a play of forces, I have distinguished between two momentums of force—the technic and the poietic—granting, obviously, that the technic momentum itself is highly diversified, embracing various, often conflictual, articulations of power. Because of these two ways of manifestation, force remains inherently ambiguous, since it can occur in either the poietic or the technic modality, materializing as either technicity or poiēsis. Perhaps we can make an analogy here between the two modes of force's appearance and string theory in physics, which maintains that strings, the most elementary constituents of the universe, come to be either matter or energy according to the frequency of their vibrations. Such strings have no "essence" or stable identity but embody differentiation, the possibility of materializing into two distinct although interchangeable modes. Force, as defined here, also has no essence but can unfold into two modes of being: technic and poietic. Whether force unfolds into a technic or a poietic manifestation depends on the kind of relation into which it enters with other forces, on the type of relatedness that gets produced as the structure of reality. Here, relationality is not understood as a link or a connection between two or more already existing forces or beings but signifies instead the very spanning or dimension that institutes relations as such. In this approach, forces do not exist prior to their relations but come to be what they always and already are *through* relating, through the tensions between forces and in conformity with the manner in which these relations, that is, the relationality underpinning the formation of forces, come to be disposed and arranged. Thus it is the modality, or the disposition, of relations, the very vector of relating, so to speak, that determines what forces come to be, whether and how they come to constitute forms of power and participate in its flows. Against the background of this specific understanding of relationality, it becomes possible to draw a distinction between the *poietic* forcework and the *technic* forcework as the parameters for our investigation of modern art. The difference between the poietic and the technic forcework would consist in the kinds of relations into which forces would enter with one another because the valence of force, its materialization as either technicity or poiēsis, depends on the momentum acquired by forces.

This distinction does not mean that all art can be simply free from power, once and for all outside power's influence, for, in fact, most of the time the kind of forcework art produces indeed becomes indistinguishable from power work and reflects the technicity of being in modernity. It only posits the possibility that art sometimes transforms this dominant form of forcework, letting relations unfold outside the forms and orders of reality determined by the metaphysics of power. If we accept the premises I have outlined above, the "same" force can materialize as different forces according to the type of relation to other forces through which this force comes into being. Perhaps this is what Adorno tries to get at when he asserts that social and political forces that contribute to and, in fact, often determine the production of art become inverted or transformed in the artwork, a transformation that, Adorno believes, opens up reality in a manner that remains inaccessible outside art: "Art, however, is social not only because of its mode of production . . . nor simply because of the social derivation of its thematic material. Much more importantly, art becomes social by its opposition to society, and it occupies this position only as autonomous art. By crystallizing in itself as something unique to itself, rather than complying with existing social norms and qualifying as 'socially useful,' it criticizes society by merely existing, for which puritans of all stripes condemn it."[15] Art becomes socially "meaningful" precisely when it breaks with the aesthetic and political functions that society establishes for it, when it alters the power formations that regulate society and that society wants to stamp or project onto artworks. Instead, what art inaugurates is a different forcework, a different disposition of forces, which means that the forces that operate in society in a technological or instrumental, overrationalized manner, as Adorno would put it, become nontechnological. They are the "same" forces, yet their modality of unfolding is different in art, which means that the relations they produce become disposed into a different mode of revealing, and, as a result, the world unfolds differently. The actual remains the same and yet it works otherwise, and art's autono-

my manifests itself in the "otherwise" of its forcework. What is certain is that the Hegelian question of art's death, to which Adorno and Heidegger respond in different yet kindred fashions, since they both insist that art retains a transformative/critical force in modernity, pivots on the possibility of such a distinction between the two kinds of forcework. This difference would define, then, the historically contemporary social meaning of art, its nonviolent forcework, a kind of nonideological version of art's social significance.

Nowhere is the importance of such a redefinition of the social significance of art more manifest than in Adorno's *Aesthetic Theory*, where he strenuously contests the idea of a thematic or cultural-political explanation of how art matters for social praxis. If art matters socially, it is precisely through the forcework to which art submits the categorial determinations invisibly stamped on reality. This forcework is reducible neither to art's social function as a cultural object nor to its social or political content. As Adorno's favorite opposition between Beckett and Brecht makes clear, this transformative moment can be explained only in terms that are specific to art and, although intrinsically connected to the world "beyond" art, are without exact equivalents in other spheres of life. What makes art *critical* in a very special sense is that its significance cannot be formulated into a set of propositions, a worldview or theory—that it eschews the socially and philosophically acceptable parameters of critique. Art is "critical" by virtue of its forcework, and it is this event of the world happening "otherwise" that constitutes art as critical in relation to society. The poietic force of art would consist, then, in an alternative, nonviolent disposition of forces, which does not mean that art becomes blind to the "real" world or that it ends up in an escapist, aesthetic limbo, but rather that it instantiates the "same" (and the only) world "otherwise." No doubt art, whether untraceably complacent or explicitly critical, as in the case of Brecht, can be ideological, but it is not this form of cultural-political critique that, for Adorno, makes art radical. If anything, such forms of critique eviscerate art's forcework, put it out of work, so to speak, and, rendering it subservient to sociopolitical forces, blunt the critical-transformative force specific to art.

Enhancement and Increase of Force

The idea of forcework articulates a crucial distinction between how relationality and difference work within technic and poietic dispositions of forces, a divergence that I explore further by distinguishing between two modes of the intensification of force: enhancement and increase. To clarify this distinction, I expand Heidegger's comments on the difference between an enhancement and an increase of force from *The Will to Power as Art,* the first volume of Heidegger's *Nietzsche.* The most interesting moment of Heidegger's reading comes when he distinguishes *Rausch,* or intoxication, from the idea of aesthetic experience and suggests that it needs to be rethought not in terms of affect or feeling but in terms of a change in the mode of relation. Heidegger explains this different (from aesthetic) experience of art as an enhancement of force (*Kraftsteigerung*), by which he understands not an "objective" increase of power but instead a change in the type of relation or bearing (*Verhältnis*), which lets be "more in being" (*seiender*):

> Such enhancement of force must be understood as the capacity to extend beyond oneself [*über-sich-hinaus-Vermögen*], as a relation to beings in which beings themselves are experienced as being more fully in being [*seiender*], richer, more perspicuous, more essential. Enhancement does not mean that an increase, an increment of force, "objectively" comes about. Enhancement is to be understood in terms of mood [*die Steigerung is stimmunghaft zu verstehen*]. . . .[16]

Force here is not a question of accumulation or capitalization of force, that is, of an objective increase in force that would translate into power, that is, produce power as an effect of the relation between "increased" force and "lesser" forces. Enhancement here is certainly not a matter of disciplining the body for the purpose of increasing its energy or the efficiency of work, for such an enhancement would be tantamount to channeling and reconstituting forces through a technology of power. As Foucault observes in *Discipline and Punish,* "Discipline increases the forces of the body (in economic terms of utility) and diminishes theses same forces (in political terms of obedience)."[17] Foucault's analysis of increase in the efficiency and capitalization of forces implies a certain economic-political trade-off, and it links the *calculative* objective of such disciplining—its measurable, "objective" increase of forces—to a technological unfolding of force into norm. The connection between increase/efficiency and technologies of power suggests that the enhancement at work in *Rausch* does not proceed along the lines of the modern disciplining of forces, either increasing their efficiency or decreasing their force of resistance; in other words, such an enhancement does not conform to the technic distribution and alignment of forces.

Kraftsteigerung is also not a matter of "overpowering" other forces, of intensifying power within a given position or site, on one side of a force relation.[18] On the contrary, it is a matter of extending beyond oneself, of being capable of a "beyond"—a certain breaking down of enclosures, and a questioning of positionality. In fact, *Kraftsteigerung* occasions an inversion of relation, and it effects a different kind of bearing among what is. Instead of accruing force to the position of the one who experiences intoxication (the subject of aesthetic experience?), it intensifies the relation itself. *Rausch* happens not as the "aesthetic" intoxication of a subject but as enhancement in the flow of forces. And that enhancement happens not to the "subject" but to the "other," to other beings that find themselves more in being (*seiender*). *Kraftsteigerung* turns out to be about letting what is other be *seiender*, that is, be more in being. It grants more force to other beings, it lets them be, or, as Heidegger later puts it, releases them into what they are. This enhancement of force, I argue, happens as poiēsis, in the specific sense of letting what is "be more," of bringing it forth in such a way that it happens "more in force" as what it is.

Enhancement should be understood *stimmunghaft*: in terms of mood, disposition, or pitch. *Stimmung*, figuratively signifying atmosphere or mood, is also a musical term that refers to tuning, key, or pitch. The verb *stimmen* means to tune or to harmonize, but it also constitutes the root meaning of a key German philosophical term, *bestimmen*: to determine, to decide, to fix, to order, and so on. As Heidegger demonstrates,[19] the idea of determination (*Bestimmung*) in its philosophical and scientific use comes out of the notion of *Stimmung*, which signifies the opening or space within which the determination of what something is becomes possible in the first place. Scientific or philosophical definitions owe their form and shape, as well as their grasping power, to a certain *Stimmung*, to a disposition of forces that predisposes them toward calculability, efficiency, and manipulation. Thus the world, even before it becomes graspable and explainable in terms of ideas, definitions, and determinations, is already in a certain pitch or disposition. Without *Stimmung* there would be no *Bestimmung*; and being, without a pitch, would not be determinable in any way. This pitch, or key, constitutes the voice (*Stimme*) or language of being prior to language, as we know it in terms of signs and signification. The decision between enhancement and increase transpires on this predeterminative level, prior to the articulation of forces into determinate practices of representation, knowing, and acting. It has to do with how forces become tuned in to a relation, and with the kind of pitch or key that relating assumes. As I have shown in the previous section, force can have a technic or a poietic pitch, and this difference can decide the momentum of force relations, that is, whether it will unfold into enhancement or increase.

One way to think of art's forcework would be to see it as enhancement and thus distinguish it from the technic formation of force relations, which produces an increase or a growth (*ein Zuwachs*) of force, measurable and objectively graspable as a form of knowledge. In the case of a technic forcework, forces become disposed into a technological modality of relations; they are channeled and organized with a view to the maximalization of force. More important, this modality forms forces into relations of power, where power is technical in its operations: it does not have any specific location or center but transpires in terms of entire formations or strategies, which produce and organize whole fields of relations, as Foucault observes in a different context. By contrast, the poietic forcework enhances forces into a relation which does not explain itself in terms of increase and cannot be measured or stated objectively. While enhancement produces a different mode of relationality that allows the other (forces) to be more in being, that is, to be more "other," the technic forcework draws forces into patterns of relations that make them conform to norms and power structures, in an efficiency-bound relationality of technopower. Both the technic and the poietic forcework involve, then, intensifications of force, but qualitatively different ones that transpire in different keys. The question of art's role in modernity can be posed, then, in terms of the possibility of two such forms of intensification, ultimately quite different: one that intensifies in order to *produce* what *is* as forms of power and bring everything in line with common criteria and norms, and one that *enhances* what is singularly *other*, what remains beyond normative discipline, what cannot be organized or (re)produced. The first of these two forms of intensification is concerned with increase or efficiency that can be regulated and exploited; the second enhances the margin of alterity, as it were, that is, it intensifies the aspect of force that cannot be calculated or "formed," since it exceeds the available forms of relation.

One of the most significant avant-garde articulations of this notion of enhancement can be found in Stein's definition of poetry: "I had to feel anything and everything that for me was existing so intensely that I could put it down in writing as a thing in itself without at all necessarily using its name."[20] Stein's writing offers a most poignant modernist challenge to the technicization of experience on the most elemental level of the everyday relations that make up the sphere of ordinary "objects, food, and rooms," as the title sections from *Tender Buttons* indicate. Although Stein is a sort of avant-garde unto herself, the particular poietic forcework that her texts comprise provides a good indication of how to approach the problem of art and technicity in the avant-garde, especially in Futurism and Dadaism, where this question gets worked out on that kind of microlevel of relations, relations that often remain below the "surface" of the formal and thematic experiments that proliferate in modernism. In Stein's version, enhancement has to do with a reworking of language, with breaking away from the power exercised by names and definitions in everyday experience. In *Tender Buttons*, naming and defining become shorthand for evacuating the intensities of everyday being into the routine of meaning. In a certain way, language has come to function technically, that is, its aim is to discipline and organize linguistic forces and flows into a coherent, efficient, meaningful picture and thus to function as an effective instrument for communicating information. One gets the sense from Stein's texts that language has become a technique of reducing the event to a name, a procedure for organizing being with a view to the norms of expression and sense, a technique that finds its most modern manifestation in the transformation and storage of being as information bytes. Stein's idea of writing pivots on turning against such technicization through her unorthodox and idiosyncratic texts, which try to release semantics and grammar from the grip that the idea of the efficiency of representation and communication has on it.

Although technological progress does not play a particularly explicit role in Stein's writing, it is her innovative approach to language that touches directly on the question of technopower. Her naming without names leads to a releasing of things into the intensity of their existence, a stripping them of their ordinary significations to enhance their singular occurrence, which is foreclosed by the generalizing norms of signification. The "intense existence" that Stein's works enact does not produce an increase in meaningfulness, clarity, or understanding. On the contrary, her works explicitly call into question the ideals of semantic transparency and communicative efficiency, which are key aspects of the modern technoinformational regimen of being. In *Tender Buttons,* things become a blur of words, a run-on syntax of everyday existence that eschews the closure of articulation. One wants to say that things work differently in Stein, that the forces composing everyday existence become reworked outside their habitual experiential and discursive relations. Objects get refigured in ways that make the incalculable and nonmanipulable temporality of existence—a phenomenon that intrigued Stein from the time of *The Making of Americans,* early in her career—come to the fore, a situation suggesting that enhancement, for Stein, means a release of things from the closure of their naming into the event of their being. The temporality of relations that Stein's works keep reproducing is poietic: a transformative event redisposing the forces of language in such a way that they no longer work according to the normative criteria of correctness and sense but let things unfold with a poietic force of intensity so that things are no longer commodities or objects of everyday use. From this perspective, Stein's texts, highly resistant to becoming artistic commodities themselves, can be regarded as enacting perhaps the most radical decommodification of things and experience. One effect of Stein's inimitable writing is that the use of aesthetic criteria for her texts becomes obviously unsuitable: the concepts of beauty, meaning, aesthetic sensibility, character, plot, theme, and even image have no particular relevance or application to works like *Stanzas in Meditation* or *How to Write.* It is as though Stein were coaxing us to reconceive writing and experience along entirely new lines, to look at writing and experience through a nontechnicist, nonaesthetic lens.

The Event as Nonpower

The distinction between the two momentums of the intensification of force—increase and enhancement—marks the critical difference between the logic of production and the artistic forcework as an alternative to the paradigm of making and manipulation. The redisposition of forces signified by forcework is not just a matter of play but of aphesis, that is, of a radical change in the mode of relating between forces, which calls into question the logic of production underwriting the operations of capital and modern social praxis. Although this part of my argument will be developed in more detail in chapter 3, in relation to commodification, I want to signal here the critical importance of the distinction between labor as production and the work that happens as forcework in art. I am suggesting here, in agreement with Adorno, that art not only unmasks the extent to which the rationality of making/manipulation saturates social praxis, including forms of counterpower and practices of resistance, but also offers an analog of relating that does not follow the logic of production. Aphesis at work in art, undermining the productionist logic, constitutes an alternative to the power-oriented operations of modern technology, a zone of nonpower, free from power and at the same time decisively different from powerlessness.

Contemporary society is thoroughly suffused with making and manipulation, its most recent form being the (re)programming and manipulation of information, ranging from practices of genetic manipulation to global economic planning. The advances in information technologies, use of the Internet, and electronic/computational "realities" confirm Heidegger's diagnosis, in the late 1930's, that modern forms of being are increasingly determined by the manipulative logic of making, by what he called the metaphysics of production. For Heidegger, metaphysics is not just a conceptual system of binary oppositions (presence and absence, subjectivity and objectivity, activity and passivity); it also signifies a manner of unfolding relations into power, a power that produces and runs through—in short, that *powers*—being, and that in the process conceals, even eliminates, any other possibility of relating: "The essence of power as machination annihilates the possibility of the truth of beings. It is itself the end of metaphysics" ("Das Wesen der Macht als Machenschaft vernichtet die Möglichkeit der Wahrheit des Seienden. Sie ist selbst das Ende der Metaphysik").[21] It is the occurrence of relations *into* and *as* power that constitutes history as metaphysical; or, to put it differently, as long as being occurs in terms of power, there is metaphysics. Metaphysics means that forces and relations transpire in terms of a certain makingness (*Mache*): "The essential in this makingness is machination [*Machenschaft*]:

the preparation for the empowerment of power, and the makeability [*Machsamkeit*] of all beings readied by power and demanded by the overpowering."[22] Machination or manipulative power: all the globally successful technologies of information gathering, processing, and (re)programming that regulate modern social commerce, purposely or not, dispose forces into relations of production in just this sense: that the various forms assumed by these relations all contribute to the accelerating increase of power, both on the global scale and in the microinformational spectrum of being. Contemporary society appears to be caught in the spiral of power, and to such an extent that almost all forms of action, planning, intervention, and so on, follow the pattern of manipulative power and thus, even when they are well intentioned and socially and politically progressive, end up extending and escalating the reach and flexibility of modern forms of power.

The insatiable intensity with which power suffuses contemporary social praxis on all levels becomes revealed with particular poignancy in art. The difference of art's forcework not only lays bare this spiral of intensification but also releases forces from the grip that manipulation has on the various forms of relations operative in modern society. In social relations, force has the value of power, that is, it comes to be formed and effectuated as an element in the overall impetus of making, manipulation, and production, which results in an increase of power. In art's forcework, however, forces are "mobilized" in an *aphetic* manner that releases and "demobilizes" them; they come to be dominated in a way that undoes domination, as Adorno remarks. To put it differently, art "works" forces in a nonproductionist mode, engaging them without manipulating, mobilizing, or maximizing them. In short, forces in art become *de-powered* in the specific sense of being allowed to have a momentum free from power, a momentum that does not participate in the manipulative, productionist logic of being and thus avoids contributing to the increase in power. This distinct momentum that art grants to force relations is what I call, working with Heidegger's terminology, "aphesis," a letting or a release—an alternative to the manipulative forming of relations effected by power. What this momentum signifies is the possibility of force having the "free" valence of letting be, unfolding, and "enhancing."

This distinction, crucial to understanding forcework as a letting be, can be illustrated by reference to two German verbs, *machen* and *lassen*, on which Heidegger relies in his critique of technology and his reformulation of the notion of poiēsis. While *machen* means "to make" or "to produce," it is also related to the German word for "power," *Macht*. Heidegger's writings from the late 1930's establish a persuasive connection between the various modern forms of production and the increasing saturation of being with power. *Lassen*, by contrast, refers to letting or allowing, but in an active rather than passive sense, that is, of accomplishing something by actively letting it come to be rather than by producing or manipulating it. *Lassen*, later associated by Heidegger with poiēsis, is a form of release from invisible entanglement within the technologies of power, a turn that lets forces unfold free from the power momentum that shapes and inscribes them into their relational context. As release from power and as letting be, aphesis is a certain active redisposition and transformation, a reorientation of forces before and beyond any act or activity, yet in no way is it to be mistaken for passivity or inaction. It operates in the middle voice, between active and passive, exceeding this opposition precisely because it signifies a mutation in the very operation of making, a release from the hold that production and power have on being and relations. Since making and power undergird and regulate the disposition of forces and relations into activity and passivity, into action and inaction, such a modulation in the productionist momentum of being reformulates this very opposition, making room for a third way, the way of aphesis, as it were. Poiēsis, rethought in the context of aphesis, can no longer signify making, creation, or production. Instead, conceived as an aphetic disposition of forces, poiēsis breaks free from the production paradigm and instantiates an alternative, nonproductionist, mode of bringing forth.

The two faces of force signified by *machen* and *lassen* reflect the turn from the concept of the agent/subject of production to the notion of force as reciprocal receptivity. Since such receptivity is conceived beyond the production paradigm, however, it is not only beyond the subject-object opposition but also beyond the dialectic of activity and passivity: force as aphesis "lets be" in the middle voice. Therefore, the notion of the "power-free" in my argument does not mean powerlessness but instead depicts the nonproductionist vector of relations, which, while confusing to the commodifying logic of capital, and unexplainable within it, remains discernible in art's forcework. Here, the term "letting" does not have the connotation of indifference or passivity, that is, of doing nothing but placidly and complacently allowing things to transpire according to their predetermined course, namely, in terms of the intensification of power. Such passivity is often mistakenly ascribed to Heidegger's notions of *lassen* and *Gelassenheit* (release), for, as he remarks in *Besinnung*, letting does not mean inactivity or indifference,[23] but, on the contrary, denotes a transformation (*Verwandlung*) in the modality of relations. This transformation is very specific, for it concerns the production-oriented manipulative unfolding of being. This is why the forcework associated with the work of art is to be understood as a kind of enabling that grants forces the space, or the opening, for a new way of relating, one that eschews production, manipulation, and thus commodification. In art, in other words, forces are "empowered" to be "otherwise" than powerful. Words like "enable," "grant," and "empower" make clear the kind of transformative work involved in art—above all, the active resignification to which art submits the very notion of "work," giving it a new valence beyond the productionist logic of action and making.

Art refashions force in a way that allows relations to gain a momentum free of power, thus opening up the space of nonpower, and a relationality that "unproduces" forces, demobilizing them into a constellation that, more radically than any form of counterpower, calls power into question. The notion of aphesis makes it possible to discern a nondialectical (neither affirmative nor negative) and yet also nonimmediate mode of relating, a forcework no longer motivated by making and power but by working as a letting-be. Blanchot, identifying the moment when the logic of making and production becomes dispersed in writing, doubts whether this turn, which I would characterize as a turn in the momentum of force, can still even be conceived in terms of power:

> Speech is this turning [where the whole withholds itself]. Speech is the place of dispersion, disarranging and disarranging itself, dispersing and dispersing itself beyond all measure. . . .
>
> What sort of power is this? Is it still a power?[24]

And, later, "What is impossibility, *this nonpower that would not be the simple negation of power?*"[25] Blanchot makes immediately clear that the modality of relation he describes as nonpower has to do with poiēsis, with the artistic forcework:

> This detour is equally irreducible to affirmation and to negation, to question and to response; it precedes all these modes, speaking before them and as though in turning away from all speech. Even if it tends to determine itself as a power to say

no, particularly in the movements that manifest themselves in revolt, this no that challenges all constituted power also challenges the power to say no, designating it as what is not founded in a power, as irreducible to any power and, by virtue of this, unfounded. Language lends itself to the movement of stealing and turning away—it watches over it, preserves it, loses itself there and confirms itself there. In this we sense why the essential speech of detour, the "poetry" in the turn of writing, is also a speech wherein time turns, saying time as a turning, the turning that sometimes turns in a visible manner into revolution.[26]

Like Heidegger, Blanchot sees the poietic in terms of resistance (the power to say no) and transformation, occasionally even revolution. Yet Blanchot is emphatic that this poetry in the turn of writing is "irreducible to any power"; and since it is not founded in a power, the poietic constitutes a challenge to all forms of power. As an undoing of power as such, it cannot be determined as a no, as a negation. To put it differently, nonpower is neither a negation nor an affirmation of power; neither is it a counterpower, a form of resistance (to hegemony) that becomes another incarnation of power, or powerlessness, that is, complicity or inactivity. In Gerald Bruns's words, "Literature is the refusal of power. It is the not-saying of language."[27] Nonpower is nondialectical without falling into immediacy; it is, to speak Levinasian, "otherwise" than power.

Radicalizing the Negative

In his text *Besinnung,* written in 1938–39, Heidegger describes such a transformative, power-free event as an originary radicalism, a radicalism beyond affirmation and negation, beyond a yes or a no.[28] Though Blanchot could not have known *Besinnung,* which was published for the first time in 1997, his remarks in *The Infinite Conversation* about nonpower never being a simple negation of power echo Heidegger's insistence in his texts from the late 1930's that being occurs "otherwise" than as power, beyond both power and powerlessness: "Being occurs beyond power and powerlessness" ("ausserhalb von Macht und Ohnmacht west das Seyn").[29] In other words, nonpower is not a negation of power, nor is it power's dialectical reversal, just as it does not constitute an unpower (*Unmacht*) or an absence of power, that is, powerlessness (*Ohnmacht*). Rather, nonpower is a realm in which power and thus also powerlessness are not operative. This realm—for Heidegger, the event or *Ereignis*—exists "otherwise" than as power: it is *das Machtlose*.[30] I translate the adjective *machtlos* as "power-free" because Heidegger's text makes amply clear that the suffix *-los* is understood in this context not as privative but as indicating a release, a freeing, or a withdrawal—in short, a desisting from power.[31] The poietic event as Heidegger conceives it is thus power-free, relieved of power and disencumbered from it, and as such emphatically different from powerlessness: "The power-free is not the power-less" ("Das Macht-lose ist nicht das Ohn-mächtige").[32] While powerlessness belongs to the same logic as power—it describes power's reversal or absence—nonpower does not explain itself in terms of power. The radicalism of such an event lies precisely in its evasion of power, which transpires otherwise than by saying no to power and therefore remains different from resistance, understood as countering power, for power can and must be countered only with another power; whereas what Heidegger and Blanchot describe, in different ways, is a radical unworking of power, which evidences a critical difference between opposing power on its own terms, that is, through power, and the radicalism of the worklessness of power, the "revolution" of nonpower.[33] The force of this unworking is not power but a renunciation of power. Heidegger writes about *Verweigerung*,[34] a declining or a refusal of power, and Blanchot describes it as nonpower: "Power, the power that is capable of everything, is able even to do away with itself as a power (the explosion of the nucleus itself being one of the extremes of nihilism). Such an act will in no way make us accomplish the decisive step, the step that would deliver us over—in a sense without ourselves—to the surprise of impossibility by allowing us to belong to *this nonpower that is not simply the negation of power*. For thought, the limit-experience represents something *like* a new origin."[35] As Gerald Bruns shows, the starting point of Blanchot's poetics is his refusal to speak, which implies the renunciation of the very conditions that form what *is* into relations of power.[36] While power is capable of everything, what it cannot do is let go of power. It can, as Blanchot indicates, explode any power, but it cannot "power itself" to be other than power, to become nonpower. This is because the "poetry" of the turn toward nonpower is not an act, not a doing or a making, not a matter of power or production. To accomplish nonpower: this turn cannot work as power. Blanchot understands this turn as an "unworking" (*désoeuvrement*), while Heidegger casts it in a more "positive" light, as a transformation (*Verwandlung*). These

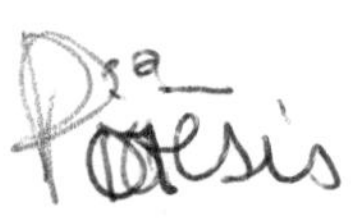

approaches are no doubt different, in Blanchot's case emphasizing the fact that power no longer "works," and in Heidegger's underscoring the transformative momentum of this release from power. Despite these differences, however, Heidegger and Blanchot both point toward the possibility of power's evacuation, the possibility associated here with art's forcework conceived, to paraphrase Heidegger, as a letting be or a release: it is a work (or an unworking) of *Gelassenheit* as a desisting from power.

What I am proposing here is that the force of art lies precisely in the way in which artworks can open up a mode of "aphetic," power-free relationality that undermines and evacuates power. Forcework seen as aphesis, irreducible to negation or absence of power, is a transformation in the mode of relations determinative of modernity: from relations of power, production, and machination (*Macht*, *machen*, *Machenschaft*) toward a power-free (*machtfrei*) form of relating. Heidegger's later texts describe this "dispowered" or power-free relationality in terms of poiēsis, which, as I will show in the next chapter, constitutes a turn within modern technicity, a turn that initiates the possibility of a different technē, a power-free poietic technē that releases forces from the grip of machination, ordering, and maximalization. Here, poiēsis no longer connotes making and production but rather designates a transformative turn in the midst of modern technology. In using the term "poietic" I indicate that the kind of transformative forcework evident in art remains irreducible to a poetics and therefore does not fall under the rubric of aesthetics.[37] This is the case because the term denotes here a certain manner of bringing forth, which is, however, not a species of making: the way in which the artwork instantiates is not of the same provenance as other forms of production, because it calls into question the very manner of fashioning and shaping that is constitutive of the logic of production.

The pivotal importance of forcework in relation to power lies in the possibility of radicalizing negativity beyond dialectics and the notion of negation. As a letting-be, the aphesis "at work" in forcework does not denote a negation of production, an unmaking or an absence of making (tantamount to powerlessness, that is, the absence or negative of power). On the contrary, aphesis as I have defined it here is "positive" and indicates a disposition of forces alternative to making, forming, and power shaping. The notion of aphesis allows us, therefore, to envision a modality of bringing forth and instantiating that breaks free from the dialectic of positing and negation. Neither positive nor negative, strictly speaking, aphesis describes a forcework that is nonproductionist, free of the momentum of making (necessary for the operation of negation), and thus no longer saturated with power. Because forcework happens "otherwise" than does power, beyond power and/or powerlessness, it "resists" and "contests" power in a radical sense, that is, it "opposes" not just this or that articulation of power (as dominant, oppressive, and so on) but undoes the very constitution of relating *as* power. Desisting from power qua power, forcework undoes the very operation of "(re)making" that is intrinsic to any manifestation of power, whether dominating or empowering. What is "radical" about this transformative forcework is the possibility of a shift in the very nature of relationality, a change of an entirely different order, as it were, from changes *within* the (metaphysical) relationality of being as it operates in terms of power. While the latter changes may alter the balance, circulation, or even meaning of power, they do not desist from power as such or call it into question. Even though such changes are often very significant, both ethically and politically, they reconstitute, metaphysically speaking, being as power. The verbs "resist," "contest," and "oppose," used here, are ultimately inadequate for describing forcework's relation to power, because they are intelligible only and already within the discourse of power. Still, I use them to accentuate the crucial point that the power-free disposition of force relations "counters" power not by changing its balance, form, or makeup but by desisting from and freeing from power. The condition of being power-free means that forces unfold without making, calculating, or being fleshed into power. It traces itself in a twofold manner: on the one hand, as the fragile trace of freedom—a freedom that remains "anterior" to the freedoms and rights of a subject or a person—already erased and forgotten by the power formation of being; and, on the other, as the silent, futural force of transformativity.

With the notion of forcework, I propose to radicalize the notion of art's critical force not only beyond the problematic of resistance and subversion but also beyond the idea of the negative as developed so powerfully in Adorno's *Aesthetic Theory*. In my reading, the transformative "unmaking" of power does not amount to power's negation, for negation and dialectics are always already in the grip of power. Adorno obviously realizes this, but the only way he can conceive of countering the complicity of dialectics with power is to arrest the dialectic in the negative. As a result, art comes to play the role of the negative imprint of what society lacks, that is, freedom, but only to the extent that it presents an image of the nonexistent reconciliation. Fearing that rationalized discourses of modern society, including aesthetic theory, always distort what art discloses as semblance into an affirmation, and thus into an implicit acceptance of the status quo and complicity with power, Adorno emphatically maintains art in the negative: art denies dialectical completion and (false) progress. As such, art becomes the figure of the nonidentical, carrying the utopian trace as the "negative" of social domination and uniformity. I propose to radicalize this negativity further here, and to see art's critical force, after Heidegger and Blanchot, beyond the negative (and thus also beyond the affirmative, which Adorno denounces as the domination of the nonidentical). What makes possible this rethinking of radical nature and critique beyond negation is Heidegger's notion of the event (*das Ereignis*), which works on a nondialectical notion of the negative as nihilation. As Heidegger writes in *Hegel*, dialectical negativity is metaphysical in its origin and operations, which means that it is based on the understanding of being in terms of beings, objects, and presence. As such, negation comes to signify a not-being, the negative or the absence of (a) being.[38] Heidegger argues that such negation derives from its unthought "origin": from the negative as the nihilation of the ecstatic temporality of the event, which exceeds the optics of presence/absence and affirmation/negation. Ecstatic temporality is the refusal of grounding; it is the "abysss" (*Ab-grund*), which, as the nihilation intrinsic to being, makes possible differentiation and consequently negation and affirmation. As the refusal of grounding, nihilation is the "highest guarantee" of the need for differentiation and decision,[39] and thus also of the possibility of critique and transformation. Desisting from the very operation of grounding, nihilation transpires as a continuous undoing and critique. Neither immediate nor indeterminate, the force of nihilation allows difference and determination to be put into play in the first place. Unlike in Adorno, where the negative as determinate negation works as the guarantee of the inassimilability of the nonidentical to the overpowering machinations of reason, in Heidegger's thought it is the nihilating force intrinsic to temporality, understood as ecstatic (that is, as instantiating and rupturing the play of the three dimensions of time), that mandates difference and nonidentity "prior to" any affirmation or negation. While negation and affirmation are always already involved in the play of power, the event's force of nihilation opens up a (spatial-temporal) dimensionality in which relations transpire as power-free.

The forcework in the work of art instantiates such an event, whose nihilating momentum is other than power and thus prior to the dialectic of negation and affirmation. To say that forces in the artwork become redisposed means that they are allowed to unfold, with the nihilating force of temporality, into a power-free event. It is in this specific sense that forcework as an event is "more" radical than negation, since it makes differentiation and thus negation, too, possible. The event's rupture is neither immediate nor mediated because it constitutes the opening up of the very site of emergence, difference, and decision, where mediation becomes possible in the first place.[40] The refusal of grounding that is intrinsic to forcework is also the refusal of and desisting from power: not a negation of power but a "nihilation" that evacuates power. In the event, to put it simply, being is nihilation (intrinsic to temporality) and not power, representation, mediation, knowledge, negation, and so on. The radicalism of art is the radicalism beyond a yes or a no, the radicalism of finitude and nihilation, the transformative force rising from nonpower opened up in the event. As power-free, forcework's transformative momentum opens up relations "prior to" their differentiation and determination in terms of power (and powerlessness). The notion of nonpower allows us to think of art's forcework beyond the notions of semblance and utopia, beyond the idea that what art displays as missing in social praxis constitutes the blueprint for the possible, yet nonexisting, change. For me, forcework *is* the space where practice becomes redefined beyond its governing optics of power. As I indicated earlier, this transformation is not limited to interaction with art but, as an altered praxis, becomes extended into modes of being-in-the-world. This altered praxis, beyond action, is a different, nonproductionist, power-free "force" (both senses are implied in Heidegger's adjective *machtlos*: disencumbered from power, and thus free of the productionist drive), a comportment that does not "make" but "releases" from the power-driven forms of representation and knowledge. Both forcework and its reenactments remain beyond negation and affirmation, beyond power and powerlessness.

As the negative of power, powerlessness is part of the broader logic of power, its verso, serving the same intensifying momentum. Conflicts and antagonisms, within the optics of power, manifest as various instantiations of the logic of negation, opposition, and sublation, that is, as circuits in the flow of power. What drives such conflicts—never truly resolvable, since they keep magnifying the very logic that produces them in the first place—is the momentum directed toward the increase of power through multiple plays of negation and affirmation: either by affirmation (of difference and its "negative" power to resist assimilation) or by negation (of the difference into a sublated, new state of affirmation). Thus neither negation nor affirmation escapes the logic of power's increase. Enhancement, as distinguished from increase (see the earlier discussion), signifies a change in the valence of force, a change that allows what is other to be "more in being" (*seiender*) as what it is: the other. Stein's notion of "intense existence" is not a simple affirmation of being, which disregards difference and conflict and thus effaces the nonidentical. On the contrary, it so "enhances" or radicalizes the difference—of everyday objects, situations, words, and so on—that their difference is neither a matter of affirmation nor one of negation, neither a reassertion of power nor an acknowledgment of powerlessness. Stein's language does not "negate" the power of grammar, meaning, comprehension, narrative, and the like, nor does it simply affirm the heterogeneity and plurality of differences flowing through the experiential/discursive field. (One could say here that the negative still instantiates power: the power of the nonidentical to remain the nonidentical, the power of objects to resist the gaze of representation, and so on.) Rather, it unfolds language beyond the dialectics of power. What I mean is that in Stein's works, the difference that is "spreading," as the opening section of *Tender Buttons* tells us,[41] is the difference of letting be—a transformation (or radicalization) beyond affirmation and negation. Indeed, one way to describe Stein's idiosyncratic language would be as a strategy of releasing words, phrases, sentences, and thus sense and things represented in the play of signification, from the power of forming the event into representation, meaning, or knowledge. But this release does not function as a negation of the above, as a way for Stein's texts to maintain their play as nonidentical in relation to power—which often ends up being (mis)read, "dialectically," as either subversive and highly resistant or, conversely, as disengaged and complicit, a reaction that captures in a nutshell the problem of understanding the relation of radical aesthetics to power. In Stein, the conflict implicit in the notion of difference—say, between a definition of the word "umbrella" and Stein's reworking of it in *Tender Buttons*, between knowledge/representation and "intense existence"—is taken to a new level, where the momentum of negation is broken with, and where the very idea of "critique" is redefined. Since it operates beyond critique, resistance, and negation, forcework transforms the momentum of power, turning power's logic into freedom from negative and affirmative, that is, into the power-free momentum of the event.

2

Ars Technica: From Futurism to Internet and Transgenic Art

The Technicity of Power

At stake in contemporary art is the question of power—not domination or oppression, or even subversion of the various forms of power/knowledge that regulate social praxis, but the possibility of a turn in power, which would open up the space of nonpower. Such a shift in the momentum of globally intensifying power is initiated in art by forcework, that is, by a redisposition of forces, which, calling into question the productionist impetus of modern relations, allows forces to assume in art valences no longer suffused with or augmenting power. Approached by way of forcework, artworks take on social relevance without necessarily having to deal explicitly with or portray a social problematic, for their importance for praxis is not in thematic critique or even in formal subversiveness but rather on the level of force relations, where artworks not only intervene or interrupt but also recode relations—rewire the connections, so to speak—and make it possible for the same forces that, within the social domain, are always already formed "in the image" of power, and *made* (that is, manipulated, calculated, and produced as) part of its intensification, to occasion a different force field. This distinctive force field, regulated by aphesis and not by power, I described in the previous chapter in terms of "nonpower" or the "power-free." But how are we to understand this peculiar sense of freedom, which comes from the transformative aphesis, and which, when conceived of on the level of force relations, that is, as operating as a work or a field, cannot be confined to matters of personal or political freedoms, which themselves remain moored to the metaphysical notions of the subject, of individual or group agency, of (counter)power, and so on? The statement that this is a "deeper," ontological dimension of freedom, while correct, does not communicate the modality in which such freedom, opened up by art's forcework, operates. The field of such freedom, that is, an expanse of nonpower, has to be traced in relation to the essentially technical character of both the operations and the forms of modern power. To put the matter differently, the question of the possibility of a power-free mode of relating, as instantiated in art, brings us face to face with the problem of technology, of the technoscientific organization of the modern world, and, above all, of the technicity of power. That is why the question posed in this chapter is whether the work of art is explainable in terms of technicity—namely, whether its forcework is another instance of the technowork that today regulates our reality on the global scale.

The idea of the technicity of power is obviously linked to continuing rapid developments in science and technology, to the global operations of biopower and information technologies, and to the unprecedented scale  of manipulation possible in today's world, from macroeconomics to microgenetics. Yet the intrinsic technicity of modern power is not to be confused with the power of technology; as powerful, commanding, and influential as technological discoveries and instruments are, the technicity of power refers to something else. It bespeaks the very modality in which power in contemporary society flows through institutions and forms of relations and regulates and mobilizes them toward further increases in power, both in reach and flexibility. After Heidegger and Foucault, the term "power" denotes the fluid array of modern productive technologies of power based on disclosure, ordering, and normalization. Power is, therefore, not a *what* but a *how*: a modality or, better yet, a disposition, that determines the value of relations among beings and phenomena in terms of production and manipulation, thus giving this relationality a distinctive momentum: an overall intensification of power. Seen this way, power circulates through different aspects of being and through various modes of relation, and this diffusion and circulation of power reflects the fact that everything that is—things, events, experiences—comes to be what it is through an accelerating mobilization of its being toward the increase of power. Even production and self-creation come to serve this escalation of power, understood here as the defining momentum of modernity. In other words, power signifies a complex and shifting interlace of articulation, production, and mobilization, whose flexible circuits can absorb even forms of resistance and challenge to power structures and can rearticulate them as sites of a further magnification of power. In this distinctive sense, modern power produces itself as a certain technology, or, to distinguish it from the instrumental conception of technology, as technicity or technics, whose fluid and expanding organization reflects the intensification of power itself.

The term "technicity" does not refer to what we commonly know as technology, whether by that word we mean modern production paradigms, instruments, and technologically produced objects, on the one hand, or technological know-how, on the other. Rather, technicity is what makes technology, in the usual sense, possible. Heidegger defines technicity as a mode of revealing, a certain manner of disposing or "tuning" (*stimmen*) relations, which tends to disclose what *is* as intrinsically calculable and as an available resource. Conceived in this way, technicity is the "power" that determines the scope and modality of relations in modernity. Technicity is to be thought of, not in terms of specific types of relations or paradigms, but in terms of the power that effects, that is, brings into being and determines, the very forms that relationality takes. It refers, then, to the disposition of relations, to the technowork that determines the shape of being, experience, and history in modernity specifically as forms of power, where power is no longer understood as domination, manipulation, or even production. Instead, the issue of power has become much more important and complicated, since it now concerns the way in which power comes to constitute the very form that beings and their relations take. When beings come to be disclosed as "resources," natural, mineral, human, or otherwise, it means that they are constituted in their very essence *in terms of power*, that is, as intrinsically disposed toward being manipulated and (re)produced and thus articulated as part of the general flow of power, or, in other words, as preprogrammed to take a form or a value that "makes" them what they are by virtue of "making" them participate in the intensification of power. Earth is disclosed as, in essence, a "standing reserve" (*Bestand*) of resources, there to be exploited by human beings, while those very same human beings are themselves also determined in the first instance as a resource in the global economy, as both producers and consumers. Beings and the relations between them are disclosed as intrinsically measurable, gauged in terms of their productive value, even when it comes to consumption, which is nothing more than the "production" of (the need for) further production.

Recent gains in genetic and information technologies have rapidly increased the possibilities for both productive and manipulative deployments of power. Heidegger's term *Technik* (technicity) indicates that modern power operates as an array of various technologies, in the manner that we know from Foucault's writings, but also reveals these modern modalities and circulations of power as technicist, namely, as producing being as inherently manipulable: "predisposed" to calculation, reworking, and digitization. Such technicity of being makes it possible to categorize experience and social relations in terms of efficiency, commodification, and exchange. The abstraction of modern social relations that Adorno decries in his writings is technicist in essence: it dominates by rendering everything transparent in terms of calculability or informational content. Even when it appears to multiply differences, as in today's "multicultural" world, technicity is characterized by a tendency toward equalization of differences, exchangeability, and convertibility, whose most recent incarnation is the Information Age, with its increasing capability, desire, and need to digitize everything, and thus to turn being into a global, continuously modifiable and expandable data bank. In this context, virtual reality becomes the virtual presentation of absolute control over the "essence" of what is, and a simultaneous disclosure of this essence as computable, digitizable, and, as such, programmable in principle.

In our reflection on the present state of technicity, we need to modify some of the terms that Adorno, Heidegger, and Foucault have used to diagnose it in their work: calculability has become computability; manipulability or instrumentality is now programmability; enframing has turned into formatting, mainframing, and Internetting; and resources and standing reserves have become data banks. Finally, technicity itself has become digitality, disclosing the contemporary world as the unstable, global flow of information. If technicity, in Heidegger, refers to such a coming into being, which discloses beings as intrinsically subject to calculation and ordering, digitality goes deeper, as it were, revealing the essence of what is as digitizable in its structure, transferable to the realm of the virtual, and open to reprogramming. Ecstatic invocations of the new world, freedom, and prosperity in the computer age, for all their truth, have to be taken with a grain of salt. It is undeniably true that electronic media, the Internet, and cyberspace have given us unprecedented freedom of access to information, new channels of expression, and ease of contact and exchange. Yet this fresh freedom is bound—dialectically, as Adorno would probably like to say—with unprecedented scope and exercise of power. While the cybernetic age has introduced a certain sense of fluidity, multiplicity, and fiberoptic speed into daily reality, it has also, and in a clearly unprecedented way, disclosed being as manipulable and programmable in essence. There seems to be nothing on this earth, or elsewhere, whose informational code, whether genetic or virtual, cannot be cracked open and reprogrammed. With the coming of the digital age, the control, reach, and saturation of power have simultaneously been extended to global proportions, penetrated to the microscopic level of genetic codes, and produced a new cyberspace mirror of reality. The freedoms that we enjoy via cyberspace are predicated on the ability to organize and digitize, that is, to convert experience, materiality, and being into a digital format. While there are clearly multiple forms of power, both creative and restrictive or negative, the fundamental conduit that renders modern being into increasingly intensifying power, power that belongs to no one and yet "powers" everything and everyone, can be described as digital. Since "to be" means today to be disclosable as, in essence, information, that is, as a code, this inherently digital disposition of being, its inclination to become convertible to digitized information and its systemic manipulability, produces modern being as saturated by power on microscopic levels. In the end, we no longer have a Platonic essence but a modern, informational one: our being becomes reducible to electronic impulses, data, and digital inscriptions. What is not convertible to information and mobilizable for the sake of power therefore appears as somehow deficient, undefinable, and lacking in being. This is why, in spite of the controversies that erupt here and there, art strikes us, especially the up-and-coming computer generation, as more and more unreal or simply as ideology.

The contemporary digital form of technicity, by disclosing everything as analyzable as information in its microelemental structures, and thus as intrinsically predisposed toward manipulation, reprogramming, (re)linking, and (re)transmitting, has allowed power an unprecedented sweep, agility, and, consequently, intensity. The accent in the operations of technicity falls on the "re-," which marks the susceptibility of being, in the Information Age, to potentially endless repetition and machination. Digitality, then, is the contemporary "mode" of power, its instant flow, fiber-optic transmissibility, and global linkage. Power, having enmeshed the "real" world with its circuits, has now colonized a new territory of virtuality, a supralayer of linkages, relays, and unprecedented velocity. Since power, in the cyber realm, is both more agile and more flexible, it is only "logical," in accordance with the logic of power, that this dimension should become increasingly important, perhaps eventually assuming the rank of the "real" world, that is, the world where power is at its most efficient and thus "truly" what it is.

To the extent that power is equivalent to technicity, the question that the work of art poses in this context is whether and how, in a world saturated by power at its microlevels and on a global scale, nonpower can be instantiated. What needs to be thought about is whether nonpower is thinkable within the flexible matrix of technicity or whether it marks a critical turn within it. To pose the question another way, is the forcework enacted by artworks merely another instance of the malleable operations of technicity, an aesthetic technowork, or does the work of art constitute a site of a radical reworking of the technicity of power?

The Avant-Garde's Technologic

This question is not new, for, as I argued in *The Historicity of Experience*, the early-twentieth-century avant-garde was already fascinated, framed, and riven by it. Breaking with the widely accepted notion that the avant-garde is unequivocally "for" technology and scientific culture, I showed that the problem of art's confluence with modern technicity is posed explicitly as the critical issue in the avant-garde, that it underlies, for instance, Dadaism and, in particular, Duchamp's work in the readymades. To this extent, the avant-garde is still important for us, perhaps even increasingly so, as our society becomes more and more technological, as the technicity that underwrites and coordinates its praxis becomes even more taken for granted and "invisible," for the avant-garde in its fascination, often intoxication, with technology becomes the very question of whether art is a form of technowork, an extension of technopower, or an autonomous and different "work," which interrogates the categorial determinations of modern being as technicist. In this way, the avant-garde allows us to keep thinking of technicity *as* a question and therefore to keep it *in* question.

Clearly, there is a pronounced tendency in certain avant-garde quarters toward an unequivocal intensification of being as a form of power, visible in particular in Italian Futurism, where being becomes expressly technicist in just this sense of mobilization. At the same time, though, there is a different current in the avant-garde, whether in Dadaism or in Gertrude Stein's writings, which takes us toward another sense of intensity, as disarticulation and release from power-oriented, technological production, and toward freedom. This current of the avant-garde represents the possibility of a turn within technicity, an arena where the technological determination of being in modernity comes sharply into view, becomes rapidly intensified but also, in the midst of this mobilization, begins to turn against itself. Side by side with the diverse political entanglements of the avant-garde "isms" and their fascination with power, what discloses itself in their artworks and proclamations—for instance, amidst the non sequiturs and contradictions of Tzara's manifestos—are forms of relationality that can be called "dispowered" or "power-free." "Dispowered" here does not refer to a utopian existence but to a turn within technicity toward relations that remain incalculable and "unworkable" and that disarticulate the very paradigm of production as the formative force of modernity. In this context, the disarticulacy of power describes an active sense of relating between forces, an event not only beyond domination but also beyond the production paradigm. Power-free occurrence signifies, therefore, neither powerlessness nor obliviousness to forms of power but rather an inversion of the technological and production paradigms that determine the history of being.

In the previous chapter, I showed that forcework constitutes the force of art, that is, its specific capacity for reworking the categorial determinations of reality into a transformative event. But this force is, in a certain way, distinctive of modern times, since the specifics of what makes up art's forcework become discernible only against technicity's determining of modern reality. The problem of the intensification of being arises as the central issue for the avant-garde movements and becomes multiply reflected in their complicated relationship to the aesthetic tradition, technology, and political power in modern society. A quick glance at the rhetoric employed by avant-garde manifestos and writings reveals a clear fascination with what might be called an intensification or radicalization of being, seen as the determining factor of modernity. This interest in the intensification of existence is reflected in some of the emblems of radical aesthetics: speed in Futurism, the "Dada" intensity and illogic of life in Dadaism, dreamscapes in Surrealism, the distorted and exaggerated imagery of Expressionism or, as already mentioned, the "intense existence" of things in Gertrude Stein's writings. What often remains ambiguous is the direction of such intensification and the role that art comes to play in disclosing it. Does such intensification result in an enhancement of being, a certain burst of nonpower or freedom, in which the other is "let be" more *as* other? Or, as is often the case, particularly in Italian Futurism, does this intensification instead produce a mobilization of being, an increase of power, that releases the destructive element within force, which is all too easily mistaken for transformation, as happens, for instance, in Marinetti's aesthetic glorification of the purifying power of war?[1] Examples of such increase or mobilization of force are numerous in modernist aesthetics; perhaps one of the most vivid is the machinist aesthetic of the Russian Proletcult poet Aleksei Kapitonovich Gastev. Borrowing from the machinist aesthetic of Constructivism and Berlin Dada, Gastev merges organic and technological imagery to produce a machinist aesthetic within which all forces become mobilized for the purpose of social engineering, producing an aesthetic blueprint for "the formation of the future world and the man who inhabits it."[2]

The distinction between intensification as enhancement and intensification as increase or mobilization may help us account in part for the complex alliances between some avant-garde movements and artists with totalitarian politics. At the same time, this distinction illustrates on what level avant-garde aesthetics can remain resistant to the formation of relations in terms of power. I am less interested here in tracing historical connections than in examining the conceptual junctures at which the aesthetic forcework of Russian and Italian Futurisms, often at the time in the 1920's when those movements themselves were no longer really in existence as artistic orientations, seemed to become coextensive with the political, if often aestheticized, mobilization of force, characteristic of the engineering of society in National Socialist Germany and Soviet Russia. There is a common thread that runs through radical modernism and the political "revolutions" of this period: the conjunction between revolutionary change and a certain radicalization or intensification of being. It may be somewhat less pronounced in political ideologies than it is in avant-garde artworks, but it is nevertheless easily detected there as well. The racist vision of Germany in National Socialism, or the Fascist rearticulation of Italy and even Maurras' idea of fascist Europe operate on the principle of strictly defining and intensifying a certain mode of being. They all constitute versions of identity thinking, which produces the fiction or the myth, as Philippe Lacoue-Labarthe and Jean-Luc Nancy refer to it,[3] of a strong, pure identity, which sustains itself by excluding or suppressing what remains different and other. To effectively accomplish such a mobilization, as Foucault points out in his analysis of fascism, fascist ideology joins the "ancient" idea of power, as the law of blood, to modern technologies of disciplining and normativity: "Nazism was doubtless the most cunning and the most naïve (and the former because of the latter) combination of the fantasies of blood and the paroxysms of a disciplinary power."[4] The modality of relations at work in such a mobilization is that of increase, in which the total body of a nation and its identity become constituted through disciplining and forming all its members in accordance with the "national" norm, thanks to which each individual in turn becomes empowered, is given a "forceful" identity. If technicity operates with a view to global mobilization of reality as a resource, in fascism such operations have a national or racial base. In both cases, forces become disposed with a view to an increase in power, and power explicitly constitutes the aim of such mobilization. While enhancement lets what is other be more in being, intensification as increase of force, in conjunction with identity thinking, can produce national or racial essentialism (biologism) and can lead, through technological disciplining and norms, to the fashioning of aesthetic-organic totalities capable of exercising, on an unprecedented scale, a form of what Foucault would call biopower, or a disciplinary power over life.[5]

Both options, enhancement and increase, are at work in many avant-garde movements, but they come to a particularly interesting and complex articulation in Futurism, even though Marinetti often blurs the distinction between them, collapsing the liberating rupture into the affirmation of power. When Marinetti, in the 1920's and 1930's, identified his idea of

Futurism with aspects of Fascism, the ambiguity and possibility of two different kinds of disposition of forces seemed to disappear from Futurism: the "revolutionary" thrust of Futurism was no longer directed toward enhancement of being but aimed at its mobilization into those forms of power that we know as fascist. We have to remember, though, that by that time Futurism no longer existed in the shape it had in the early 1910's, and that its radical aesthetic rupture was largely confined to the years before and during World War I. As Giovanni Lista argues at length in his recent study *Le Futurisme*, Marinetti's nationalism had its roots in the nineteenth-century Italian movement of Risorgimento, and his firmly anticlerical idea of national unity found its expression in the notion of Futurism, understood as a complex cultural revolution aimed at radically changing and modernizing Italian society in ways similar to those in which Futurist artworks revolutionized art and aesthetics. Thus, even with respect to the 1910's, Marinetti's nationalism should be distinguished from the conservative positions advocated by the Nationalist Party. It also needs to be remembered in this context that Marinetti always advocated an international, even transatlantic conception of the avant-garde, inclusive of various orientations and aesthetics aimed at revolutionizing modern art and culture. Equally significant for understanding Futurism is the fact that Marinetti's bellicosity and his form of nationalism, whose subsequent differences from and confluences with the emerging Fascist movement Lista carefully examines, were opposed almost unanimously by the other artists in the movement, who had largely leftist and anarchist leanings.[6] In effect, any simple identification of Futurist art with the glorification of war is historically inexact and simplifies beyond recognition the complex Futurist aesthetics of dynamism, depriving it of its most radical avant-garde momentum. An examination here of the complexities of force relations within the Futurist rupture, of the tensions and alliances between art and technology as they took shape within Futurist aesthetics, allows us to flesh out more concretely the possibility of distinguishing forcework from the technowork of modern power, and to make this distinction pivotal for thinking about art's alternative force.

There is a two-pronged desire in Futurism: to make art technological, to make it speak the dispassionate, mechanical language of technical inventions; and, conversely, to render technology artistic, to have it acquire the vitality of life and the vibrancy of art. A quotation from Mari-

netti's 1912 "Technical Manifesto of Futurist Literature," which he frames as a dictation he took from a plane propeller while flying over the chimney pots of Milan, provides a good illustration of this tension: "We want to make literature out of the life of a motor, a new instinctive animal whose general instincts we will know when we have learned the instincts of the different forces that make it up."[7] What "dictates" modern literature, what it should listen to and follow, is the rhythm or the life of the machine. Getting fresh energy and guidance from technology and the new forces it brings into existence, modern art should destroy the *I* or the subject in art, "to substitute for human psychology, now exhausted, the lyric obsession with matter."[8] Interestingly, technology is not opposed to nature or human subjectivity but supersedes them, takes into itself their forms of life and reformulates them into a thoroughly modern, technic organization of forces. Marinetti presents the motor on which Futurist literature is to be modeled as a new animal, a force that, although different from natural forces, acquires a "biological" dimension of its own, a technological life, so to speak, with new kinds of instincts and powers.

Such examples of the animization of technology in Marinetti's manifestos could easily be multiplied, which suggests that, consciously or not, underneath the insistent rhetoric of the glorification of technological progress, these texts approach technology beyond the worn-out oppositions of nature and culture or nature and technology. This "naturalization" of technology in Futurism is never just a reflection of the modernist mixture of the modern and the antimodern, the technological and the natural—for instance, the simultaneous fascination with technology and with Russian and Asian folk tales and myths in Velimir Khlebnikov's work—which later became so characteristic of fascist aesthetics.[9] In Futurist texts, technology signifies more than the technoscientific revolution and its effects on the modern world, since it points also to a new force, or, better, to a new disposition of forces across both the natural and the cultural-historical spheres. Underneath the often childlike fascination with technological inventions and gadgets, underneath the "automobilism" for which Wyndham Lewis so forcefully chided Marinetti, Futurist works begin to draw out a new, unprecedented understanding of the mobilizing, disciplining, but also transformative, impetus of technology. Ultimately, it is not just the question of modern dynamism, or of technological imagery and vocabulary, that gives distinctness to the Futurist preoccupation with technology. In fact, Futurism provides a glimpse of something like the technicity that Heidegger sees as the force of revealing, which is constitutive of being in the modern world. When Marinetti suggests depsychologizing literature, he wants to substitute a lyric (poietic?) preoccupation with matter for the idea of expression, which implies that Futurism never simply idealizes technology but sets out to reformulate both the natural and the social world in terms of a certain technicity and dynamism of forces. As Lista argues, "Carrà, Boccioni, and Russolo want to evoke the live intensity of the phenomenon, even its emotional and lyrical dimension, and not just devote themselves to a simple optical reconstruction of movement."[10] Futurist dynamism never simply foregrounds the intensity of movement and the speed of modern life with its multiplying technological inventions but discloses the vitality inherent in phenomena. The intensification and acceleration of experience brought about by technology reveals being in both its "natural" and "produced" realms as essentially a field of energy, as vibrations of forces. Understanding phenomenality in terms of force fields leads Futurist painters toward a denial of the fixity, materiality, and limits of objects, in the name of a continuous flux of being. Their paintings aim toward an abstraction motivated not merely by painterly considerations but also by an attempt to reflect being as an "abstract" configuration of the relations and pulsations of forces beyond their momentary, and illusory, immobilization into things and phenomena.[11] Thus, in Futurist art, technology brings out the technic dynamism, the energy field, intrinsic in being. In Lista's words, it materializes the infravisible by reconstructing optically the becoming of form in space.[12] For Futurism, in the end, nature—itself a form of technē and an intensification of forces—is as technic as technology and modern social praxis. One of the corollaries of this approach is the critique of anthropocentrism, that is, of the central role and power of the human subject conceived as the master of being. Technicity, which manifests its force in the triumphs of technological progress, functions for Marinetti as a release from the "binds" of the human subject and his domination of the world, as an opening onto a new "numerical sensibility" that would reflect the "universal vibration" of forces on the level of microrelations, "expressing the infinitely small and the vibrations of molecules."[13] Paradoxically, in Marinetti's manifestos, technology does not signify the culmination of human power but rather the recovery of an intrinsic technicity of being, of which humans, aspiring in their art to the mechanical, technic rhythm of being, become a part. Technology is not just a tool at the disposal of the human subject but an emblem of transcendence beyond the subject and the anthropocentric notion of being, and toward technicity conceived as the determining ground of modernity, its future, and its power.

It is therefore easy to paint a one-sided picture of Futurism as unequivocally embracing and propagating the blessings and revitalizing force of modern technology, and as insisting on an even faster and more radical reconstitution of art and life on the model of the overall technicity of being. One should not, however, downplay the internal ambiguity that both fuels and complicates this Futurist idea of technicity: is "futurist" art to be simply a reflection of technicity, which has already come to the fore in scientific discoveries and modern technologies, or is art itself supposed to perform such a reformulation of forces? Is art's forcework technic, a mobilization and maximalization of all forces, whether "natural" or "technological," or does it take the form of poiēsis, as the idea of "the lyric obsession with matter" seems to indicate? Very often Marinetti's texts tilt decisively toward what looks like a technic intensification of force, a production of a new futurist life of power, and yet these texts almost immediately counter themselves—for instance, when Marinetti proposes that poetry "should be an uninterrupted sequence of new images," which would infinitely forestall such a closure. Even as Marinetti's artistic manifestos concern themselves with revolutionizing art so that it might disclose the modern "life of matter,"[14] his polarized, simultaneously vitalistic and mechanistic rhetoric continues to raise the issue of whether modern life unfolds as a technic disposition of forces. The texts seem to leave open, almost in spite of themselves, the possibility that modern, "futurist" art can point to that volatile aspect of relating where forces could work as aphesis, where, instead of producing orders of power that determine "the life of matter" as a technologically calculable and available resource, they would "capture the breath, the sensibility, and the instincts of metal, stones, wood, and so on. . . ."[15] Marinetti's call for a machinist aesthetic aims, in fact, to reach beyond technology and science and to invert itself into a specifically artistic or poietic "grasp" of forces, into a new relation to the materiality of being: "matter whose essence must be grasped by strokes of intuition, the kind of thing that the physicists and the chemists can never do."[16] The way in which Marinetti's works gather and dispose forces does not ultimately form a technowork, for the logic it follows turns technicity inside out, strangely transforming it into a futurist "poiēsis" of matter. Giovanni Lista remarks that Futurist dance, in exalting "the impersonal and geometrical pulsations of machines," aimed not only to exclude human subjectivity but to dematerialize or "surmaterialize" experience, thus disclosing the rhythm of movements and forms, in a sort of an ontological dimension of dance linked to universal dynamism.[17] Marinetti's words-in-freedom behave like unsyntaxed forces and reflect a modern dynamic of being that cannot be grasped by technoscientific means. It is as though modern technology, whose praises he continuously sings, had participated in Marinetti's attempt to free being from the kind of technological mobilization of forces described earlier. Marinetti's futurist imagery contains that unmistakable moment when the "lyric obsession with matter" ruptures the increasing technologization of being, changes its vector, and gives it a new, nontechnic intensity. A parallel with certain aspects of Gertrude Stein's *Tender Buttons* and its "intense existence" of things seems unavoidable here.

Among Futurist literary forms, Khlebnikov's revolutionary transformations of literary language into *zaum* constitute a kind of culmination of the tension between the technic and poietic formations of forces. *Zaum* is the idea of an extended, "transrational" poetic language, generated by Russian Futurists, primarily Khlebnikov and Alexei Kruchenykh, but also practiced in somewhat different inflections by a lesser known poet, Iliazd (Ilia Zdanevich). *Zaum* is a compound composed of the Russian preposition *za* (beyond, behind) and the noun *um* (mind, reason), and indicates a space or a modality of thinking beyond reason or understanding. The adjective *zaumnyi* derived from this compound noun is often paired with the word for language, *yazik*, and has been translated as "beyonsense" language: a field of language in which relations take place otherwise than in the conventional sense, or beyond its scope. As practiced by Khlebnikov, *zaum* is a language in a different key, neither representational nor determinative. It is a language that becomes disposed, not with a view to the production of meaning and understanding in accordance with the dominant rules of sense, but with a view to transformation. In *Zangezi*, Khlebnikov's most complex work, the elements of *zaum* constitute a language of forces outside the play of signification, a language that spaces and builds relations: "Planes, the lines defining an area, the impact of points, the godlike circle, the angle of incidence, the fascicule of rays proceeding from a point or penetrating it—these are the secret building blocks of language."[18] *Zaum* describes, then, the temporal (non)ground of all relations, the event whose temporal "language" marks the openings of freedom in the midst of the finite materializations of history—the field of nonpower. In *Zangezi*, Khlebnikov recasts language so that its primary disposition, its *Stimmung*, if you will, becomes a nexus of transformative language relations, which keeps opening words, letters, and grammatical paradigms to combinations and inflections that remain foreclosed in normative language uses, including uses associated with aesthetic and literary conventions. To this extent, it is possible to see *zaum* as the exploration of the aphetic, releasing key of language, a beyond-rational discursive remapping of relations.

But, as in Marinetti, there is a strong countercurrent to this direction of *zaum*, a constant struggle in Khlebnikov's work to scientifically determine the forces of history and language, to give them a calculative, mathematizable form. His notorious calculations from *Tables of Destiny* attempt to construct, with the help of mathematical equations, a calculative picture of the temporal relations between the major events and forces of history, a kind of a calculus of being. Such a calculus, Khlebnikov leads us to believe, would be a version of *zaum*, a transrational *mathesis* of being and historical forces, a technicity beyond the scope of anything made possible by the technoscientific revolution. These calculations find their literary counterpart in a strain of Khlebnikov's linguistic speculations on the possibility of constructing what could be called a translingual language of alphabetic verities, a system of meaningful units recognizable across various languages: "The goal is to create a common written language shared by all the peoples of this third satellite of the Sun, to invent written symbols that can be understood and accepted by our entire star. . . ."[19] As idiosyncratic as Khlebnikov's mathematical and linguistic calculations may be, they articulate something of the ambiguously shifting and self-erasing internal divide between the two faces of technē. As Khlebnikov pushes the technē of his mathematical-historical and linguistic calculations toward what seems at times to be reminiscent of a Platonic, atemporal form of reality, its grand mathematicolinguistic equation, the makeup of forces that he brings into play changes from calculative to poietic. The calculations, the master patterns, and the language verities become retuned, thrown off into a different pitch by the unexpected reverberations and continuously transformative extensions of *zaum*. What emerges in *Zangezi* is a modern work of art constituted as intrinsically transformative, a work that embodies not aesthetic ideals or mathematical orders but the transformative force of temporality. Forces, in Khlebnikov—and his discourse about history and meaning in *Zangezi* is explicitly articulated in terms of forces—become composed into a transformational event of the *zaum* language, whose forcework is its ability to extend language and work beyond its technoinstrumental modalities.

Khlebnikov's inversions of technicity into artistic forcework are symptomatic of a much larger twentieth-century artistic phenomenon, known as radical, experimental, or avant-garde aesthetics. These aesthetic ruptures, which continue to reverberate today despite the often bland eclecticism of postmodern art and a powerful return of the realist aesthetic, should never be construed simply as a rebellion against worn-out aesthetic and literary conventions, for they also, perhaps even primarily, constitute a response to the parallel phenomenon of an increasing mathematization of being in modernity. The technic constitution of being finds its most powerful expression not in information technology but in the underlying determination of being as intrinsically "informatizable": the modern tele-electronic incarnation of "essence" as information. Anything can be transformed into, and its essence faithfully captured as, information because each being, occurrence, or phenomenon, natural or artificial, organic or inorganic, has an informational core, a kind of ontological genetic code. This "code" provides a blueprint for an intrinsically technic, orderable and manipulable, disposition of forces. I would argue that aesthetic "experiments" like Khlebnikov's concern the possibility of inflecting just such a technic disposition of modern reality, an attempt to unfold experience in the aphetic valence of its forces, which necessarily remain *za*, behind or beyond, their technic determinations. At issue is the disposition of forces, the *Stimmung* or pitch of experience and of what counts as real in it.

This explicit interest in presenting reality and reconceiving the space of representation in terms of forces constitutes perhaps the most characteristic feature of Futurism, which sets it apart from other avant-garde orientations. In one of the polemics between Italian Futurism and Cubism, the Futurists, responding to an attack that claimed the superiority of

Cubism in achieving pure, timeless representation, accused the Cubists of clinging to the idea of the object and continuing to paint a static, frozen, and motionless reality.[20] If Apollinaire's remark that Cubism attains a transcendence of time in a presentation of pure forms is correct, then Futurism would indeed constitute something of an opposite of Cubism, since its main preoccupation is the dynamic of the forces that constitute modern reality. Sometimes the Futurist representation of force remains on the literal level of portraying the dynamic of movement, as in Balla's painting of a dog in motion, in which the dog's legs reproduce the circular motion of a plane propeller in a way that resembles slow-motion photography. But in Umberto Boccioni's two versions of the triptych *States of Mind,* force is no longer just a matter of speed or physical movement but reflects the complex temporal dynamic of experience. It represents the Futurist idea of the complementarity of images, the interpenetration of the temporal and spatial planes and lines of forces, through which painters express the dynamism of matter.[21] Harking back to Impressionism, the triptych presents the force lines constitutive of modern reality by way of depicting the experience of a train station, one of the favorite modernist icons of technological revolution. The first version of the triptych is more fluid, and its repetitive and rhythmic articulation of lines, from the swirling lines in *State of Mind I: The Farewells* to the horizontal lines in *States of Mind II: Those Who Go* to the vertical, undulating lines in the third painting, *Those Who Stay*, produces what Butler calls "dynamic Impressionism."[22] The second version reintroduces some mimetic elements and uses abstract, Cubistlike planes and structures so that, as Boccioni comments, "the mingled concrete and abstract are translated into *force lines* and rhythms in quasi musical harmony."[23]

Even though Apollinaire claims that Futurist paintings, unlike the pure Cubist forms, remain bound to the idea of subject matter, Boccioni's triptych, rather than portraying a specific modern theme, that is, the train station, tries to present experience in terms of the flow of forces. What predominates in Boccioni's paintings are the force lines that figure the rhythm of happening, the coursing of force through the various modern "states of mind" or forms of experience, reflected through the prism of the train station. The title *States of Mind* appears to indicate a collective psychological experience of modern society but also has a transhuman connotation. Marinetti's call for depsychologizing art indicates that Futurism abandons individual or collective psychology for a portrayal of the modern disposition of forces, of the "matter" of modern existence. In Boccioni's triptych, the force lines that organize the representational space of the paintings flow through the contoured human figures as they do through the abstract and incomplete planes of the train, the platform, the rising steam, and so on. The kinetic arrangement of these lines suggests more than the celebrated dynamism of technological change, which the middle painting of the second version remarks in the prominent geometrical contour of the engine and its number: 6943. The dynamic these paintings bring forward is that of the temporalization of experience, which is certainly heightened and highlighted by the speed of modern life and reflected in its modernist emblems: trains, automobiles, and planes. But, like Marinetti's manifestos, *States of Mind* also raises the question of the disposition of the forces whose lines it traces: technological, social, psychic. The rhythm that metamorphoses through the paintings is, as Boccioni remarks, musical, and the force lines that choreograph their space impart intensity to the scene: they literally draw out and enhance the temporal contours of the event that the triptych describes. The German term *Stimmung,* which Heidegger uses to describe the disposition of forces in his comments on Nietzsche's notion of intoxication, indicates that enhancement should be understood in terms of a disposition or a pitch. Boccioni's comments point to a similar way of thinking about art in terms of how it "tunes" or disposes the lines of forces, of what kind of pitch force is granted in the artwork. As emblematic of modernity and technology as the train station is in modernism, Boccioni's force lines work in a different key, projecting "states of matter" that release or enhance what is: the forcework in his triptych instantiates not the mobilization characteristic of technicity but also aphesis. The differences between the shapes of the force lines in each painting, playing off the limited palette and often largely monochromatic tones of large sections of the paintings, suggest an intrinsic diversity of configurations. In each case, however, such diversity registers the rhythm of happening: a general disposition or type of relationality according to which specific forces—psychic, technological, social, artistic—unfold.

In Futurism of course, and in other avant-garde movements, there was a lot of enthusiastic and sometimes naive aestheticization of technology, which later easily spilled over into aesthetic glorification of the technological organization of modern life in totalitarian states, in the form of parades, mass rallies, militaristic discipline, monumental architecture, and gigantic labor projects. And the aesthetic and vitalistic pull of such a totalizing mobilization of forces into revolutionary "modern power" drew Marinetti to embrace fascism, as, on the other side of Europe, it led the early Futurist Vladimir Mayakovsky to become, at least for a while, a fervent supporter of Soviet Russia. The disciplined "marching" of Mayakovsky's verse, so different from his early poems in the way in which it tries to evoke the euphoria and pathos that accompanied the engineering of a new socialist Russia, can be seen as a reflection of that moment when the Russian revolution turned against its own emancipatory manifestations and began indiscriminately to mobilize everything into a giant resource for building a totalitarian state. What came with it, as was also the case later in fascism, was the elimination of avant-garde art, whose aesthetics the Soviets used to advertise their revolutionary transformation and spread their power across Russia. Because of this tangled aesthetic and political history, there will always be something problematic about Futurism, but problematic also in a "good" sense because Futurism problematizes the technicity of modern being itself and points toward the possibility of a different disposition of forces. To forget or simplify this ambiguity that traverses Futurism is to annul the most worthwhile aspect of this avant-garde movement. More important, it is to risk covering over the problem of the two faces of the intensification of force, which insistently signals itself through the belligerent Futurist rhetoric. This would mean foreclosing what seems to me a crucial point of entry into the problematic of modern art, of its historical raison d'être vis-à-vis the intensifying technicity of being in modernity. Without acknowledgment of this ambiguity, art often ends up represented as *forceless*—socially isolated and condemned, or forcefully and disingenuously kept alive as an expression of political critiques and aesthetic fancies.

This excursion into the aesthetics of Italian and Russian Futurisms brings to the fore the link between radical avant-garde aesthetics and forcework. The ambiguities that criss-cross Futurism, and its different manifestations in various European countries, reflect the fundamental equivocation still discernible at the heart of modern technology, that is, an equivocation recognizable, if often just barely, as the effect of art's forcework. This equivocation concerns the character of technicity as the contemporary modality of power, its mobilizing and intensifying momentum, and the possibility of a different forcework, which I have explained as aphesis, that is, as an interesting inversion of manipulation and making into a release and a letting be that allow relations to register as power-free. Futurism thus marks the possibility of thinking about the artwork otherwise than as technowork, and of designating an alternative momentum, which art grants to forces that otherwise would remain in-formed by power within social reality. This alternative impetus of avant-garde work becomes even more pronounced in the works of Dadaism, particularly in their emphasis on the tangibly nontechnicist form of the event that temporality assumes in them. The protohappenings, the nearly instantaneous configuration of Dadaist works that underscores the irreducible singularity of each moment, mark the eloquent force with which Dadaist art calls into question the calculative, globally connective, and desingularizing momentum of technicity. It is thanks to the avant-garde that we have this alternative to both the glamorization of technology and its opposite, demonization, which often produces a sentimentalized, naive escape from the operations of modern technopower. The avant-garde does not fall under either of those categories but instead maintains in its artworks, throughout the twentieth century, a critical and transformative tension between forcework and technowork.

The *Gesamtelewerk,* or the Avant-Garde in the Twenty-first Century?

The critical importance of the avant-garde lies in preserving, against the progressing saturation of all aspects of modern reality by technopower, the possibility of what I have termed an "aphetic forcework." The avant-garde forcework thus allows us to formulate the parameters of the question about art's role in an age when power in-forms being to such an extent that everything that *is* becomes disclosed in its microstructures as information, which is characterized by being analyzable, calculable, and repeatedly processable. Today power discloses its potency and elasticity as the informational structure of being, as the digital technicity of existence, where all that is has become intrinsically penetrable, comprehensible as information, and thus exposed not only to compression as data and to global transmissibility but also to seemingly boundless manipulation and reprogramming. The end of the last century saw an exponential quickening of the accessibility of information technologies and of their influence on the daily commerce of society. Art began to respond with comparable alacrity, swiftly extending beyond video- and computer-assisted art to enter the domain of the Internet and, most recently, genetics, and thus to establish new realms of aesthetic interactivity and transgenic art—potentially new fields for avant-garde activities. Though it is hard to evaluate these new directions opened for art by advances in information technologies, it is clear that the World Wide Web, in addition to providing a disseminating and interlinking function, has given art an unprecedented flexibility with respect to involving potential audiences not just in appreciation but, above all, in collaboration. Thus it is no surprise than most of what might go by the name of Web or Internet art, whether the Web projects of Seiko Mikami, Ken Goldberg, Knowbotic, Eduardo Kac,[24] or many other artists who construct their Web sites and programs either solo or through multiply expandable linkages with other artists and collaborators, has been—so far, at least—predominantly interactive in nature. Thus, for instance, the description of the virtual spider in Mikami's *Molecular Clinic* project on the Web places the emphasis specifically on the creative role of Internet viewers who also become the participants in the ongoing evolution of the cyberspace project:

> The SPIDER functions as an interface of cyberspace. Users can, from various angles, zoom in to view SPIDER on the molecular level; select an "atom" and download it, in the sense of peeling off a piece of skin, to one's own computer; and then users can move the transformed molecule back to its original place. Affected as they are by such manipulations, the body of SPIDER, as well as the whole space, are transformed.[25]

This is no doubt not just a new form of art but perhaps even an entirely new direction for art as a collaborative and interactive, rather than individual-oriented, medium. While it is too early to pass such judgment, it is important to keep this problematic of collaboration/partnership and interaction/participation as a key component of the critical optics for the barely emerging art of the twenty-first century. In basic terms, this "inter" orientation of new art has to do with the changing notion of agency, which implicates not just group or interlinked authorship but also open-ended and collaborative projects, often involving, as in the case of Mikami's *Molecular Clinic,* nonartists interested in art and even "accidental tourists."

Art thus becomes intrinsically opened not only to boundless accessibility and transmission but, above all, to random participation by unknown audience-artists. In its most interesting manifestations, as in Eduardo Kac's Web/museum project *Teleporting an Unknown State,* the Internet enables, in Kac's words, "a new sense of community and collective responsibility."[26] This "biotelematic interactive installation," as Kac calls it, became the venue where participants could access photons registered by cameras at remote sites and transmit them, via the Internet, to a gallery where a seed had been planted in a dark installation space. The teleported light was then re-emitted onto the seed by a projector, making possible the germination and slow growth of a plant. In this work, Kac set the parameters for a potentially Webwide audience, whose communal effort and coordination became indispensable to the plant's existence. With works like Kac's, or like Goldberg's *The Telegarden,* it becomes clear that never before has any medium allowed for such a wide scope, and such a degree of unpredictable interaction and modification, as has become possible with artworks installed on the Web, using programming that allows the audience to participate in the evolving artwork. Likewise, never has the line between reception and creation been so thin and easily crossed. No doubt these and other changes associated with art's going digital will call for new ways of thinking about artworks, reception, creativity, interpretation, and so on. Without playing the game of anticipation with regard to future directions of art, it is still possible, and important, to examine whether these quickly evolving parameters of art, in addition to allowing for the introduction of new artistic forms and the modification of traditional ones—for instance, "visual" Web poetry, with moving, disappearing, and flashing words[27]—are affecting the avant-garde problematic of art's relation to technicity.

Beyond the obvious expansion into animation, video, digital processing and programming, interactivity, and global linkage networks, the question is whether the relation of art to technology has undergone a substantial change since the days of the early avant-gardes and, further, how such a change affects the way in which we can (re)conceptualize contemporary art in its aesthetic and social dimensions. Through the last century, technology has expanded and evolved in evident ways; as I suggested in the previous section, technicity can now be thought of in terms of digitality, to underscore the expanded reach and elasticity of power flows and formations immanent to contemporary social praxis. And yet the momentum characteristic of technicity—intensification of power—has not changed; it has only increased its pace geometrically, a pace that has become reflective of the speed with which humans today calculate, transmit, and manipulate. Thus the question has, in many respects, remained the same: can art affect the power momentum of the society of which it is itself a product and in which it most often plays the function of an aesthetic object and/or commodity, and, if so, how can it do this? While it is impossible to quickly gain an overview of Web-fueled developments of art—this arena is, like the Web itself, simply too large and too rapidly growing and metamorphosing—some of the tendencies mentioned above are clear. Perhaps the most intriguing aspect of "Internet art"—it remains to be seen how viable this term will prove to be—and of the continuing opening of possibilities associated with the World Wide Web is the notion of a telematic artwork, a notion often linked with the tendency to resuscitate the old dream of the synthesis of art, of the notion of the total work of art. Inspired by Wagner, this notion of a new Web-based *Gesamtkunstwerk*, integrating not only various media but also artists and audiences, appears to represent one of the most prominent directions facilitated by the new technologies. This development should come as no surprise, since such an integrationist concept of the artwork stems directly from the unprecedented degree of interconnectedness and "real time" interactivity made available by information technologies, a concept that is both a product of and a new global circuit facilitating the increase of technopower.

To understand the relationship between the idea of the telematic artwork and the technicity of power, I propose to examine here the collectively produced Web document, revealingly titled *The Telematic Manifesto: A Hypertextual Collectively-Generated Net Document Organized by Randall Packer*, available at http://www.zakros.com/manifesto/index1.html. The manifesto has multiple links and becomes a labyrinthine text, impossible to survey here. The introductory page has eight hyperlinks, marked in red on a black background and titled as follows: DISEMBODY, which leads to AGENCY, which in turn branches into SYMBOL, AUTOPOIĒSIS, and ZERØ, with three additional links to the right, namely, MONADOLOGY, RHIZOME, and GESAMTELEWERK. This matrix of links leads to various interconnected pages generated either collectively or by individual artists and employing many quotations, paraphrases, and references to twentieth-century art. Two aspects of this hypertext are of particular importance for considering the relationship between contemporary art and technicity: the manifesto's claim to revitalize and recontextualize the ambitions of the avant-garde, and the idea of telematic art developed in the manifesto. The link called AGENCY guides one to the page that "advertises" the concept of telematic art as having collective agency, which inherits and rearticulates the radical aesthetics of the twentieth-century avant-gardes in the context of contemporary technological and communicational developments. The text I quote below is framed by quotations from El Lissitzky, Ma Group, Pierre Lévy, and Douglas Engelbart:

Telematic Art as Collective Agency for Cultural Transformation
Call-to-Action

The Telematic Manifesto is a participatory, collectively-generated Net Document that articulates a vision for the future of Telematic Art as a socio-cultural force in the twenty-first Century. This project investigates Telematic Art as the synthesis of art, culture, and global telecommunications, and its promise for a revitalized artistic expression resulting from an inherent interconnectedness catalyzing aesthetic, technological, philosophical, and cultural transformation.

The Telematic Manifesto recontextualizes the ideologies and ambitions of aborted avant-garde movements whose efforts to bring about artistic, cultural, and political change through collective action—from the Italian Futurists to the Surrealists, from the International Faction of Constructivists to Fluxus—lay dormant as unfinished business at the close of the Century.

History has also shown that the evolution of computer science has tended towards collective action: the dream of a free exchange of information and new forms of human and technological collaboration. From Norbert Wiener's seminal theories on the science of "Cybernetics" to J. C. R. Licklider's research in "Man-Computer Symbiosis," to Douglas Engelbart's creation of a networked information space designed for the "Augmentation of Human Intellect" that would "Boost the Collective IQ," these visionary scientists laid the groundwork for an emerging medium that is now transforming every aspect of human expression.

In an effort to define and engage these artistic, scientific, and cultural forces of change, the Telematic Manifesto serves as a conceptual framework articulating the collective, cross-disciplinary ideologies of a group of artists, theorists, critics, curators and scientists at the transition into the Millennium.

Throughout the ZKM Net_Condition exhibition, an email list and threaded discussion introduced a series of themes intended to frame historical, philosophical, technical and aesthetic issues surrounding Net Art. The email dialogue was uploaded daily into an automatized writing space/bulletin board viewable by exhibition visitors on the Web.

The resultant texts have been organized, archived and published as the Telematic Manifesto, a hypertextual, Web-based Net Document that provides a Millennial record and collective statement proclaiming the future implications of Telematic Art: its transformative properties, aesthetic issues, virtualizing forces, historical significance, and potential for generating a new artistic sociopolitical ethic in the broad context of a rapidly evolving networked culture.

Much like the avant-garde manifestos we know, *The Telematic Manifesto* is a call to arms, to the technological arms of the almost instant, real-time communication and transmission of information. The global networks of such transmission and communication become the interlinking grid for new collective aesthetic action, with social and historical implications. The manifesto advertises telematic art as the engine behind the new twenty-first-century art, which claims as its inheritance the "ideologies and ambitions of the aborted avant-garde movements," from Futurism and Dadaism to Fluxus, Situationism, and Pop Art. As was the case in Italian Futurism, *The Telematic Manifesto* testifies to the artistic desire to keep abreast of and develop the means of communication offered by the new technologies, looking toward the future in which experience is becoming changed by global and instantaneous relays of communication and interaction.

As the manifesto defines it, "To be telematic, is to be embedded within a network semiotic composed of abrupt information transfers and instantaneous, more or less, communications." And on another page: "Telematic can be understood as a reference to the popularization of cultural codes having to do with acceleration and the industrialization of perception, as described by Virilio. It is a rather poor indexical term for categorizing technology enterprise or anything else for that matter. Telematic is a descriptor to the function of language, not things." What constitutes the backbone of telematic art is the ability to communicate and interact in nearly real time, made possible, maintained, and developed by networks of telecommunications technologies. In other words, at the core of telematic art lies technicity in its most contemporary incarnations: information, telecommunication, global reach. As the second quotation indicates, the term "telematic" describes the "language" of this new art: not expression, representation, or meaning but the instantaneity of communication and interaction. What underlies much of the text of *The Telematic Manifesto* is indeed the notion of enabling communication in its global reach and instantaneous realization. The new telematic "workings" of art, as David Ross remarks, reopen the possibility for the telematic art form to be

> the harbinger of a set of radically innovative social structures and practices—all of which are within a set of technologies evolving at an unprecedented and unpredictable pace even in an age defined by its passion for velocity and unpredictability. It is an integral set of production and distribution tools directed by aesthetic propositions, varying from hyper-hermetic, ontological concerns to the overtly political, to the broadly comic and self referential. An art form evolving within a system that is so fully totalizing and global that it contains within it every other known mass medium on the planet.[28]

In his clearly optimistic picture, Ross may well be right that the telematic artwork can indeed become the harbinger of new forms of social praxis, with its emphasis on telecommunications speed and global distribution. Interestingly, though, the words that appear with notable frequency on the various pages of the Net manifesto are "global" and "totalizing." In fact, one of the pages goes so far as to propose that telematic art might become the total telework of the twenty-first century:

> Telematic Art: Gesamtelewerk for the Twenty-first Century?
>
> The Gesamtelewerk proposes a resurgence of the optimism of previous efforts to formalize the Gesamtkunstwerk (Total Art Work), to devise an integrated medium which blends all the arts and engages all the senses. Introducing telematics into the equation suggests an art that in addition seeks a global embrace, a collective vision to which the artwork, artist and viewer aspire. This aspiration has gradually [taken] form as a matrix of interaction in the wake of recent networked art: from the satellite works of the 1970s to the experiments in collaborative telematics of the 1980s to the emergence of Internet art in the mid-1990s. The latter is now advancing at a prodigious rate, forcing the establishment artworld to take notice of a rapidly developing new movement.
>
> Will Internet artists revive the hopes of previous avant-garde with the power to distribute their message instantaneously and globally?
>
> Does the notion of a *Gesamtelewerk* suggest the possibilities for social transformation resulting from forms of collective art that engage audiences through involvement, inclusiveness and participation?
>
> Can the *Gesamtelewerk* serve to defragment cultural separatism, specializa-

tion, and the isolationist tendencies within our institutions, encouraging rather a cross-disciplinary interaction between individuals in all fields and walks of life?

The questions asked here seem largely rhetorical, indicating, in fact, the revival of the hopes and ambitions of the twentieth-century avant-gardes, reenergized and strengthened now by the "power to distribute their message instantaneously and globally." Emblematically enough, this text appears between two columns of quotations, the two most telling ones in this context coming from Wagner (on the total work of art) and Deleuze (on rhizomatics). Without engaging here the question of whether rhizomatics might be compatible with the notion of *Gesamtkunstwerk*, one quickly notices the outspoken tendency toward globalization and totalization, much in agreement, one might say, with the trends in economy, capital, and power. I have no intention of downplaying the indisputable possibilities, on the aesthetic, social, and political levels, that Internet art appears to offer for the future. What interests me, however, is the extent to which the very concept of Internet art, its "essence" as a telematic work, implicates itself in the increasing technicity of contemporary being. When the manifesto claims that telematic art revitalizes the hopes and ambitions of the avant-garde, one might ask which ones: are we talking here about the increase of power (even the power to communicate, interact, cocreate) or about aphetic enhancement? In other words, what kind of forcework takes place in telematic art?

The terms employed by *The Telematic Manifesto* identify the work done by twenty-first-century telematic art specifically with its telematic character: instant interlinking, communication, and interactivity. What underlies such aesthetic telematics, then, is the power of information technologies, their global ability to link and communicate instantly. It is therefore not surprising that among the chief characteristics of the telematic artwork are globalization and totalization: a kind of absolute connectivity and inclusion. What seems to become, for the first time, possible in telematic art is a complete and total gathering of all differences, a kind of global inclusion. As thrilling as this possibility truly is, Adorno would most likely want us to examine the other side of the "web": the unprecedented reach and access of power on a global scale, an essential element in the planetary intensification of power. The Internet may be, paradoxically, the great dream of communication, but one in which links between all possible differences become frighteningly actual as the instantiation of the uncontrollable global expanse of power. The latter appears to be the reverse of the former. The telematic work triumphantly signals the revival of the Wagnerian dream of the integration of all art forms, now possible on an unprecedented scale and with instantaneous communication and even interactive input. But this dream seems to forget Nietzsche's warning about the manipulation intrinsic to the concept of Wagnerian artwork, the admonition so important to Deleuze, for the total—or, should we say, "global"—work of art appears to be the mirror image of the totalizing technicity diagnosed in the twentieth century by Heidegger, Adorno, and Foucault.

Interestingly enough, *Gesamtelewerk* loses *Kunst,* that is, art, from its makeup, emphasizing its other components: totalization, telematics, and work. This linguistic slip may indicate precisely that what is being eliminated from the telematic work is nothing less than art itself: art not defined aesthetically but understood in terms of forcework. There is a distinct possibility that in the telematic (art)work, the artistic merges without difference and thus disappears, as such, into the technical: art becomes indistinguishable from technicity. If the "essence" of telematic work is speed of communication and interaction, then it is just another instantiation of technicity. As such, it is capable, as Ross suggests, of developing new forms of social structures and practices, but such a praxis, Adorno would probably say, would be only a novelty and not truly anything new that could thus become critical of what has been. In other words, what telematic art may make possible would be proliferations of "new" forms, links, interactions, and so on, yet all these forms, even if nonexistent before, would be actualizations of an ever-expanding technicity and its increasing flows of power rather than a critique and negation of categorial determinations of social relations.

The analyses of Adorno and Raymond Williams have already diagnosed the merging of the aesthetic and the technological, evoked again in our different circumstances by telematic art, as characteristic of modernist art. Instead of the revolution that the avant-garde intended to bring about in the social domain, avant-garde aesthetics became incorporated, with time, into the mass commodification characteristic of late capitalism, which effectively closed the gap between *aisthesis,* or sensory experience, and use value.[29] In an effort to continuously create new demand and to supply ever more products, the practice of the culture industry is to erase the distance between *aisthesis* and use value, between aesthetics and consumption, since its products and marketing practices effectively assimilate avant-garde techniques to a whole range of mass-produced commodities. This progressive integration of the avant-garde into the very culture it has tried to oppose inevitably blunts the critical edge of radical aesthetics, turning the transformative avant-garde praxis into the parameters of consumer appeal. At the bottom of this assimilation of the avant-garde for the purposes of the intensification of commodity culture, as is already evident in Adorno's thought, are a certain technologization and instrumentalization that structure modern experience and form the practices of everyday life. As a result of the intensification of technicity, the shock and dislocation characteristic of avant-garde art has been subsumed and neutralized by the shocklike aesthetics of popular culture, which, especially with the advent of the new electronic media, has become the standard of what might be called the electronic paradigm of representation: multiple frames, mobile and constantly alternating advertising images, collagelike electronic surfaces, new and sometimes unexpected but always multiple hyperlinks. In such an electronic environment, dislocation, newness, and freedom of the unexpected become, paradoxically, inverted into the very principle of linking, of ever-increasing reach and interconnectedness. Difference, strangeness, and alienation become transformed into the obverse side of a global network of connections and relays and come to be used as the negatively energized engine of expansion and ever-nuanced marketability. It is no wonder, then, that the avant-garde, on the one hand, and telecomunications and popular culture, on the other, appear, in fact, as Williams suggests in *The Politics of Modernism*, as the two faces of the same modernism:

> Thus the very conditions which had provoked a genuine Modernist art became the conditions which steadily homogenized even its startling images, and diluted its deep forms, until they could be made available as a universally distributed "popular" culture.
>
> The two faces of this "modernism" could literally not recognize each other, until a very late stage.[30]

Radical Modernist art thus finds itself, against its own revolutionary impulse, complicit with the powers that be, at play in the technoinformational age. Doubts and dissatisfaction with the avant-garde, frequent proclamations of the death of the avant-garde, and the general inability to think differently about its art are symptoms of what Williams calls "the long and bitter impasse of a once liberating Modernism."[31]

Telematic art claims to reenergize, with the help of new technologies, the aspirations of the avant-garde and radical modernism, to recharge its drive toward transformation and the new. Yet the parameters of the telematic artwork, its "essential" telematic technicity, indicate that the new in the "total telematic art work" may end up being a quantitative addition rather than a qualitative change, for the telematic work understands transformation as the vector of new information technologies and electronic communications, as changes brought about through the widening scope of technicity rather than as a transformation in the very momentum of technicity toward the intensification of power. If this diagnosis were (unfortunately) correct, then telematic work would confirm the "corporate merger" of art with technology, of artistic technē with technopower. As such, it would also fuse avant-garde art with technology, erasing the tension between art and technicity that is so fundamental to avant-garde artworks, their fascination with technology notwithstanding.

In an interview published several years ago in *Le Monde,* the French performance and body artist Orlan made a remark that captures very well this trend in contemporary art and its relation to technological forms of power: "The avant-garde is no longer in art, it is in genetics."[32] In the interview, Orlan makes the case for locating the radical avant-garde momentum no longer in art, as was apparently the practice in the twentieth century, but instead in the latest developments in genetics and information technology, thus giving priority to recent genetic and telematic art. In other words, Orlan, reflecting, perhaps even magnifying, the sentiment implicit in *The Telematic Manifesto,* announces a certain sense of the end of art by postulating that art, in order to preserve any sense of radical momentum, has to merge with and follow technology. Despite Orlan's claim, there is, on one level, nothing new in her statement, granting, of course, the newness of the recently developed forms of genetically based or telematic art. As attested by the work of Eduardo Kac—for instance, his *GFP Bunny* (the acronym stands for "green fluorescent protein") or his more recent project, *The Eighth Day*[33] (which presents genetics as the eighth day of creation)—what we are seeing now is the next, undoubtedly radically innovative, chapter in the story that is at least as "old" as the early-twentieth-century avant-garde, which, in Francis Picabia's words, claimed the identity of art and technology, for the unspoken assumption underlying Orlan's statement says precisely this: poiēsis is technē, art is technology, the avant-garde is genetics. But in what sense, exactly, could one pose a sign of equivalence between art and technology? What makes Orlan's remark possible is the fundamental idea running through the history of art: that art is equivalent to making, that poiēsis is a form of production or creation. And if art is a genre of making, then the most radical and innovative form of making in modernity is technology, and, currently, genetics. Hence the conclusion becomes possible that it is in genetics, and not in art, that the contemporary avant-garde is located. It does not matter, ultimately, whether we examine the work of a Kac or of an Orlan from the point of view of "high" aesthetics or postmodernism, or in terms of the historical, material, and cultural situatedness of artworks; while those approaches remain recognizably different and bring to light distinct important aspects of art, what remains uninterrogated, in all those cases, is the fundamental idea, surfacing in Orlan's claim, that poiēsis works the way technē does: that what takes place in the work of art constitutes a form of making, production, or manipulation. This idea is a correlate of the broader notion that firmly links aesthetics to metaphysics and technology, namely, that being is, in its essence, preformatted for making, remaking, and manipulation. The correlation between being, conceived in this way, and the forms of technology developing in modernity constitutes the index of rapidly intensifying power as the emblem of modern civilization. Thus, in spite of the various claims made either by artists or by critics, of poststructuralist, postmodern, or cultural studies provenance, we have not really advanced, nor have we somehow radically improved on the horizon of questioning opened up by Heidegger and Adorno. Rather, what we are seeing, whether Information Age technology, the Internet, telematic art, or genetics and genetically based art, is a much more visible and palpable confirmation of the fundamental technicity at work at the basis of modern culture.

Undoubtedly, as Orlan suggests, contemporary art has to take account of the rapid transformation in genetic and information technologies and their effect on everyday life and culture, but this does not necessarily mean that art employing the most recent technologies—multimedia, informational, telematic, or genetic—is, by virtue of these technologies, somehow more important or avant-garde than more traditional forms of art—say, avant-garde poetry or music. Obviously, such new forms of art utilize recently acquired technologies to affect and transform experience, sensibility, and consciousness. Art has always used, and will use in the future, newly available materials, production processes, and technologies in constructing innovative forms of artworks that will be, for those reasons, unprecedented. Indeed, telematic and transgenic artworks undoubtedly change radically the way art is done, disseminated, and received, and our critical discourses have not yet quite caught up with the rapid changes such developments have been introducing into the world of art, literature, and, more broadly, into culture. *Aisthesis* in the broadest sense has been profoundly affected by them, and, as a result, aesthetics has been evolving as well, with new types and forms of aesthetic experience initiated by art that uses computer, Internet, or genetic technologies. Yet, though such technologies are new and unprecedented, their impact on art forms is, in a way, parallel to the manner in which the technologies of speed, film, recording, and radio revolutionized art and culture at the beginning of the twentieth century, producing the first wave of avant-garde manifestos, artworks, and performances, or the way in which video and computer programs influenced visual arts and music in the 1950's and 1960's. To put it very simply, technological novelties translate into new art forms and a variety of fresh and innovative aesthetic experiences. Thus, if we pose the question of telematic and transgenic artworks in aesthetic and technological terms, the answer will clearly be that such art is new and different, and that it uniquely expands and modifies the horizon of aesthetics, introducing—through interactivity, telematics, and genetic manipulation—creative and contemporary genres of aesthetic experience. And these new genres are absolutely critical to the further historical development of art and to the continuation of art's critical function in modern society. Similarly, theoretical and philosophical reflection on art and literature needs to keep pace with these developments to be able to understand if and how such new forms of art retain or alter the transformative force of art brought to the fore by the twentieth-century avant-garde. But this is also why it is insufficient to pose only in aesthetic and sociocultural terms the question of the new trends in contemporary art that are taking shape at the intersection of art with science and technology. Aesthetically and culturally, such art forms are historically transformative and innovative; yet the question of the transformative momentum of contemporary art needs to be asked on another level: are the works that employ new technologies, whether they involve multimedia, technoperformances, telematic, or genetic works, indeed transformative, not just of the aesthetic rules and cultural practices associated with art's function in society—almost always the case when new technologies, materials, or communication channels are employed—but of technicity itself, that is, of the ways in which relations and forces today tend to become increasingly disposed and formed into constellations of technopower? In other words, do the changes in the very forms of art introduced by telematic and genetic artworks also signify a turn in the technicist momentum of the relations that are formative of modernity?

Re-turning Technē

The distinction between novelty and transformation is the matter of art's forcework. In *Aesthetic Theory,* Adorno keeps gesturing toward the possibility of such a different, nonproductionist and violence-free forcework: "The critique exercised a priori by art is that of action as a cryptogram of domination. According to its sheer form, praxis tends toward that which, in terms of its own logic, it should abolish; violence is immanent to it and is maintained in its sublimations, whereas artworks, even the most aggressive, stand for nonviolence."[34] Both action and production, the cornerstones of social praxis, reflect in their operations the "secret" and deeply ingrained patterns of domination and violence subtending modern instrumental rationality. Thus any counteraction, if still exercised within the paradigms of power, simply rechannels and remaps domination without changing its overall principle of mastery. This is why the telematic call to action appears to be more of an extension and reformulation of the rapidly growing telematic technicity underpinning and structuring social practice. As such, it would carry over in its practices, no matter how new or innovative they become, the stamp of domination, for contemporary domination is exercised not so much by oppression as, in most developed and democratic countries, through the ways in which telematic technicity organizes, facilitates, and connects everything into a total work of power. Establishing new networks of "informational" freedom, telematics in the same move constitutes itself into the modern conduit of power. The paradox of telematics, and thus also of telematic art, is that this kind of free-

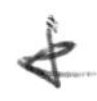

dom (on personal, group, and perhaps even social levels) becomes, on the plane of force relations, coextensive with the flow of power: new possibilities, links, and interactions are always already co-opted into the expanding network of informational power, confirming and instituting being as information. The notion of such freedoms is called into question by the fact that what remains unexamined in the idea of telematic art is the way in which communication itself has already been implicated in domination and power. Adorno had already contended that contemporary art, in order to "communicate," has to call communication into question and thus "speak" through its own silence. Communication, and certainly the means and conduits of today's telecommunication industry, reflect and put into practice the determination of being as, in essence, information, basing itself on the convertibility of experience into data, which ensures the possibility of its calculability and reprogramming. The multiplication of differences, the introduction of new forms of (hyper)links and channels of interaction, does not as such disagree with or alter the informational matrix of relations underwriting today's society. Since difference has itself become globalized and commodified, it not only does not call into question technopower but also often serves to ensure its spread and investment in regions, structures, and practices hitherto inaccessible to capital and the flow of modern power.

What is needed, therefore, is a radical questioning of the very form—technic, digital, telematic, and so on—that power has assumed in the contemporary world: questioning on the model of forcework that I have developed in the preceding chapter. With the help of this notion, I have sketched out the terrain and the terms on which we need to address the problem of the force of art at the turn of the new millennium. Some of these terms—those involving aesthetics, technology, power, and freedom—are not new, but their configuration changes substantially within the optics opened up by avant-garde art. Aesthetics is no longer thought of in terms of sensibility, pleasure, subjective expression, or the twin logics of production and consumption but instead is understood as an event that transforms relationality beyond the terms of power. If the term "technopower" describes the matrix of relationality that remains characteristic of modernity, then the term "poiēsis" refers to an event in which the vector of technicity changes from power to freedom. Adorno describes this turn when he claims that "art mobilizes technique [*Technik*] in an

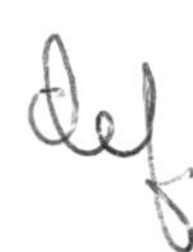

opposite direction than does domination."[35] Freedom, as the transformative relation between technē and poiēsis that encodes the relation between the social and formal aspects of art, becomes a matter not of an amplification and expansion of technicity but of a continuous and critical turning of technicity against itself. Within this turn, the poietic is not simply the opposite of technicity but rather a way of disarticulating technicity from within—not an escape, but a transformation. This turning is also not a dialectical reversal or negation but instead a fold that marks an opening of a beyond to technicity within the technological organization of power. Thus this beyond or "otherwise" is neither post-technological nor outside the reach of technology but constitutes a certain "outside within," whose force consists in manifesting the poietic modality of relating within the technic paradigm of modernity.

Such a transformative shift is at work, for instance, in Karlheinz Stockhausen's *Helikopter-Streichquartett*, one of the latest instances in which the work of art undertakes a certain reformulation of technology into a musical composition. What is interesting about Stockhausen's rather unusual quartet, with the use of four helicopters in which the separated quartet members play their respective parts, is that it does not use the sound of the helicopter blades as background sound/music or as musical material that becomes incorporated and rewoven into the string composition. In other words, the *Helikopter-Streichquartett* is not just one more repetition in the well-known mantra of the aestheticization of technology/experience; instead, it is something of a reversal in what has been happening with aesthetics' gradual incorporation and disappearance into technicity. The *Helikopter-Streichquartett* incorporates the sound of the four helicopters as that sound enters the cabins in which the members of the Arditti String Quartet are playing. The piece literally works with the technological sound, or the sound of technology, beginning to draw out its melody, to bring out and rework the musical structure embedded in the technological noise. The notes played by the musicians pick up on the technological noise, reshape it, and turn it into notes, disclosing a musical, aesthetic structure at work in technology. Drawing out a poietic technē from the by-product of technological progress, that is, noise, the complex play between the helicopter and the quartet sounds opens up a beyond within the technological technē, a poietic technē, rephrasing and remodulating the technic relationality into the poietic relationality of an artwork.

Among the most recent developments in technologically facilitated and inspired artworks, it is the transgenic art of Eduardo Kac that explicitly renders visible, plays with, and questions the increasingly thin and problematic boundary between art and technology. While most discussion of Kac's recent work has focused on the social and ethical implications of genetic manipulation, what is most significant about his projects from the point of view of aesthetics is his exploration of the fluctuating, sometimes vanishing, boundary between art and technology. At the same time that some of his works appear to fuse art and technology, to erase the border between aesthetics and science, they also, on other levels, reopen this very debate and remark all the more forcefully the significance of this difference. At its most "extreme," Kac's art renounces the ideas of representation and mimesis and moves toward associating artistic with biological creation. In fact, Kac goes so far as to end his essay describing the parameters and goals of his *GFP Bunny* by equating the creativity of the new art with the literal creation of life: "At last, transgenic art can contribute to the field of aesthetics by opening up the new symbolic and pragmatic dimension of art as the literal creation of and responsibility for life."[36] The "artistic" production of Alba, Kac's "green fluorescent protein bunny," genetically engineered through transfer of the gene responsible for fluorescence from a jellyfish into an albino rabbit, therefore seems (notwithstanding Kac's insistence that the key element of the artwork is the important social and ethical discussion generated by Alba's creation) indistinguishable from the scientific, technological deployment of the powers of genetic engineering in the service of creating new, transspecies forms of life. The social, ethical, and aesthetic issues raised by transgenic art are far too numerous and complex to address here; there has already been a flood of essays, articles, and responses to Kac's provocative works and statements, both in artistic journals and in the popular media. The discussion so far does indeed testify to the importance, innovation, and suggestive character of Kac's *GFP Bunny,* but it is quite telling that most of it has centered on ethical and social questions regarding integration of and respect for new, transgenic forms of life, as opened up by the breeding of a unique, fluorescent rabbit. That is, the "aesthetic" question—the question of whether and how *GFP Bunny* is (or is not) a work of art—has been relegated to the background instead of occupying a central place. One could also ask whether art is actually needed in order to generate the kind of discussion, no doubt crucial and imperative, that has been going on around

Kac's work, or whether those questions do not in fact arise from the very premises, objectives, and capabilities of genetic technology. Kac's work has clearly energized and accelerated the pace of such discussion, and it has contributed new insights that the scientific community itself perhaps would not have provided, but this in itself does not make *GFP Bunny* a work of art. Where *GFP Bunny* remains indisputably critical is in its manifestation of the fragility of the boundary between technology and art, between technoscientific and artistic powers. In a way, Alba is a new icon for the possibility (inevitability?) of art's fusion with technology, which was already tantalizing the Italian Futurists almost a century ago.

In the context of this thinning boundary, it seems legitimate and necessary to ask whether and to what extent transgenic art is complicit with the manipulative flows of power or whether, on the contrary, it exposes, complicates, or perhaps even contests them. In *Aesthetic Theory* and other writings, Adorno analyzed the complicity with and contestation of commodification by modernist art. Now that art has moved directly onto the level of genetic manipulation, the question of its complicity/contestation has been transferred into the heart, so to speak, of contemporary technical manifestations of power. Is the awareness of the uniqueness of the "created" animal, the context of its social needs, a complication or a contestation of the very manipulation the artist used to create Alba? To make the engineering marvel into an artwork, is it enough to debate, in the context of *GFP Bunny,* the significance of interconnections, social acceptability, and intersubjectivity?[37] Is the rapprochement between art and science/technology in Kac's work dissimilar from the momentum of Duchamp's ready-mades? Obviously, the technology is notably different—from mass-produced objects to the possibility of mass production of engineered/altered life forms—and so are the ethical and political dilemmas associated with it. Yet, aesthetically speaking, are we not still within the horizon of avant-garde questioning about whether the forcework at stake in art—in spite of, or perhaps because of, art's fascination with modern technology—remains different from and critical of the technological deployment of power that is regulative of modern life? Without adjudicating these questions, I would like to focus the discussion on the boundary between art and technology, and on the possible turn within technicity intimated by Kac's work. Kac's art remains critically important here because, even beyond the explicit intentions stated in his texts on *GFP*

Bunny and *Genesis* (discussed below), it keeps this question open and thus keeps technicity in question by pointing to the intrinsic possibility of a turn within it.

This questioning, as already suggested, is evident in *Genesis,* another of Kac's transgenic artworks.[38] *Genesis* uses a constructed "art" gene to interfere with and literally illuminate the process and the powers at work in genetic engineering. To "create" his "art gene," Kac took the famous statement from the biblical book of Genesis about human domination over the world—"Let man have dominion over the fish of the sea, and the birds of the air, and all creatures that crawl upon the land"—and translated it through a double process into a DNA sequence. First he transposed the sentence into Morse code, and then, converting the Morse code into its equivalents in the genetic alphabet of Adenine, Guanine, Cytosine, and Thymine, he retranslated the passage into a DNA sequence. The "art gene" was then inserted into fluorescent *E. coli* bacteria living in a petri dish, whose mutation was further influenced by Internet users who could turn on and off a light source illuminating the dish. The dish was then placed in an art gallery, with its magnified projection on one wall, the DNA sequence of the "art gene" displayed on another, and the biblical passage quoted on a third.[39] An Adornian question posed to Kac's *Genesis* would probably read like this: does the "art gene" create/mutate in a way that undoes the domination and manipulation at the very basis of genetic technology? No doubt Kac's gene, much like the techniques of genetic engineering itself, "creates" a new being, but in its manner of creation it also discloses technoscientific manipulation and even calls it into question. Since the "art" gene is produced from the biblical quotation that gives humans the directive to control, manipulate, and exploit "nature," Kac's *Genesis* begins to function as a parody of the anthropocentric conception of being, with the manipulative power placed at the center of existence. Moreover, Kac's gene cannot help recall Tristan Tzara's idea, from his Dada manifestos, that Dada is a virgin microbe. For Tzara, Dada was the invasion of a radical avant-garde poiēsis into rationality and logic, an outbreak of a-logicality which called Enlightenment rationality into question, interacted with it, and transformed it beyond recognition, thus "freeing" life from its "organic disease"—logic. Kac's "art gene" is art literally inserted into genetic material, "illuminating" it (through the fluorescence of the bacteria and the projected lighting) and transposing it from within. While

Dadaism tried to alter the very momentum of relationality, transforming the overly "logical" and "rational" charge of experience, *Genesis* literally "manipulates" and modifies the technological manipulation of being. It demonstrates and enacts the extreme closeness between the power of information technologies and genetic engineering, on the one hand, and artistic power, on the other. At the same time, the "art gene" not only lays bare but also, using literal genetic transposition as its conduit, alters the very modality of power that makes possible and operates *in* genetic engineering, giving genetic power a different momentum. In a way, the power is still the same—it is the power to transfer genes and engineer transgenic life forms—and yet its momentum appears to be different: geared no longer just to manipulation, that is, to further intensification of the reach of power into the microelements of being, but rather to the possibility of a different, "artistic" disposition of forces. The most important and interesting aspect of Kac's work is this constant highlighting/erasure of the boundary between artistic and technical technē, between genetic engineering and the "art gene," which, beyond the celebration, excitement, and fears brought about by the information and genetic "revolutions," keeps alive—literally, in the case of *Genesis*—the possibility of a critical turning, which remains intrinsic to technicity even in the midst of its modern, seemingly limitless, deployments of power.

What is at stake in this turn are the mode or valence of relation and, more specifically, the question of whether such relationality has the momentum of power. To engage with this problem, I reformulate Heidegger's question about technology in the following way: do relations in the technological age take—necessarily, as it seems—the form of power relations and thus participate in the continuing intensification of being's manifestation as power, or do they point to a turn in technicity toward a different disposition of relations, one that withdraws from the productionist logic of power and does not contribute to its increase? The key, if undeveloped, element in Heidegger's reflection on technicity is the idea of a fold or turn within technē itself. Heidegger's notion of technicity does not refer to what we know as technology, such as instruments or technological means of production, but to a mode of revealing that discloses what *is* as intrinsically calculable and available as a resource. When beings come to be disclosed as "resources," natural, mineral, human, or otherwise, it means that they are constituted in their very essence *in terms of power*, that is, as inherently manipulable, and thus subject to calculation, reworking, and numerification. Technicity makes it possible to categorize experience and relations in terms of efficiency, commodification, and exchange. Technicity's most recent incarnation, characterized by the tendency toward simultaneous multiplication and equalization of differences, exchangeability, and convertibility, is the Information Age, with its increasing capability to digitize and turn being into a global, continuously modifiable data bank.

In this context, I propose to think of art as the possibility of a turn in technicity, and to argue that art is "real" as a transformative event in which technical relationality comes to reflect upon itself and calls itself into question. Art's forcework would then be not a matter of modifying or reworking telematic relations but of calling into question the power momentum instantiated by them. Relations in the contemporary world are no longer just abstract, as Adorno analyzed them in conjunction with abstract art, but "infomatic," that is, based on reducibility and on conversion to information, and on the instant transmission of such information. Therefore, the work of art needs to be thought of precisely in relation to the informational paradigm increasingly dominating modern life: never limited to celebrating the opening of new artistic possibilities associated with the new information media, as much of Internet art seems to be doing, but interrogating the momentum that this informational paradigm is giving to praxis. If this momentum, as seems to be the case everywhere, amounts to a new "telematic" agility and expansiveness of power, then the artwork needs to disclose the formation of modern relations into power on the level of infomatics and telematics, and to call this paradigm into question. Such a way of rethinking the relation between art and technē emerges from "The Question Concerning Technology," where Heidegger indicates that the possibility of a turning in technicity depends on a rethinking of modern art beyond aesthetics and the notion of production:

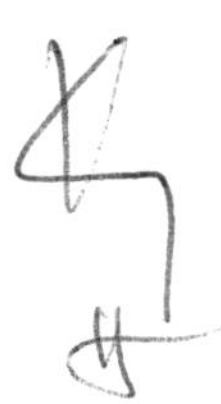

> There was a time when it was not technicity alone that bore the name *technē*. Once the revealing that brings forth truth into the splendor of radiant appearance was also called *technē*.
>
> There was a time when the bringing-forth of the true into the beautiful was called *technē*. The *poiēsis* of the fine arts was also called *technē*.[40]

Technē is characterized by the ambiguous play of two faces—a technical technē and a poietic technē, I would add, by the tension between technopower and aphesis. If technicity, for Heidegger, is a mode of revealing that "challenges forth" (*Herausfordern*), calculates, orders, and organizes being into resource, poiēsis, by contrast, is a transformative event that changes relations into an "unproductive" modality of letting be. Like technicity, art, too, disposes relations but, as Adorno remarks in *Aesthetic Theory*, with a radically different result: "Through the domination of the dominating, art revises the domination of nature to the core. In contrast to the semblance of inevitability that characterizes these forms in empirical reality, art's control over them and over their relation to materials makes their arbitrariness in the empirical world evident. As a musical composition compresses time, and as a painting folds spaces into one another, so the possibility is concretized that the world could be other than it is."[41] Following the patterns of domination and power at work in technicity, art takes over the relations between forces in society and transposes them into its own force field. But this transposition changes the vector of relations between forces away from domination, commodification, or exchange of information.

It is in terms of such a turn in technicity that I would like to propose here, by way of closing, a few observations on Bill Viola's remarkable video installation titled *The Crossing*.[42] My question here is whether the crossing in Viola's installation represents a transformation in technicity or a turn within the same. In the video, two elements, fire and water, are portrayed as destructive and at the same time transforming: the fire consumes, or purifies; the water drowns, or cleanses. In both cases, the crossing has to do with the disappearance of the subject, enacted by a male figure that vanishes into the flames and the cascading water. That *The Crossing* hinges on this ambiguity between annihilation and transformation is of crucial importance to my argument. It manifests, in a way, the double valence of force that I discussed earlier, the ease with which forces can take the form of power and violence or enable release and freedom. This metamorphosing of force depends on how it comes to be disposed, on what kind of relationality it draws out—in other words, on whether forcework becomes disposed artistically or in terms of power. *The Crossing* draws out relations in terms of stillness: between the dark background and the figure advancing in slow motion; between the figure's raised hands and the rest of the body, as well as the unilluminated background; between the slowly moving body and the flames and water that engulf it. But this stillness, underscored by slow-motion photography and articulated through the contrast between the movement of the body and the motion of the flames and water, is not mute. The aim, in Marjorie Perloff's words, is "to slow down the viewer's attention and witness what has always already been there but never quite seen."[43] As a result, what has always already been there begins to articulate itself to our eyes and ears; it speaks, precisely in the sense in which Heidegger invests language with the ability to speak. Language speaks not so much in words as between words, through a form of relationality that opens the space for and disposes words. Beyond signification, words, and images, it is forcework, the key in which relations unfold and become disposed, that speaks in Viola's work.

For Viola, video art looks for "an image that is not an image" and makes us dwell within what does not enter the scope of visibility: the temporality of experience. The slow motion in Viola thus "tells" time, or "says" temporality itself, which, irreducible to calculation and measurement, to information and the telematic forms of its circulation, comes into focus, as it were, in the blurred movements of the body. The sequenced running of *The Crossing,* though itself programmed, repeatedly communicates the importance of the turn in increasingly programmable experience, the importance of being's irreducibility to a programming or informational code. Viola, using the latest technology to manipulate time—to "dominate" it, as Adorno would say—turns this artistic disposition of forces against technicity, specifically against the foreshortening of the irreducibly futural projection of temporality to processable and programmable information. Against the backdrop of measurement and digital manipulation, *The Crossing* opens experience up into its transformative futurity, the futurity that marks the present and expands its "here" beyond the linear dimension of presence. Employing digital technology as a counter to technicity, Viola's art "makes visible" a fold within technicity between its increasingly power-ful deployment of calculative/digital relations and its power-free poetic sculpturing of experience. Instead of a telematic, total work of art, Viola redeploys forms of modern technology to free the event from its increasing compression into the informational paradigm. Viola's works point the way to a transformation within the "infomatic" operations of contemporary technicity: the models and means of disciplining being into informational streams and exchanges are invoked in his works in order to perform a "crossing" into noninformational, power-free event.

In the approach I am proposing here, art's force is its ability to bring us face to face with the power at work in technicity. This power operates beyond the obvious power of the new technologies, since it constitutes the very momentum of how the complex of relations forming modernity develops and becomes an intricate and differentiated matter of power. Art's importance, in this context, lies in its work on the possibility of the turn within technicity and power. The forcework characteristic of art shows the other face of technē, marked in modern technicity as the possibility of a different future. This tension within technē, which is internal to art, recodes the dialectic between formal, "aesthetic," and social aspects of art, reformulating their continuing conflict in terms of forcework and its transformative turn within technicity. Modern technē reveals its face as manipulative technicity, which unfolds the world in terms of a programmable and manipulable network of relations, as a kind of global computer matrix. Technicity, manifesting itself in the form of multiplying informational relays and the increasing reach of digital technology, discloses the essence of being as an informational code, thus intensifying the global sense of power. Art, by contrast, shows technicity its other, "ethical" face, as a revealing that could "let be" and enable relations to unfold free from power. Perhaps the critical difference here is between the character of modern technicity, "in essence" manipulative and programming, and the enabling technē, or forcework, of art. The power of art, the transformative force of its rupture, lies in opening up a nexus of power-free relations. To put the issue differently, what becomes transformed in art is power itself as it is changed into what perhaps can no longer even be referred to as power, since the forcework at stake in art, though it is a kind of force, does not contribute to the intensification of power. Letting be, it undermines the power formation of relations in the modern world, changes their momentum, and opens up a certain "otherwise" to power. My suggestion here is that this turn or change marks the avant-garde vector of art.

3

Beyond the Subject-Object Dialectic

PART I: ART "OBJECTS"—FROM COMMODITY AESTHETIC TO PUBLIC EVENT

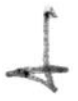

> The immanence of society in the artwork is the essential social relation of art, not the immanence of art in society.
>
> —Theodor W. Adorno, *Aesthetic Theory*

In contemporary discussions there are two main lines of thought concerned with the social function of art: the first, the post-Heideggerian/ Nietzschean approach, in its attempt to move beyond the "economic" understanding of power, focuses on the broadly conceived technologies of power, where technology stands for the dominant paradigm of social relations; the second, represented by different versions of Marxist thought and the Frankfurt School, in its attempt to diagnose historical mutations of capital, gives priority to commodification and exchange as the dominant forms of power. The difference between these two orientations lies primarily in their respective understanding of power: technologies versus economies of power, and not necessarily in their conceptions of art. By shifting attention to art's transformative force, this book examines art's social function vis-à-vis both of these notions of power, showing their convergence and collusion in modernity with its signature technoeconomy of power relations. In the previous chapter I discussed art's position in relation to technology; in this chapter I will focus primarily on the problem-

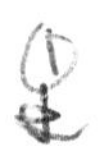

atic of commodification, which will enable us to revisit the question of the form/matter distinction and the object status of artworks. Ultimately, this discussion moves the understanding of artworks beyond the notions of objects and commodities, in order to rethink the "public" character of art in terms of the event.

The definition of art in terms of forcework and aphesis, that is, release from power, prompts the reconsideration of the artwork's social significance not only in terms of technology but, this time, also in relation to commodification and consumption and their evolving functions within modern technological society. To the extent that production, commodification, aesthetic objects, and consumption are all historically related within the social sphere and function as part of the technoeconomy of power, the idea of nonpower at work in art makes it both possible and necessary to reassess art's social significance outside the customary aesthetic and cultural debates about art's cultural capacity, and to rethink the categories of separation/integration, aesthetic formalism/cultural inscription, complicity/resistance, and so on, that structure such discussions. The approach I propose here owes much to Adorno's description of art's social relation in *Aesthetic Theory*, especially its final section, "Art and Society," even though, as I indicated in the previous chapter, my view of art reformulates the dialectical terminology and radicalizes the notion of the negative operative in Adorno through the Heideggerian optics of the event. Perhaps more important, I rearticulate the concerns with reification and power encoded within the notion of form central to Adorno's *Aesthetic Theory* in terms of art's forcework and its power-free configuration of forces.

Between Aesthetic Object and Commodity

A great deal of ink has been spilled over the reification of the subject, but what about the problem of the reification of art's work, its congealment into an object and commodification? Art's struggle with its reification into an aesthetic object, and its attempts to articulate the artwork beyond the metaphysical paradigm of the subject-object relation, constitute perhaps the single most important aspect of the history of art in the twentieth century. It is in the context of this refusal of art to remain an aesthetic object that I continue Adorno's aspiration to liberate the object, but suggest that to do so art has to be taken, as the avant-garde shows us, beyond the idea of the object. Dadaism and Futurism not only parodied and critiqued art's reification but also emphasized the ways in which the technicity characteristic of modern experience revealed a new dimension in art: the artwork as a transformative event. Discovering art to be first and foremost an event, Futurism, Dadaism, and Surrealism played a critical role in switching attention from art's character as an object to its "event work." 

This shift from object to event necessitates a reconsideration of art's relation to commodification and exchange: since art resists or "objects," as the title of this chapter hints, specifically by refusing to be an object, the most important aspect of art's social relation is the dissolution of the related logics of the aesthetic object and the commodity, the dissolution implied in the avant-garde's "discovery" of art as an event. By opening up the space of the power-free, forcework in art inscribes *and* critiques both aesthetics and commodification as the twin forms of art's incorporation into the technoeconomic operations of power. Aesthetics and commodity are two ways in which art's language of nonpower becomes mistranslated and distorted into the power-instantiating idioms that reflect and intensify modern technicity. Historically, the changes in capital and society in the eighteenth century produced this split logic, according to which artworks come to be constituted as aesthetic objects existing within the jurisdiction of affect and taste and by the same token also become subject to the operations of commodification and exchange. This double life that artworks are presumed to live forces them to be autonomous, subject only to their own "aesthetic" rules, and at the same time heteronomous, obeying the external laws of the market. Paradoxically, the "autonomy" imprinted on the work of art as a result of its constitution as an aesthetic object both allows art to gain a significance seemingly irreducible to or untranslatable into the mechanisms and discourses operative in society and, in the same gesture, threatens art with irrelevance and separation from society as a result of art's incomprehensibility within the rationality governing the social domain. Simply put, if there is something inexplicable about art, something that cannot be grasped and explained within the discursive fields through which society understands its own historical existence, then the artwork can be judged irrelevant, socially irresponsible, and even complicit with the powers that be. Or, as has been the case more recently, if the social standards of comprehensibility tend to become increasingly 

"average," mediocre, or plainly low, artworks can easily be denounced as elitist or esoteric. In the end, this aesthetic autonomy turns out to be spurious, since it only confirms art's subordination to the social operations of power: art is certainly allowed a critical voice, but only to the extent to which this criticism has already been foreseen, anticipated, and regulated by society's own, if unconscious, vision of itself. When art's critique of consumer society is brought into the light of day, interpreted, and discussed, even though it appears new and revolutionary, it has in fact already been envisioned and accommodated within social praxis as a kind of replicating "self-criticism," which remains perfectly permissible within the flexible extensions of the modern operations of power. In a word, despite appearances to the contrary, there is nothing new about such criticism, as Adorno would say. New aesthetic vogues find their parallel in the new products of the computer, automobile, or entertainment industries, while the "anything goes" aesthetic characteristic of postmodernism replicates the multicultural logic of contemporary consumer society. In a kind of worst-case scenario, the more art tries to be critical of society while also conforming to the aesthetic categorization of artworks, the more it ends up reproducing the logic of commodification, the twin companion of aesthetics within the productionist organization of modern society.

This paradoxical convertibility or "exchange" between the logics of the aesthetic object and commodification finds its explanation in the metaphysics of production, which underpins the historical development of modern society. It is the understanding of art within the overall Western productionist scheme of being—that is, according to the logic of making, manipulation, and power (*Macht* and *Machenschaft*)—that determines art's "work" as both aesthetic and commodifiable. In "The Origin of the Work of Art," Heidegger explains the specificity of artworks in terms of their "workly character" (*das Werkhafte*),[1] which distinguishes them from things, objects, and instruments. It is specifically this idiomatic, workly character, or the "work-being," of artworks that calls into question the aesthetic categorizations of art, which, first, constitute the artwork as *an object*, and, second, understand the aesthetic object in terms of the relation between matter and form: "The distinction of matter and form is *the conceptual schema which is used, in the greatest variety of ways, quite generally for all art theory and aesthetics*. . . . Form and content are the most hackneyed concepts under which anything and everything may be subsumed.

. . . if in addition the subject-object relation is coupled with the conceptual pair form-matter; then representation has at its command a conceptual machinery that nothing is capable of withstanding."[2] The idea of objects and, by extension, artworks as formed matter, reinforced in the Judeo-Christian tradition with the notion of creation, becomes the universal matrix for understanding being, and the cornerstone of the productionist metaphysics of power: "The inclination to treat the matter-form structure as *the* constitution of every being receives an additional impulse from the fact that on the basis of a religious faith, namely, the biblical faith, the totality of all beings is represented in advance as something created, which here means made."[3] The productionist notion that artworks are objects, that is, formed matter, comes to aesthetics not from artworks themselves but from the concept of equipment, produced for the sake of use and reliability. In other words, the cornerstone of the aesthetic conceptualization of art is the notion of production, the metaphysics of *machen*, which intrinsically ties aesthetic objects to the making of commodities: the logic of production is the basis of the cultural formation of art into aesthetic objects and, at the same time, of commodification. It is therefore no wonder that artworks, understood aesthetically, immediately submit to the operations of commodification, since this process is the extension of the very logic of machination (*Machenschaft*) that underpins aesthetics. As Heidegger suggests, the machinery of productionist metaphysics is so nimble and powerful that it becomes capable, in its great variety of operations, of forming what *is* into relations of making and power. Whether *Machenschaft* operates in terms of the subject-object structure, as modern technicity, or, more recently, as information and telematics—with all the obvious technological advancement and social changes that such progression brings—it still produces relations as a network of conduits for power.

To understand the work of art as an aesthetic and cultural object, subject to the laws of aesthetics, cultural transmission, and commodification, is to effectively foreclose art within the operations of making and power and thus to sap and annul the very force of art, that is, forcework understood as the transformative redisposition of relations otherwise than in terms of power. But to discern the level on which this forcework transpires in art amounts to calling into question the very notion of power and its proclivity to shape relations and beings in its own image: into forms of making and power. It entails rethinking relationality in terms of "letting be," that is, in terms of *lassen* rather than *machen*, power, or manipulation. The pivot between power and nonpower, between manipulation and letting be, is the artistic forcework. As such, forcework is a "forceful" critique of the idea of art as aesthetic object and commodity. While artworks obviously often play the function of aesthetic objects and commodities, what makes them art—that is, forcework or aphesis—cannot be understood within aesthetics and the logic of commodification, because art's force effects a transformation within power that reworks power's manipulative logic, on which both aesthetics and commodification are based. What constitutes the (force)work that makes art art, namely, the power-free space into which art releases and transforms relations, remains beyond both the idiom of aesthetics and the language of commodification. Aesthetics and commodification, even when disguised in the language of beauty, feelings, and desire, are instantiations of the operations of production, making, and power. If power, through production, has "colonized" the productive forces, through commodification it has infiltrated the realms of fantasy and desire, by co-optation but also by endless expansion and production. In a way, commodification and consumption can be seen as extensions or evolutions of the metaphysics of production, as techniques that continuously upgrade and expand the flows of power.

This is why art's forcework cannot be understood aesthetically in terms of an object. As Adorno explains, still renegotiating the aesthetic conceptuality of the subject-object and form-content dialectic, which Heidegger so forcefully criticizes:

> Object in art and object in empirical reality are entirely distinct. In art the object is the work produced by art, as much containing elements of empirical reality as displacing, dissolving, and reconstructing them according to the work's own law. Only through such transformation, and not through an ever falsifying photography, does art give empirical reality its due, the epiphany of its shrouded essence and the merited shudder in the face of it as in the face of a monstrosity. The primacy of the object is affirmed aesthetically only in the character of art as the unconscious writing of history, as anamnesis of the vanquished, of the repressed, and perhaps of what is possible. The primacy of the object, as the potential freedom from domination of what is, manifests itself in art as its freedom from objects.[4]

Art's "object" is, in fact, not an object or a thing at all, but rather its *work*, its work-being, as Heidegger remarks in "The Origin of the Work of Art." Art guards the freedom, the otherness, of things and objects in the reality external to art precisely by refusing to be reduced to or representable as *an object*, in this way calling into question the powerful machinery of representation. Art's forcework, free from objects (objectification, representation, aesthetics, and so on), spells out a transformation of empirical reality: art, inscribing in its works the elements of social reality, especially its power-oriented relationality, redisposes forces into nonpower, into freedom.

It is this dimension of nonpower, or of the power-free, that has been progressively vanquished by modern society: not a specific object, thing, or, entity, or even their constellations, but rather the very "form" or mode that beings assume within the multiple relations that "make" them what they are, that is, the form of objects, resources, information, and so on; or, to put the matter differently, all the various "power forms" into which being comes to be rendered in contemporary society. Forcework stands for a power-free relationality, which has been repressed but which remains perhaps still possible, as Adorno suggests, echoing Heidegger's statement from *Being and Time* that history is not a matter of the past but of the silent force of the possible. This force of the possible, manifested in art's release from technicity, writes the sedimentations of history, that is, the various layers and forms of relationality through which power intersects and mobilizes modern reality. It is thus in its forcework that art remains eminently historical, not only in the sense in which art inscribes in its works the history of the formation of forces into power but also in the specific sense in which nonpower instantiates the historicity of being as an event irreducible to historical representations and significations, that is, to the sociocultural space of historicism. Art's force is the very historicity of happening, the temporal impetus of *ekstasis* uncontainable within the notions of presence/absence, of sequential and measurable time, or of historical narrative. It is in this sense that Heidegger speaks of art as "grounding history": "Art is history in the essential sense that it grounds history."[5] Heideggerian "grounding" is always a kind of ungrounding, a letting go of any ground, which opens up the abyss (*Ab-grund*) in which the historicity of being is shown to be not at all about "grounds," "reasons," or "first principles" but instead about the "silent force of the possible."[6] In Heidegger's later writings, this historical force becomes linked with the critique of power and technology and signifies the possibility of a release, intrinsic to the unfolding of temporality, from dominant social rationality. In this way, the force of art is seen to instantiate the force of history: the silent force of the possible, which opens up the space of relationality no longer operative in terms of power. It is as such an event that art is "radically" significant for society.

One of the most significant implications of art's "force of the possible" is its displacement and dissolution of the logic of commodification, so spellbinding for contemporary consumer culture. When it becomes a commodity, an object's form comes to inscribe the power modality of relations into the object's existence as a commodity. Commodity is a form in Marx that, in its tendency toward fetishization, encodes social relations beyond the abstract labor invested in the object, as well as beyond any natural or physical properties of the object:

> The mysterious character of the commodity-form consists therefore simply in the fact that the commodity reflects the social characteristics of men's own labour as objective characteristics of the products of labour themselves, as the socio-natural properties of these things. . . . the commodity-form, and the value-relation of the products of labour within which it appears, have absolutely no connection with the physical nature of the commodity and the material [*dinglich*] relations arising out of this. It is nothing but the definite social relation between men themselves which assumes here, for them, the fantastic form of a relation between things.[7]

Marx concludes, therefore, that commodity fetishism has its origin in "the peculiar social character of the labour which produces" commodities.[8] The commodity form assumed by produced objects reflects the codes of social power, imprinted on the use and exchange value that the objects carry. This is why Adorno focuses his analysis of art on what he calls "form" as the cipher of a radical, nonexistent praxis, which calls into question the social relations that obtain in the historical forms of production. Just as is the case with other produced objects, artworks, too, carry the stamp of social relations through the social character of the labor that creates them. In the case of commodities, however, these social relations tend to assume a phantasmatic existence, which the commodities not only sustain but also tend to expand and reinforce, relying on the deferring operations of desire. In a way, commodities remain essentially passive in relation to the social imprint they bear, for they display the tendency toward amplifying and reifying those relations, presenting them as obtainable and controllable objects. While social relations come to be imprinted on a commodity, in fact come to constitute its very form and often lead to its fetishization, the work of art critiques and transforms social relations through its forcework. What in this context distinguishes artworks from commodities, and thus also counters the social tendency to commodify art, is their contestation of the forms of social relations impressed on them. A work of art bears such a mark only to call it into question and, in the process, transform the very relations that fashioned art and stamped it with their own productionist thrust. Art's forcework refigures these imprints of the essentially technological character of social relations, thus calling into question not only commodification but also the technological disposition of relations operative in society. Since the relations impressed on the work of art reflect the manipulative, "technical" essence of modern power, art's forcework amounts to a reworking of the power form of social relations. If, as Heidegger has shown, aesthetics is firmly embedded in the logic of making and power, then forcework's critique of the metaphysics of production cannot be accounted for within the terms made available by aesthetics and aesthetic theory. In the same gesture with which it critiques the logic of production, art's forcework calls into question the practices of commodification and the commodified form that artworks themselves assume when categorized and "misrecognized" as aesthetic objects. This is why commodification in relation to art becomes possible only when art no longer "works," that is, when its forcework has been covered over or erased, and the artwork has congealed into an object; for the commodity form imprints itself on objectified forms of labor, and if art's "object" is its work, then this very forcework undoes both the notion of the object and the commodity form that artworks inherit in the process of being created. The way in which, for instance, Stockhausen's *Helikopter-Streichquartett* reworks technicity implies not just a re-forming of technological noise into musical sound forms, that is, not merely a change in form, but a reworking into poiēsis of relations that, on a deeper level, constitute being in terms of technicity.

As a power-free event, the work of art frees itself from commodification and consumption, both corollaries of manipulative power, and opens up a space for freedom from the logic of commodity and exchange, a space that pervades contemporary reality. Precisely to the extent that art's work remains irreducible to production, commodification, and consumption is art critical of reality. This critical element of the forcework, its manner of relating otherwise than through power, remains an enigma to the productionist logic of *Machenschaft*: it is unexplainable, often illegible, within the discursive operations of power. Adorno explains this enigmatic aspect, essential to art's relation to society, by way of a certain fetishistic admixture in art:

> The truth content of artworks, which is indeed their social truth, is predicated on their fetish character. The principle of heteronomy, apparently the counterpart of fetishism, is the principle of exchange, and in it domination is masked. Only what does not submit to that principle acts as the plenipotentiary of what is free from domination; only what is useless can stand in for the stunted use value. Artworks are plenipotentiaries of things that are no longer distorted by exchange, profit, and the false needs of a degraded humanity. . . . A liberated society would be beyond the irrationality of its *faux frais* and beyond the ends-means-rationality of utility. This is enciphered in art and is the source of art's social explosiveness. Although the magic fetishes are one of the historical roots of art, a fetishistic element remains admixed in artworks, an element that goes beyond commodity fetishism.[9]

The social truth of artworks is their refusal of heteronomy, of the principle of exchange central to the operations of modern power. In their truth, artworks decline to participate in the practices through which experience becomes infused with power. This is the sense in which Adorno understands domination, namely, as the flexibility with which power infiltrates, ingrains itself in, and co-opts various forms of existence and relation. Art's "social explosiveness" lies in its liberation from the technicity that shapes modern social relations. Adorno associates this explosiveness with a fetishistic element in art, with its enigmatic force, incomprehensible within the technological rationality of today's world.

Adorno's analysis implicitly differentiates among the notions of aesthetic object, commodity, and the force of art. One could say, reformulating Adorno's argument, that in a consumer society art is socially meaningful because its forcework remains irreducible to aesthetic object and aesthetic categories, on the one hand, and to the laws of exchange, commodification, and commodity fetishism, on the other. Caught between aesthetic object and commodity, the work of art explodes the logic of production encoded within both the processes of commodification and the aesthetic conceptuality. This explosion—the transformation of "making" and "manipulating" into "letting be"—is the instantiation of the enigmatic force of art, which remains emphatically different from, if sometimes mistaken for, commodity fetishism, for while the commodity fetish invests the object with the life of social relations external to it, the force of art explodes, in the rupture of its event, the very paradigm of relationality that structures the social sphere into multiple formations of power. Undoing manipulation and domination, the work of art exhibits a different quality of force, a force that, in the process of artistic creation, manages to free itself from the paradigm of making, thanks to which it comes into being. This force explodes silently, acting as the plenipotentiary of what becomes power-free. Enciphered in the work of art, nonpower, by virtue of its radical "difference" from and "critique" of the operations of power, exerts its enigmatic—because power-free—force of "letting be" on society.

Duchamp's ready-mades remain among the most eloquent examples of this triangulation characteristic of the positioning of the modern artwork at the intersection of aesthetics, commodity, and forcework. On the one hand, the ready-mades ironically invoke and parody the aesthetic assignments given to art: the notions of beauty, sublimity, aesthetic affect, experience, and so on. It is enough to remark upon the starkness of the bicycle wheel or the bottle rack, or to note the playfulness of the urinal/fountain, to understand the extent to which Duchamp explodes not only the aesthetic conventions of the past but also the very categorization of artworks as aesthetic, on the one hand, and as objects, on the other. What changes in Duchamp's work is nothing other than the very *element* in which art works: it is no longer *aisthesis*, playfully ironized and refashioned by the ready-mades, but, I would venture, technicity, which underpins modern sensibility, aesthetic affect, everyday experience, and so on. The inverted urinal, serving parodically as the new "Fountain" of art, evokes, by way of their absence, both the aesthetic of the beautiful and the notions of originality and genius. Nevertheless, the ready-mades appear readily to inscribe themselves into the very processes of commodification and consumption that art, according to its aesthetic categorizations, is supposed to resist. Employing mass-produced functional objects for everyday consumption—shovel, urinal, bicycle, bottle rack, and so on—the ready-mades engage directly with the production/consumption paradigm on which modern society is based. Yet the ready-mades are as parodic in relation to commodities as they are vis-à-vis aesthetics. The mass-produced objects that serve as the "material" of the ready-mades are dramatically "unmade" through artistic creation: they are disencumbered from the very functionality and usefulness that defines their being as technological objects of everyday consumption. In a way, these contraptions lose their status as objects and come to form part of the forcework constitutive of art as redefined by Duchamp.

Duchamp's ready-mades are among the best examples of the modernist critique of art as commodity: the shovel, as a work of art enshrined in a museum behind the ubiquitous rope, cannot be touched or handled and thus becomes deprived precisely of what it is meant to do in its existence as a commodity; the bicycle wheel is disassembled and inverted, perhaps a motionless and mutilated parody of the motion and technological speed so exalted by the Futurists. The shovel constituting the ready-made titled *In Anticipation of Broken Arm* signifies precisely by virtue of being useless; propped against a wall, it exposes—to scrutiny, or even critique?—the notions of usefulness and reliability functioning as the structuring principles of the exchange society. The "broken arm" suggested by the title is not only the arm possibly broken as a result of the anticipated fall on the uncleared snow but also the "technicist arm" that has become so habituated to using, employing, and manipulating that it no longer notices the extent to which it has grown to be the extension of the very power it purports to possess and control. The broken arm signifies the artistic breaking open of the logic of production, the exposition of the mechanisms that form forces into the processes of commodification and consumption. In a parallel gesture, *The Fountain* literally turns a urinal on its "head," performing a minirevolution in the entire social nexus of relations bound by production and usefulness. In this act of "breaking" or inverting, the ready-mades transform the social relations that imprint themselves on commodities: the famous Duchampian signature "R. J. Mutt" on *The Fountain* literally rewrites the imprint of social relations on the processes of mass production and the strategies of consumption, replacing their impression with the mark of art's different force. The signature thus not only parodies, as is widely and correctly asserted, the notion of artistic originality and uniqueness but also, in the same stroke, explodes the practices of making and manipulation, both tributaries of the social flows of power. It is tempting to think here that the inversion to which Duchamp submits mass-produced commodities is itself a play on the famous image from Marx's *Capital* that describes the commodity as a table with its legs upside down.[10] If commodities invert use and exchange value, then in Duchamp's work they are submitted to a further turning, which allows the artwork to function in its uselessness as the plenipotentiary of the stunted use, to recall Adorno. What appears upside down, inverted, or broken in Duchamp's art is not only aesthetics but also, and perhaps above all, technicity as the matrix of modern relations. The ready-mades thus expose the intrinsic link between aesthetics and commodification, both effects of those practices of Enlightenment rationality that underscore mastery and manipulation. Duchamp's works problematize not only the aesthetic "form" of art and its corollary, commodification, but also the logic of manipulative power in which both are grounded. Neither aesthetic objects nor cultural commodities, and yet bringing both forms into interplay, Duchamp's ready-mades register the dramatic, often ironic, difference of forcework. This force frequently speaks in Duchamp through playfully "violent" inversion, breaking, or dismantling, which all come to form part of the transformative work that takes upon itself the task of "unmaking," side by side with aesthetics, the very logic of making that powers modern technicity.

Beyond the High/Low Divide?

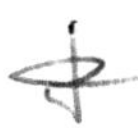

The understanding of the work of art on the level of forcework, as the unmaking of the aesthetic and commodity "skins" of art, provides a new, critical way to contextualize much of the debate about the role of aesthetics in contemporary mass and consumer culture. This new definition of the *work* performed by art makes it possible to demarcate the range of aesthetic questions and their relation to issues of consumption and mass culture, and to situate them vis-à-vis the problematic of radical art. The question of aesthetics in mass society, even though it remained unasked in this form for a while, had already begun to mark itself when the split between aesthetics and commodification arose in European societies, raising concerns about relations between aesthetic categories: on the one hand, the notions of the aesthetic object, beauty, judgment, affect, and experience, and, on the other, the increasingly accessible productions of "low," mass, or popular art/entertainment. A great deal of ink has been spilled, and many arguments for and against have been raised, about what has come to be known as the divide between "high" and "low" art.[11] What is clear from these exchanges is that the line between artistic objects and the products of mass culture becomes blurred almost as soon as this line begins to emerge, at least in part because aesthetics is inseparably entwined with commodification, since both are offshoots of the more extensive practices of what I have described as operations of manipulative power. Recently the debates between the partisans of high and low art seem only to have intensified with the rise of information technologies and computer and Internet art. Because of their scope and complexity, I do not intend to engage with these debates here, but merely to show what bearing the notion of forcework may have on how we understand the role and the significance of aesthetic questions in the increasingly technologized society of consumption.

To the extend that forcework remains beyond the province of aesthetic questions, since it is critical both of the aesthetic conceptualization of the artwork and of the aestheticizing logic of consumption, the high/low divide does not appear to touch on the problem of art's force. This is the case because the very distinction between high and low art presupposes the aesthetic formulation of art, with its conceptual scaffolding, as well as its paradigms of perception, judgment, and valuation. Just to ask whether something can be considered high or low art, it has to be assumed that the object in question is (a) (reducible to) an object and (b) definable and understandable in terms of *aisthesis*. Thus the value judgments pertaining to art objects and products of popular culture presuppose, in the end, the technicist framework of being that art's forcework calls into question. In short, aesthetic judgments do not employ the criteria that would allow them to address the problematic of forcework, remaining bound as they are to the procedures dictated by the entwined logics of aesthetics and commodification. What I am proposing instead is a reconsideration of the relationality enacted by art, which would approach artworks beyond the purview of aesthetic concerns in order to flesh out the ways in which art inscribes in its work the determinants of social relations without submitting to their technicist momentum. As Duchamp's ready-mades make amply evident, the confusion that seems to reign with regard to the limits and value of aesthetics in relation to popular and mass culture reflects the points of attraction and tension between aesthetic objects and mass-produced commodities.

The partisans of popular art as aesthetically valid and important—for instance, Richard Shusterman in his recent *Performing Live*[12]—highlight postmodern theories of the exhaustion/end of art and focus on explaining, in terms of aesthetic criteria, the relevance of mass-consumed products of the entertainment industry. In his persuasive argument, Shusterman goes so far as to claim, in the face of the "end of art," that when contemporary artworks appear disconnected from wider audiences and mainstream culture, it is indeed the popular forms of art—from the work of performance artists and rap and country musicians to the "arts of existence" manifesting themselves in the plethora of self-help books and manuals dealing with how to live one's life (postmodern pop-culture versions of Aristotelian *Nicomachean Ethics*?)—that carry the hope of revitalizing art and aesthetics. He argues that popular forms of music produce genuine aesthetic experiences, which have implications for both the moral and political spheres of life:

> The recent flourishing of alternative aesthetic forms outside the sacralized modernist realm of fine art provides a good argument for the persistent presence of an artistic impulse beyond the confines of modernity's compartmentalizing ideology. Since the power of these alternatives seems to wax with the waning of art's modernist paradigm, one could venture that the end of modernity's artistic monopoly augurs some vibrant new beginnings for different forms of art. The two most prominent sites for today's aesthetic alternatives are clearly the mass-media popular arts and the complex cluster of disciplines devoted to bodily beauty and the arts of living as expressed in today's preoccupation with aesthetic lifestyles.[13]

In these aesthetic alternatives, aesthetic perceptions and affects are extended into the domain of activity, integrated with "everyday living."[14] On the other side of the high/low divide, one can notice various efforts to revitalize the traditional aesthetic notions, such as the beautiful and the sublime, and, in more general terms, the idea of aesthetic experience. Two recent books—*The Future of Art*, by Marcella Tarozzi Goldsmith, and *Radical Aesthetics*, by Isobel Armstrong—set out to perform just this task. *The Future of Art* reconsiders the problematic of the sublime, one of the most

important vectors of postmodern art, and finds in its disclosure of the new the vehicle of future art, whereas *Radical Aesthetics* argues for the continuing social relevance of aesthetic experiences.

While the idea of art as an aesthetic object remains alive and undergoes fresh transformations in these debates, such discourses do not engage with what I see as constitutive of art beyond the aesthetic and commodity functions assigned to artworks in modern society—that is, forcework. To the extent to which artworks keep having imprinted upon them both aesthetic categorizations and commodity form, discussions of aesthetic questions and their place in mass culture doubtless retain a great deal of relevance for the types of considerations I am proposing in this book. Although the notion of art's forcework is critically entwined both with aesthetic values and with commodification, this notion is intended to shift the focus of discussions about art. It seems to me less important to continuously revisit the shifting boundaries between high and low culture, to keep reassigning aesthetic categories and values across this divide, than to radically reexamine the very effects that aesthetic formation has had on works of art and their participation in the dominant mechanisms of social life. My interest lies, therefore, not in reformulating and revitalizing aesthetic categories, or finding aesthetic alternatives in mass-produced popular art, but in obtaining *an alternative to aesthetics*, without, however, reducing art to the parameters of social, cultural, or political analysis. What needs to be questioned, as I have tried to argue in the first two chapters, is the very notion of art, in particular the force with which art subsumes into itself and refigures the reality external to it. Rather than tracing the outlines of aesthetic experience within the products of both high and low art, we need to rearticulate the way in which art's forcework—its event of poiēsis—transforms, as I show in *The Historicity of Experience*, the very modality of experiencing that art inherits from its sociohistorical context of origin,[15] for what can be regarded as high art, according to some aesthetic criteria—an opera or theater performance, for instance—may not be of any importance or relevance at all when it comes to forcework. Opera productions in this day and age can largely be classified with high-quality works of the entertainment industry: both tend to be aesthetically good, accomplished, and interesting. In fact, often the products of the culture industry can be said to be much more aesthetically challenging and au courant—for instance some music videos, electronic games, or Web pages, which occasionally even achieve subversive qualities in relation to dominant aesthetic and cultural discourses. In such cases, and in aesthetic terms, one could view "high" opera art as "less" valuable than "low" products of the entertainment industry. High cultural productions, certainly these days, appear more readily to offer a comfortable replication of the status quo, a consumer product for the "higher" echelons of society, apparently having nothing to do with the kind of critique and transformation at issue in forcework. To this extent, high art can indeed often remain complicit, not necessarily with political or aesthetic ideologies, but with the underlying technicity of relations. In this context, Shusterman may be right to claim more vitality and aesthetic radicalism for some adventurous creations of hip-hop music, which appear to be more in tune with the avant-garde critique of art and society and thus closer to the idea of art as radical forcework, than are many examples of what, judged aesthetically, qualifies as high art.

Yet an aesthetic endorsement of the works of popular culture in the epoch that has witnessed the avant-garde critique of aesthetics does not address the most critical, in its double sense, question about art's social significance, for there is a crucial difference between avant-garde artworks and performances and the subsequent incorporation of avant-garde aesthetic strategies into mass consumption and popular culture. One of the most frequently invoked arguments in confirming the death of the radical avant-garde cites numerous examples of incorporating aesthetic aspects of avant-garde art into consumer culture, from advertising collages to music videos and Web pages. As Andreas Huyssen points out in his discussion of Adorno, the commodification of the aesthetic ends in the aestheticization of commodity.[16] The counterargument could be that when avant-garde art is appropriated—as has often been the case, for instance, with Magritte's paintings in advertising, or with montage techniques in video clips—it becomes aesthetically impoverished or degraded. A far more interesting and difficult question, however, would be whether in the practice of citation and reuse so characteristic of postmodern aesthetics, both in its artistic and its commercial manifestations, the kind of forcework performed by the elements of avant-garde artworks is also at work in the new contexts, regardless of whether the artistic work is carried over into popular culture or used to aestheticize commodities. As I argue in *The Historicity of Experience*, Dada manifestos and performances are never "merely" aesthetically radical and playful but also instantiate a most severe critique and reinvention of experience in the face of what the Dadaists regarded as corrupt Western logic and rationality.[17] As Tzara suggests in his manifestos, Dadaist art operates on the assumption that logic is an "organic disease" that infects the "Dada" manifestations of life.[18] One could argue, therefore, that Dadaism, even when it seems to be merely clowning and playing, or just borrowing the techniques and elements of popular culture and entertainment, continues to take aim at the nerve center of modern culture: the calculative and manipulative operations of power. Consequently, the forcework that figures in Dada performances or Duchamp's works carries with it an explosive social charge, which, beneath and apart from any explicit social commentary or irony, detonates on the level of force relations, transforming the very momentum of power that modern technorationality confers on contemporary reality. When the elements of avant-garde art are patched onto a new aesthetic surface, whether that of a popular work, a video clip, or a commercial advertisement, and yet are not "figured" in a way that allows them to work with their critical enigmatic force, these elements remain merely aesthetic (or aestheticized) and are thus deprived of the critical charge of forcework. They become part of an aesthetic recycling operation instead of working as a triple challenge: to aesthetics, to commodification, and to power. Thus mass culture can be said to successfully "evacuate" the avant-garde's critical impetus only if one confuses the forcework of the avant-garde with the aesthetic skin of the artworks themselves. In other words, the claim that avant-garde works have lost their historically radical nature is based on a fundamental misunderstanding of or lack of attention to their forcework. It only confirms the restrictive enclosure of the artwork within aesthetic categories—precisely the very procedure that the avant-garde so forcefully called into question.

The issue of whether and in what way popular or mass art is indeed art and can be capable of producing aesthetically valid experiences continues to be of the highest importance with regard to the intensifying technologization and parallel expansion of the commodification of contemporary culture. This question needs to be posed differently, however: no longer in aesthetic terms, and with reference simply to aesthetic and cultural categories, but instead through considering forcework, that is, the work's ability to engage with and critically redispose relations beyond the parameters of power. Works that can be aesthetically challenging and innovative do not necessarily work transformatively with regard to the imprint of the social relations they bear, as might arguably be the case with some avant-garde artists, such as the Italian Futurists or Francis Picabia. As Duchamp's ready-mades make clear, such works need also to be examined beyond the scope of aesthetic questions and cultural analysis pertaining to the processes of production and consumption, that is, beyond the divide into high and low art. While artworks by their very nature as produced works keep restaging the divide between high and mass culture, between aesthetics and consumption, what makes them artworks reaches in its transformative force beyond the social and technicist determinations of power that make possible the constitution of being into objects, whether of aesthetic appreciation or of commercial consumption. Instead of invoking or criticizing the high/low divide and perpetuating the aesthetic debates, it is more important, at least from the point of view of art's significance in contemporary consumer society, to seek an alternative to the aesthetic formation of art, which could help us understand whether and how art can be radical in relation to technicity. The alternative *to* aesthetics proposed in the notion of forcework can perhaps also facilitate the transition beyond the difficulties produced by the firmly institutionalized forms of the "great divide," which continue to fracture cultural debates and critiques. As is already implicit in *Aesthetic Theory*, though on that point Adorno is most often misunderstood, the critical divide exists not between high and low art but instead between radical art and objects that, though clearly of aesthetic value, do not have the transformative force characteristic of art. Beyond the controversial and continuously belabored aesthetic partition between high and low art, there remains the "postaesthetic" question critical to the future of art: can art in its aphetic forcework instantiate a modality of power-free relations alternative to the intensifying momentum of power, that is, the technological index of modern times?

The Public Face of Art

Art's significance, conceived in terms of forcework, can no longer be fully explained in terms of commodification and exchange but has to be articulated as an unconventional and distinctive "antagonism" of nonpower in relation to power. Art not only reflects and sediments in its form and content existing social antagonisms but also instantiates as its forcework the concealed "alternative" of nonpower. Forcework, letting forces unfold into power-free constellations, is not indifferent or oblivious to the conflicts and antagonisms that continuously ripple through society. It is not quietism but a quiet—or silent, as both Adorno and Heidegger might say—instantiation of relations into a modality that desists from power. The "antagonism" between power and nonpower expressed in art remains masked in society, which, circumscribed and regulated by power, admits only of conflicts between various forms of power, whether those conflicts are balanced, asymmetrical, or configured in terms of power and powerlessness. By contrast, the radical nature of art's refusal of power lies in its instantiation of an alternative to power, and to power's twin, powerlessness, which leads to the uncovering of a power-free "otherwise," suppressed and often erased in social relations. Art does not rectify or critique specific conflicts, antagonisms, or injustices; while such conflicts can be expressed thematically in art or even transposed into its formal configurations, art's forcework exposes instead the underlying "antagonism" of nonpower with regard to the power-driven relationality determinative of modern society. As Adorno suggests, art "transcends" specific struggles and conflicts not by abandoning or forgetting them but by reinscribing and critiquing them through a radical revision of "the domination of nature"[19] characteristic of modernity. The paradox of art lies, for Adorno, in art's capacity to artistically "dominate" domination and revise it into nondomination, a notion that resonates with Heidegger's idea of desisting from power and disclosing the alternative of nonpower. Art is not a matter of addressing this or that form of power, empowerment, or domination but instead of pointing to the release of relations from the circulation of power, within which relations come to be formed in terms of power to begin with. Thus Samuel Beckett's plays, for instance, do not criticize or oppose any specific forms of domination but, in an inverse move, present a world trapped without exit in the routines of power, power that empties the physical and psychic landscapes of his texts of anything save (near) meaningless repetition. And in Stein's texts, power is shown to operate on the level of syntax, to form the grammatical grid of language, thus bringing everything already within the orbit of power in the very act of disclosing experience in words. For Stein, the structuring of reality into a gram-

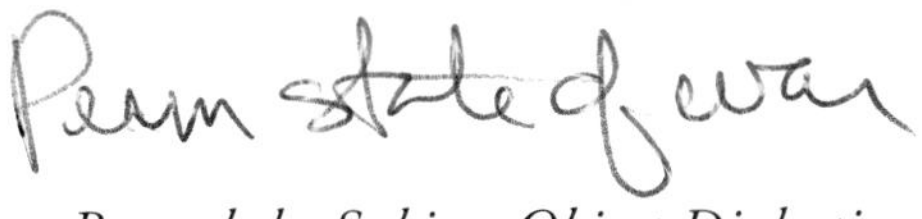

mar determines being and experience as always already a matter and a field of power. In texts like "Patriarchal Poetry" or *Stanzas in Meditation*, Stein's playful distension, repetition, and rewiring of grammatical connections between words and phrases shake relationality loose from the grammatical grid of power and undercut that grid's ability to produce (and reduce) being into meaning. It is a uniquely radical attempt to drain power from the flow of being, and of language, and to open the very interstices of experience as a power-free zone of relating. Art's critique is thus more radical than forms of social or political critiques in just this sense: that artworks call into question the very determination of relationality in terms of power, which functions as the source of domination pervading social practice. In this uncovering of nonpower, art transforms the power-bound space of social relations, letting this transformative event continue to reverberate in society, and sending the echo of nonpower, and thus of the possibility of a radical "otherwise," through the social domain. Even though modern relations are highly diversified and multiple, and as such can allow for the preservation of difference and otherness on various levels, they consistently come to be constituted into "power-ful" forms—they constitute a permanent state of war, as Heidegger remarks in *Die Geschichte des Seyns*.[20] To call into question the "uniformity" with which relations come to be constituted into forms of power, resistance, or counterpower is not enough, for these forms of active critique are always already made into the elements of the overall flow and intensification of power. It is in this specific sense that power-free forcework's instantiating can be seen as more radical than critique, as more "negative" than the negative.

The social significance of art lies, then, beyond politics and social relations, within the radical nature of the "otherwise" to power. Adorno explains:

> If in art formal characteristics are not facilely interpretable in political terms, everything formal in art nevertheless has substantive implications and they extend into politics. The liberation of form, which genuinely new art desires, holds enciphered within it above all the liberation of society, for form—the social nexus of everything particular—represents the social relation in the artwork; this is why liberated form is anathema to the status quo. . . . Today the socially critical aspect of artworks has become opposition to empirical reality as such because the latter has become its own self-duplicating ideology, the quintessence of domination.[21]

Beyond function, and thus also beyond functionlessness, beyond sense and nonsense, art's language is power-free. Of course, art can be made to speak, often quite easily, the idioms of power, to conform to aesthetic standards—including the historically changing precepts for aesthetic radicalism and subversivesness—as well as to the principles of objectification and the laws of exchange. In other words, artworks are always already prescribed as aesthetic objects and commodities, for aesthetic, cultural, and social discourses on art themselves work as fields of power, as conduits for inscribing art and its various aspects into the determinative, both subtle and supple, power matrix of contemporary society. The citation from Adorno leaves little doubt that what he calls "empirical reality," that is, the reality external to art, is a self-duplicating formation of power, an intensifying metaphysics of production working toward the constant, self-fulfilling increase of power, to recall Heidegger. Its ways of explaining art—whether through aesthetic theory, sociocultural critique, or philosophical reflection—unconsciously tend to perpetuate the power impetus of modern technicity. This is why nonpower is often "said" or "communicated" through silence, beyond or between words, marked on the hither side of discursive fields, as Adorno's analyses of Beckett or Heidegger's discussions of the unsaid in Friedrich Hölderlin demonstrate.

The event of this "otherwise," as I suggested in the previous chapter, can be seen as more radical and more "negative" than the negative, for both the positive and the negative constitute parts of the operations of power. Therefore, nonpower is, strictly speaking, neither antagonism nor negation of power. This is the case because forcework, which brings about nonpower, occurs outside the perimeter of power, so to speak, and this means that its force is more radical than negation, in the sense of being beyond or otherwise than negation (without, however, becoming affirmation) and more contestatory and critical than antagonism (without leading to utopian reconciliation). It prompts the revision of the dual optics of affirmation and negation, of the dialectic underlying binary schemas of relation (in this context, it is interesting to note that the Information Age is based on a binary logic, which forms the very basis for the calculability of being). Adorno's *Aesthetic Theory* understands form as both a repository of the historically sedimented technologic of modern society and as a transformative force reworking, in accordance with the artwork's own laws, the categorial determinations of being operative in and as history. It

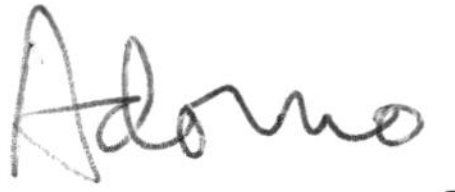

is in this reworking that the productionist logic underlying the modern society of mass production and consumption comes into view in its historical ascendancy and becomes disclosed as the "modern stage" in the intensifying progression of power. Adorno charges form with the capacity to disclose, as the negative of the social, what kind of dynamic of relations remains absent, lacking, or impossible within the historically determined parameters of existence. The starkness of Beckett's plays, the simultaneous irony and desperation of their many empty, repetitive gestures, signals for Adorno the stale repetition of the same logic of technopower, which tries to disguise its unchanging momentum toward domination in the appearance of novelty, innovation, and technological advancement. Art's difference is marked in this context by the way in which form does not replicate this drive toward domination but indicates the possibility of a different momentum of relations: freedom or nonpower. The social significance of artworks lies, then, in the manner in which, inscribing the logic of power that underpins and regulates society, they refuse to serve the same momentum as the cultural contexts that produce, incorporate, and attempt to regulate art. Artworks' social meaning is their refusal to be "social," that is, their unwillingness to subsist on the terms prescribed for art by the social operations of power that regulate cultural and aesthetic discourses. It is already implicit in Adorno that, "frozen" in the negative, artworks refuse to follow the logic of negation and affirmation, modifying the valence of the negative: negation no longer has the momentum toward eventual affirmation, which would prolong the dialectical movement and participate in the ongoing intensification of power. Rather, the negative becomes more radical than negation, since it works otherwise than the repetitive rhythm of affirmation and negation, disrupting the productionist momentum of relations. The production of the work of art, while it sediments in its processes the development of forces and relations of production operative in society, differs in its very momentum from the society that produces it. It is not that the artwork (re)produces itself as critical or resistant to its sociohistorical context but rather that in artworks the very logic of production sustaining the matrix of relations constitutive of social practice is called into question, unraveled, and transformed. This displacement and transformation constitutes the very forcework that distinguishes artworks from things and commodities.

Such forcework needs to be understood in relation to informational and digital forms of technicity, which, together with the telematic operations of power discussed in chapter 2, make up the vectors indicating the manner in which contemporary being comes to be constituted into historical and social relations. Beings, occurrences, and relations are disclosed today as informational in their structure; they are effectively produced as data, whose essence is to be intrinsically susceptible to reprogramming and manipulation. It is therefore no surprise that information has become both the most important commodity and the fastest conduit for the dissemination of power. In the digital age, information appears to be the most efficient and farthest-reaching way of rendering what exists calculable and manipulable and thus making it available for and conducive to the intensification of power. Information, digital technology, and telematics can be seen as the contemporaneous culmination of the logic of *Machenschaft*, that is, of machination and manipulative power. In them, the productionist logic of *machen*—of making, manipulation, and power—reaches the unprecedented flexibility of operating simultaneously on the micro and macro scales of existence. The paradigm of production thus penetrates to and regulates the levels of digital commodities, informational data banks, and telematic circulation. As Michael Hardt and Antonio Negri observe in *Empire*, contemporary social reproduction transpires increasingly in terms of immaterial labor, where conventional forms of material production have been replaced by new, immaterial processes of production associated with analysis and manipulation of information, with cooperation, and with communication.[22] The determination of being, production and social reproduction in terms of information and its manipulation implies not only a different speed of transmission and exchange but also a specific modality of relating, geared to maximizing the convertibility of "experience" into data, reflective of the intrinsic technicity of being. In the epoch of information technology, when computer-related immaterial labor and leisure tend to become increasingly indistinguishable or at least tend to occupy the same temporal and spatial territories, the pervasiveness and significance of technicity are reflected in the array of information-based forms of relations that regulate society.

It is such information-based modes of relating that come to be deployed, in Bill Viola's work, against their own propensity for efficiency and maximalization. Viola's video/sound installations both highlight and "manipulate" technology's own tendency toward manipulation, only to turn it against itself, so that from the vehicle of acceleration and efficacy, technology becomes, as in *The Crossing* or *The Greeting*,[23] a medium—or, better, a venue—for a meditative disarticulation of power and manipulation. The slow-motion photography taken almost to its extreme in *The Greeting* not only expands our capacity to see, functioning as a technological prosthesis whose possibilities Walter Benjamin celebrated in "The Work of Art in the Age of Its Technical Reproducibility," but also, and primarily, opens up normally unseen or unnoticed spaces of relating and interacting, which tend to become covered over by the generalized acceleration of life that is characteristic of modernity. Beyond the expressive images and visual commentary in Viola's work, its importance is concentrated in the interstices of relations, where his artworks deploy the powers of contemporary technology against the increasing technicity of relations in order to redirect their very momentum and orientation away from calculative transparency and manipulative efficacy. The slowing down in Viola's work does not celebrate the additional, technologically mediated, prosthetic ability to better see and grasp what our imperfect senses cannot register but instead draws our attention to the dimensions of relating that become progressively evacuated in the rush, reflective of contemporary society, to accelerate and optimize. Each element of gesture, each flutter of clothes, and every nuance of light in *The Greeting* is simply allowed the space to be and the time to occur, thus exposing the extent to which technicity constricts and compresses being into forms that are meant to ensure calculability, conversion into data, and optimal efficiency, often at the expense of the complex spatial-temporal nexus of relating that is constitutive of the rhythm of being. Viola, using technological facility to augment the human power to control and manipulate surroundings beyond our bodily capabilities, somewhat perversely draws out another impetus intrinsic to technology—that is, its poietic ability to reveal—which becomes juxtaposed with the technological power to grasp and manipulate. In Viola's work, technology is always two-faced: one face reflects the continuous increase of power, manifested in the progressively perfected ability to technologically produce and manipulate images, culminating today in virtual reality; the other face retains the ability to disclose the poietic momentum of being. In music, what comes to mind are the microtonal works of Giacinto Scelsi or, more recently, the acoustic and computer-assisted sonic explorations of Iancu Dumitrescu, which, frequently with the help of computer technology, expand and extend sound, opening up spaces, often close to noise, that are, as it were, internal to sound, hidden under the surface of the sonic spectrum of the modern day. Such art is eloquent testimony to the possible turn within technicity—to the poietic reserve, so to speak—that technology maintains even in the midst of the rapidly intensifying Information Age. Perhaps, and here we discern an echo of Heidegger, it is in the face of such informational "mobilization" and manipulation of being that, today, the other face of technē, that is, poiēsis, might unexpectedly come into view. Playing the two faces of technē against each other, art's forcework not only "critiques" but also inflects the operations of power on the level of the modality of relating, that is, in the interstices of force relations, which is where art's social significance lies today. What the work of art transforms is the manner in which the immaterial productionist logic of contemporary social reproduction disposes entities into relations that tend to intensify power by rendering beings and events into graspable, manipulable, and exchangeable objects. Through such a transformation, artworks give forces a different valence and momentum, disclosing a power-free relationality alternative to the technicity that shapes and regulates even the immaterial labor increasingly characteristic of contemporary society.

Amiri Baraka's collection *Funk Lore* illustrates how artworks can deliver their most forceful critique on the microlevel of force relations, beyond the accepted practices of critique and social commentary. While Baraka never shies away from abrasive criticism and explicit, militant social commentary, on issues ranging from the transnational operations of modern capital to racism to American politics and elections to African American history to vignettes about Malcolm X, Spike Lee, O. J. Simpson, and Clarence Thomas, his poetry suggests that it is not in these thematic layers that the most critical impetus of his art lies. As Adorno would say, the language of social commentary and critique is already compromised by its adoption of the very idiom that makes the existence of the criticized situation possible in the first place. The critical edge of the commentary is thus blunted by the acceptance and repetition of the very relations, inscribed in the operations of discourse, that are to be critiqued. Baraka is certainly aware of the problem and, while he accepts the risks involved in presenting poems written in straightforward language and in offering a clearly spelled-out message, he quickly complicates his direct commentary by lending his most vociferously critical texts a "jazzy," repetitive, variational rhythm.

Baraka's strongest "critique" manifests in the way in which his poetry calls into question and reworks the very paradigm of production and manipulative power that regulates the society he so scathingly attacks in his commentary. The production paradigm, the idea of social self-creation through labor, as Paul Gilroy argues in presenting the Black Atlantic as the counterculture to modernity, cannot serve as the universal model of emancipation, because it cannot address the modes of emancipation at work in the struggles of slavery and racial difference. Gilroy, critiquing production as inherently tied to enslavement and power, instead identifies poiēsis and poetics, and in particular music, as the alternative paradigm for liberated forms of relations.[24] Baraka expounds a similar position, fiercely critical of the metaphysics of production (and exploitation), which informs contemporary forms of capitalism and mass culture, and he points instead to an alternative mode of being, imaged in the funky rhythm of jazz. This jazz rhythm, a characteristic aesthetic icon of Afro-American liberation, is both the condition of eventual freedom from the heritage of slavery, and thus the condition of the liberated African-American voice, and the possibility of a turn within the very paradigm of modernity. Poems like "JA ZZ : (The 'Say What?')," "Art Against Art Not," and "J. said, 'Our whole universe is generated by a rhythm'" develop the poetic forms of jazz rhythm as an instantiation of a different "universe" between the lines, as it were, of the bloody and violent world of capitalism, class inequality, and racism. The jazz rhythm of the universe is the rhythm brought into the open by art; it is the poietic rhythm, which Baraka opposes to the "efficiency" rhythm of modern technicity, opposes, that is, to transnational capital, big business, finance, and so on: "The Universe / is the rhythm / there is no on looker, no outside / no other than the real, the universe / is rhythm, and whatever is only is as / swinging."[25] This quotation from "J. said, 'Our whole universe is generated by a rhythm,'" the opening poem of *Funk Lore,* frames Baraka's reflection on the "rhythm" of modern being, for it is in terms of the rhythm, of the timing and scansion of relations, that Baraka proposes to reenvision the world and call into question the operations of power that stratify and polarize it.

"J. said . . ." immediately penetrates to the level of the modes of relations in modern society, to their technicist, calculative beat, and proclaims that indeed our entire world is generated, structured, and regulated by a rhythm. What kind of rhythm it is decides the types of relations, beings, forms of existence, production, power, and so on that history and society will take in the present. The difference here is between the technicist measure, that is, the dualities and polarities underlying the productionist logic of modern society, and the jazzy rhythm of the "degrees of the swinging": "There is no such thing as 'our / universe,' only degrees of the swinging."[26] The technicist rhythm is a falsification of the jazzlike occurrence of being, which produces dualities and oppositional values (negative/affirmative, good/bad, black/white, and so on) where there are in fact only degrees of swinging. What exists is only "as swinging," that is, as motion in between, as degrees of extension, never reducible to polarizable fixities. The rhythm of being is one of degrees and in-betweenness. The polarization intrinsic to the operations of power, to the manipulative and calculative momentum of modern being, disfigures the jazzy, snakelike occurrence of being, which Baraka associates, in "Art Against Art Not," with the poietic rhythm of art, whether music or poetry: "Black snake the tongue of the world. . . . // The electrical 'Yes' / of livingness eternal as truth, beyond ourselves / yet in which we will always be part of however!"[27] The final image of the opening poem, "J. said . . . ," evoking the vision of a camp where inmates are trained to worship dualities, makes explicit the connection between the productionist rhythm of being and the power relations manifested in racial, economic, and social inequalities: "Dualism is a quiet camp near the outer edge of the forest. / there the inmates worship money and violence. they are / learning right now to sing. . . ."[28] Some of the poems that follow, in particular the tellingly titled "Sin Soars," extend and reinforce this idea of the rhythm that determines the shape and scope of relations structuring the contemporary world. Multinational corporations, the ceaselessly metamorphosing alliances of transnational capital aimed at the increase of wealth and power, come into progressively sharper contrast with the snaky, poietic rhythm of jazz.

This alternative rhythm of relating, the jazz pace of being, comes into relief in the closing poem of *Funk Lore*, "JA ZZ : (The 'Say What?')." The poem regathers and reiterates the leitmotifs of the collection, reworking them into a spatial and sound composition whose rhythm opens up an alternative to the social world, disclosing a different universe generated by a jazzlike, snakelike, rhythm of the degrees of swinging:

Yes Bees !
God-Electric
Come Coming
Fire Jism
S H A N G O
CANTO JONDO
Eternity Power
Living Happiness
S P I R I T L I F E
WORD SHIP
The Soul's Soul[29]

Baraka refers to this different universe as "the body of is,"[30] the story of being as shaped by the rhythm of interrelations based on freedom and letting be, a universe that has tended to disappear under pressures from power-oriented forms of life. Through music and poetic language, Baraka draws this universe out through the cracks in the edifice of global production, which has determined the relations of modernity in terms of manipulation and exploitation. Raging one moment against transnational corporations and the next against political and economic inequalities, Baraka dramatically changes his tonality, amplifying a different tune about relations released from the "dualisms" of power, relations that are barely audible in the rapidly intensifying pace of technological modernity. *Funk Lore,* literally jazzing up being, tries to inflect the rhythm of modernity: from self-organizing rhythms and globalized flows of power to the snakelike, flexible, jazzy rhythm whose force lies in instantiating the very disarticulateness of power: "The snake was music the visible thought / the answer, as the Sea crawls in waves / the waves of is' story. . . ."[31]

Like Heidegger, who directed our attention to the *Stimmung*, to the pitch or disposition, to *metron*[32] and *rhythmos*,[33] that is, to the measure and rhythm of being, Baraka energizes his critique on the level of the measure of relations, of the meter or cadence of being, which become responsible for the momentum that relations take. In both cases, what is at stake is an alternative to the intensifying technicity of the contemporary world, which functions as the often concealed matrix of power. In this context, art's significance is measured precisely by its ability to mark a turn within technicity, to recalibrate relations in terms of the "degrees of swinging." The difficulty and importance of such forcework in art is increased by the fact that technicity, understood as diversified and multilevel constellations of the modern flows of power, is not homogeneous or unified in any simple way; in fact, as its informational phase clearly bears out, it thrives on diversity and multiplicity. This flexibility of modern technē necessitates a rethinking of power and of a possible "counter" to it, that is, nonpower, beyond the notions of universality and particularity, unity and fragmentation, oneness and multiplicity. In the contemporary world, it appears that multiplicity is no longer really subversive, for globalization does not require total homogenization, since it transpires not in spite of but, it seems, with the help of multiplicity. The multiplicity characteristic of modern flows of power allows for more flexibility and a wider reach of technicity and capital without becoming "subversive," that is, without ever really being outside the fray of power. Therefore, both subversiveness and resistance, which remain imperative within the dominant optics of the power formation of forces, need to be rethought. Let me say as clearly as possible that replication of power into a counterpower, an empowering of difference(s), is critically important and necessary within the power-driven mechanisms that dominate social relations but does not open up any alternative to technicity, which constitutes the index of modern society and its increasingly immaterial forms of production. Within the hegemonic perspective of power, art—and here Adorno was truly perceptive—does not have commonly accepted social or political "meaning," or has it only at the ultimately fatal price of abandoning the very thing that makes it art and of becoming a political billboard—in short, propaganda—whether of the right, the left, or the middle. To put it briefly, art does not have a directly political meaning, not because it is not important or relevant to social praxis but because it does not, in essence, speak the language of power that is determinative of politics and society at large.

Among works by contemporary artists, Krzysztof Wodiczko's projections, vehicles, and instruments aptly illustrate this double bind of modern art, in which artworks both find themselves embroiled in the operations of power characteristic of today's reality and point beyond them. Wodiczko, inspired by the early avant-garde and by Situationism, utilizes contemporary technology to produce "public art" in the context of the postmodern culture of late capitalism. Like Viola, Wodiczko employs various new technologies—from industrial design and video to computer technology and electronic media—to bring into focus and then critique discourses of power in the economic, political, and symbolic spheres. From the beginning of his career in Poland, Wodiczko's art projects have adapted industrial design and communication technologies to produce vehicles, projections, and, more recently, performative instruments, which come to be deployed in public spaces and on public/official buildings and monuments. Publicness is thus inscribed into the very mode of existence of these artworks. Whether we are talking about objects produced for such projects as *Homeless Vehicle* or *Poliscar*, about the use of computer technology in *The Alien Staff* or *The Mouthpiece,* or about his widely known video projections, Wodiczko freely uses technological and industrial products to create artworks that address silences and exclusions from public spaces, discourses of power, and official histories.

Wodiczko's projections—for instance, his projection on the facade of the Hirshhorn Museum Building overlooking the Mall in Washington, D.C., critiquing George Bush's 1988 presidential campaign,[34] or *The Hiroshima Projection*[35]—unmask the workings of power in the symbolic, psychosocial, and economic domains by demonumentalizing public buildings and undercutting their stabilizing role in modern urban landscape. Modifying and redescribing buildings as institutional sites of the discourses of power, Wodiczko lays bare the silent, often imperceptible ways in which power both structures and stabilizes urban landscapes into a fixed and repeatable reflection of the prevalent social and institutional relations that decisively shape historical memory and attitudes toward otherness. As he puts it, "the building is 'sculptured' to operate as an aesthetic structure, thus assisting in the process of inspiring and symbolically concretizing (reflecting) our mental projections of power."[36] Frequently citing Benjamin's thoughts on history, Wodiczko frames his own works, whether projections or performative instruments, as he calls them, in terms of confronting and interrupting official history in order to open room for "the memory of the nameless" and "the tradition of the vanquished."[37] At the same time that his projections try to undo exclusion and forgetting, and thus to instantiate a different form of relation to the other—in his essays and theoretical statements, Wodiczko has frequent recourse both to Levinas's rethinking of alterity and Kristeva's notion of the stranger in ourselves—Wodiczko is careful not to err in the other direction, as it were, and monumentalize the vanquished and the forgotten.

The Hiroshima Projection is exemplary in this case, since Wodiczko chooses to commemorate the anniversary of the atomic explosion over Hiroshima by temporarily "resculpting," through his projection, the A-bomb Dome, the building that stood directly under the impact point of the bomb that exploded on August 6, 1945. Remembering those who died in the aftermath of the explosion, Wodiczko projects, onto the riverbank between the building and the river below, images of the hands of interviewed survivors and their families, accompanied by the sound of their voices telling their stories. In addition to these Japanese survivors and second-generation victims, however, Wodiczko includes slave laborers brought from Korea, who were themselves victims of Japanese mistreatment during World War II. The logic here seems to run parallel to Levinas's thought, since the "others," in this case the Japanese, are not only commemorated in their otherness and their suffering but also called to account before their own "others," the Korean slave laborers. In this instance, the Koreans become the other's other, exemplifying the open-ended character and multiple vectors of ethical relations. What is clear in *The Hiroshima Projection* is that Wodiczko is not interested in monumentalizing the victims but rather in unveiling and critiquing the very notion of victimization. Within the victimization of the Japanese at Hiroshima, Wodiczko inscribes, in a provocative gesture, the victimization, oppression, and exclusion of the other as inflicted by Japan. Thus what is denuded in the projection is the assumption of power vis-à-vis the other, the very formatting of one's attitude to what is different, other, or foreign, in terms of power. Wodiczko chooses to celebrate the monument commemorating the Hiroshima bombing by demonumentalizing it, by opening the now sedimented discourse of official history and memory to its own unspoken exclusions and silences.

The various projections that Wodiczko has produced over the years in different cities around the world seem to have in common the project of undoing the very idea of the monument and questioning the manner in which monuments and public buildings imprint existing power relations, and their formative influence on history and memory, onto city architecture and urban landscape: "The strategy of the memorial projection is to attack the memorial by surprise, using slide warfare, or to take part in and infiltrate the official cultural programs taking place on its side."[38] "Resculpting" various monuments and public buildings, Wodiczko unmasks and ironizes the very operation of monumentalization, the idea of understanding and forming history in terms of monuments: "The memorial projection will become a double intervention: against the imaginary life of the memorial itself, and against the idea of social-life-with-memorial as uncritical relaxation."[39] His projections suggest that writing and conserving history in terms of monuments is an approach intrinsically underwritten by power, both reflecting and cementing its operations within the symbolic, political, and even economic domains, for it is not to be forgotten that monuments serve as political and cultural commodities: they not only generate revenue for their own preservation but, more important, they sell, and thus further reinforce, the official power relations structuring the public sphere and historical memory.

What we can trace in the variety of Wodiczko's works and projects is a double logic, which, in a refiguration of the iconoclastic gestures of the early avant-garde and the provocations of Situationism, on the one hand brings into the open and often literally gives voice to the forgotten and the vanquished and, on the other, tries to clear space for a different dynamic of relating. This particular attempt to enable a new modality of encountering otherness is characteristic above all of Wodiczko's vehicles and their evolution through the years: from the initial 1973 Polish *Vehicle* through *Homeless Vehicle* in New York in the 1980's and the recent "immigrant instruments." What strikes one in these artistic ventures is Wodiczko's interest in enabling the other, and with it the subject, to experience relations "otherwise." Here is how Wodiczko described, on one occasion, *The Alien Staff* of 1992:

> No aliens, residents, nonresidents, legal or illegal immigrants have voting rights, nor any sufficient voice or image of their own in official "public" space. . . . *The Alien Staff* is a piece of storytelling equipment and a legal and ethical communications instrument for immigrants. It is an instrument that gives the singular operator-immigrant a chance to "address" directly anyone in the city who may be attracted by the symbolic form of the equipment, by the character of the "broadcast" program, or by the life presence and performance of the operator. *The Alien Staff* resembles the biblical shepherd's rod. It is equipped with a mini video monitor and a small loudspeaker.[40]

As Wodiczko notes elsewhere, "The stranger equipped with the immigrant instrument will be able to speak back to all of those strangers or nonstrangers who would like to cast the stranger in some preconceived mold of an individual or collective identity."[41] The performative instruments are designed to interrupt the "said," as Wodiczko suggests, citing Levinas, and open room for the "saying": by giving immigrants a technological instrument for making themselves heard and understood in the public sphere, a performative instrument is designed to endow the migrant with "new rhetorical power to wrestle with the power of the 'said.'"[42] This invocation of Levinas indicates the direction in which Wodiczko's immigrant instruments—alien staffs, mouthpieces (*porte-paroles*), and, more recently, "Æegis: Equipment for a City of Strangers"—point: the other as the instance of undermining or, even more radically, evacuating power. Levinas associates otherness with rupture of the subject's power, with stoppage in the circulation of power and its operations. The relation in which the subject acknowledges and welcomes the other is characterized by an evacuation of power: it is a relation that transpires "otherwise" than through power.

Wodiczko calls the project of designing various performative instruments *Xenology: Immigrant Instruments,* as though suggesting that the otherness foregrounded in the project may afford us a certain knowledge (logos) through the unusual dynamic of relations that it instantiates. In *Xenology,* the logic of the relation to the other, and thus the logos/knowledge it opens for us, may be understood in terms of its characteristic evacuation of power and the enabling of a relation that is power-free. Wodiczko's own descriptions of how the immigrant instruments work underscore the interest in enabling and facilitating a different modality of encounters and exchanges with the other: "The proposed design should not be conceived as a symbolic representation but as a performative articulation. It should not 'represent' (frame ironically) the survivor or the vanquished, nor should it 'stand in' or 'speak for' them. It should be developed *with* them and it should be based on a critical inquiry into the conditions that produced the crisis."[43] At stake here is not a different, less biased representation of the other, or a form of speaking for the other, but working *with* and enabling the other to relate differently to the surrounding culture. This transformation happens not through manipulation, intervention (speaking for the other), or making (a new representation of the other) but through releasing existing relations from the grip of power and enabling a different dynamic. The conditions producing the crisis are the often invisible operations of cultural, technological, and economic power, and their influence on daily life. The immigrant instruments, making these conditions visible, inscribe electronic technology and modern relations of production into an artistic project that unworks the very operations of power and thus questions the pervasive influence of the production paradigm and the various technologies it both deploys and makes available. As the titles of many of Wodiczko's works reveal, technology in these works becomes a critical vehicle or a performative instrument for bringing into the open the invisible lines of power relations and, as is most obviously the case in the immigrant instruments, transforming such relations in order to enable different attitudes toward and exchanges with others.[44] The use of technology is thus serious and ironic at the same time: it is a deployment of technology that calls for a rethinking of "productivism" beyond the metaphysical paradigm of production and power. As Wodiczko puts it, behind the suggestion of producing new equipment for immigrants "there is perhaps a more general call to a postprogressive, interrogative design, leading to 'productivism' of a new kind."[45] My suggestion here is that this "'productivism' of a new kind" can be understood in terms of an enabling forcework, that is, as an art event where relationality becomes free from power and its productionist framework.

Wodiczko's artworks, in their performative aspect of "public" art events, exhibit the social valence of the contemporary avant-garde in its multilayered complexity: from critique of the object/commodity status of artworks to questioning of the underlying technologic of modern power relations and its cultural and economic effects. As Wodiczko makes clear in his pronouncements, he is interested in continuing and thus transforming the avant-garde practices of "public art" in ways that would be almost hyperaware of their relation to the social domain and its contemporary technological, economic, and political effects: "How close are we all to the ground? How much contact do we have with the social terrain when pacing or enjoying that creative freedom?"[46] By making his art events literally and directly in public spaces, from monuments, official sites and buildings to streets, parks, and airports, Wodiczko makes works immediately engaged with the social sphere, both in its architectural dimensions but also in the symbolic, political, and economic relations that organize and stratify it. In this way, Wodiczko unmasks and projects onto public spaces the invisible technological/productionist operations of power that underwrite and maintain, even "monumentalize," the social sphere. This gesture of exposing the flows of power is paradigmatic of the avant-garde challenge: it enters into the thick of power relations and often ends up producing a counter to its operations. But Wodiczko extends his artworks beyond the operations of power, and it is in this gesture that his art becomes a critique of the fused paradigms of power, production, and commodification. He often speaks, perhaps again thinking of Benjamin, about healing or redeeming urban landscape and public spaces. But what would "healing" signify in the contexts of his projections and performative instruments? an event that enables a different relation to others? one that would interrupt the operations of power and free the encounter from it? What becomes visible and dramatized in the project of *Xenology* is, if I can put it this way in the context of the conception of forcework, the foreign "logic" of the power-free event. It is a novel "xenologic" of relations, in the service of which Wodiczko enlists the latest technologies, thus bringing into view the tension between the technicity of power relations and the xenological event. What Wodiczko's performative instruments perform, is, so to speak, a xenologic of relations, a logic that gathers its force not from the subject and its placement within power relations but from the other, and the "foreignness" of this force comes from the way the event disencumbers from power the relation to the other. In Wodiczko's works, the avant-garde imperative of social critique takes the form of a "public" event that enables the power-free "xenologic" of relations.

Wodiczko shows that what is socially and politically significant in art is not directly translatable into the language of politics or into socially acceptable and practiced discourses. And it is expressly not translatable because art calls into question the very language—always already a language of power—in which society represents itself to itself, no matter whether such representation is socially critical or not. Art's significance lies instead within the strange and baffling artistic idiom of forcework, within the silent language of the power-free event: "Artworks exercise a practical effect, if they do so at all, not by haranguing but by the scarcely apprehensible transformation of consciousness. . . ."[47] Art's relevance is "otherwise" than politics because it calls into question not just various political forms of power but rather power itself; that is, it transforms the power-intensifying forms of relations and production, and it does so more radically than any politics, whether by social, aesthetic, or institutional means, can do, for politics is always already a matter of power, permeated with power's language, organized and traversed by power's intensities, formed into power's constellations. It breathes and breeds power. In Baraka's poetry or Wodiczko's art projects, therefore, it is never enough to critique, attack, or resist, though their works obviously do that and find it important in the face of a general discursive and political complacency; that is, it is never enough to "perform" the political in accordance with the social determinations of what counts as politics. Side by side with their militancy, avant-garde artworks gain social and political significance as a result of the artistic transformation of the very rhythm of relations. It is through such transformations, whether in musical composition, poetic language, visual projections, art events, or interrogative designs, that art instantiates the "radically" emancipatory, that is, power-free forcework.

PART II: SUBJECTIVITY AFTER AESTHETICS

Forcework is a mode, an event, not an object or a thing. Since forcework is an event, how it unfolds is not a matter of "experience," strictly speaking, and thus it does not transpire in terms of the subject's relation to an object that is experienced. It is not only the subject, whether individual or collective, that comes into play in the creation and reception of art, but also, on the level of forcework, the event of the redisposition of forces. An encounter with forcework thus claims the subject on a new level, or, better, in a different mode. This "experience" transpires as an event, as a rupture and reconfiguration of relations below, as it were, the threshold of representation and meaning, apart from images, forms, and content, at ground zero, where artworks "unfold like forces in infinitesimal physics," as Adorno puts it.[48] Form and content participate in and figure the rupture of forcework, yet forcework remains "unthinkable" in aesthetic terms, occurring on another level or in a different modality, which does not work on the dialectical principle that underpins the relations of form/content, subject/object, activity/passivity, and so on, but touches on the infinitesimal, fractal flows of power. This new mode of art's work—a rupture and transformation of the subject-object dialectic—leaves the subject behind, but it does not transcend to the realm of "objective" collective experience or to the domain of social or historical truth, for forcework is not an objectified form of the experience of the subject (in art): it is an event "anterior" to the subject/object dialectic, an occurrence that foregrounds its own temporality and historicity. Playing with Tzara's terminology, one might say that forcework is the moment or the instant, the instantiation, of Dada, for Dada is not, in spite of much misunderstanding on this point, a particular state of chaos, disarray, or anarchy; the term "Dada" refers instead to a nonsubjective, nondialectical, and nonmetaphysical mode in which being occurs in the temporality of the event, different from instant to instant, never fully graspable, never really there, neither present nor absent—in a word, Dada. In this occurrence, the human being is not the subject, experiential (particular) or social (collective), and the (force)work of art is not an object. Consequently, to explain what happens in art's event, it becomes necessary to move beyond the subject-object dialectic and its corollary notion of aesthetic experience.[49]

Forcework has the rhythm of the "degrees of the swinging," to borrow from Baraka, disrobing the subject of the very relations that constitute it as a subject and, in the same gesture, make what it encounters into an object, positioned in such a way that its "essence" is to be experienced, appropriated, represented, or manipulated by the subject. There is, in Baraka's words, "no 'our' [subject] universe" [object], only degrees of the swinging. The mode of relating that forms the event into the structures of subject/object, identity/difference, activity/passivity is modern technicity, which fashions the site of such relationality into power. What art's forcework does, in this context, is not only to disclose the power momentum that shapes these relations but also to rupture and transform it so that the changed mode of relating, the new way of drawing things together, no longer gives being the momentum of power. The subject-object dialectic, which is one of the primary vectors of power, the very matrix of making and manipulation, becomes transformed by forcework from its productive and power-ful form into the relationship of letting be. "After aesthetics," historically speaking, the subject within art's forcework, that is, "prior to" the aesthetic dimension of the artwork, is no longer a subject, and the matrix of difference and identity, of activity and passivity, which still constitutes the template of our discussions about social and cultural issues and differences, is called into question. Forcework offers the possibility of a different logic of relating, a new way of thinking difference on the model of poiēsis, understood not as making or producing but as letting be or aphesis. The question that forcework raises is how to think this (non)subject of aphesis, how to understand "subjectivity" no longer in terms of action, production, or power.

As I explained in chapter 1, forcework brings about a displacement in all the usual ways of doing, knowing, prizing, and so on—that is, in the very dynamic of the relations that constitute (the nonsubjective sense of) experience. It gives a different momentum to those relations, in effect altering how things come to be, become related, perceived, done, and so on. Thus what is affected by forcework is the very way in which beings come to be, when this "coming to be" is disentangled from the metaphysics of subjectivity. In Heidegger's "Letter on Humanism," one of his most sustained critiques of subjectivity, in which he faults humanism for not being radical enough to disclose the temporal, eventlike character of the occurrence of being, he describes such transformation in terms of a letting be that "enables." Production and power, as well as the notions of activity, critique, and negation, because they are bound to and limited by the metaphysical discourse of subjectivity, are not radical enough to disclose the kind of "doing" and "acting" that happens in forcework. The "acting" in forcework does not have the character of making (and thus of power) but instead of enabling. Heidegger describes this dynamic of enabling through the relation between being and thinking. Being enables what is, lets it occur, and thus also enables thinking. Being enables thinking to remain within the element of thought, that is, within the event of being, and, through this attentiveness, to allow being to come into language and thought. Being enables thinking, but, without thinking, being would not be brought forth as that which enables and thus would not, in truth, enable. Heidegger makes clear that this enabling is different from making the potential into the actual,[50] from converting the possible into the definite, or from bringing essence into existence. Thinking belongs to being and participates in it precisely by way of "favoring" (*Mögen*, enabling, permitting) being, that is, by enabling being to disclose itself. This enabling is the "activity" of thinking, its deed. It is nothing practical, not an effect or a result; it does not produce a thing, an entity, or a being but simply enables what *is* to be *as* it is. In short, enabling here becomes tantamount to the instantiation of "letting be," to *lassen* understood as a transformation within *machen* and *Macht*. As such, this enabling is not passive or contemplative but instead participatory and transformative. It is a "quiet force."[51] The enactment of this "quiet force" in forcework is precisely what makes art what it is: "It is on the strength of [*Kraft*, by force of] such enabling by favoring that something is properly able to be." It is "on the strength of" forcework that something is properly able to be, enabled, and granted the capacity to be what it is rather than be drawn, through the multiple operations of "making"—production, representation, empowering and overpowering, domination, and so on—into the intensifying flow of power. Such force, actuated in art, works against the dictatorship of the public realm, which is constituted technologically. It displaces and transforms technicity from within, by altering the momentum of being from "making" to "enabling" and thus opening up a different, power-free register of force.

It is abundantly clear that this modulation in the momentum of relations, from making to enabling, is not the act of a subject, nor is it a matter of dialectical tension or inversion between subjectivity and objectivity. "Man is never first and foremost man on the hither side of the world, as a 'subject,' whether this is taken as 'I' or 'We.' Nor is he ever simply a mere subject which always simultaneously is related to objects, so that his essence lies in the subject-object relation. Rather, before all this, man in his essence is ek-sistent into the openness of Being, into the open region that clears the 'between' within which a 'relation' of subject to object can 'be.'"[52] Heidegger is thus interested in a mode of relating (*Da-sein*) anterior to subjectivity, which opens up the space for the subject-object relation, and clears the "between" that determines the valence and momentum of relating. How the between (that is, the spacing of relationality) comes to be formed is critical here: whether the between becomes constituted into the terms of power and production or works as "enabling." The composition of the very paradigm of relationality depends on the valence of this between. Since Heidegger makes clear that the between is beyond the province of subjectivity (and objectivity) and action, the alteration in the momentum of relationality from power to the power-free is not, therefore, a simple matter of action or praxis. Rather, this transformation is brought about as nihilation, which unfolds beyond the reach and the gaze of the subject: "Nihilation unfolds essentially in Being itself, and not at all in the existence of man—so far as this is thought as the subjectivity of the *ego cogito* Dasein in no way nihilates as a human subject who carries out nihilation in the sense of denial; rather, Da-sein nihilates inasmuch as it belongs to the essence of Being. . . ."[53] Heidegger is quick to point out that nihilation is not negation in its dialectical sense, for in dialectics it is still will that wills itself and "in this willing Being as will to power is still concealed."[54] In other words, negation still masks in itself power, which in its modern form operates as technicity. By contrast, nihilation, the quiet force instantiated in art's forcework, "nihilates" power: not negating or canceling it into powerlessness but enabling power-free relations beyond the productionist optics of technicity. What nihilates—that is, enables—is neither subjective action nor objective power but the quiet force of the event, but only when it is allowed to unfold and transpire as such. The difference between negation and nihilation, between subjectivity and aphesis, is the difference between the "power" of acting and making and the "quiet force" of enabling. Where subjectivity negates, acts, or makes, aphesis lets be, that is, capacitates. In this way, forcework transforms the dialectical formations of being, denuding the subject, divesting it of power (and powerlessness), and thus enabling a new sense of "acting" in the middle voice: acting seen not as making or effecting but as letting and favoring, in short, as aphesis. Forcework thus takes us beyond the intrinsically conjoined paradigms of subjectivity, aesthetics, and power, changing the optics for thinking difference, identity, and action as well as the power-oriented formulas of relation.

The Alternative Praxis of Nonpower

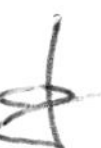

As a changed valence of force relations, forcework points to a different modality of praxis, to an alternative to what Adorno, in *Aesthetic Theory,* calls the false sense of praxis. What counts as practice in modern society is reflective of how relations come to be formed, distributed, and configured—namely, in accordance with the multiple modes of the operation of power. Thus social practice and the notions of action all come to be determined in terms of power, that is, as versions of power in its different modalities: dominance, resistance, critique, counterpower, ideology, powerlessness, inaction, and so on. Because these terms are set and regulated by and as forms of power, what desists from power *is not*: it does not *exist* and thus does not count as viable in terms of practice or action. Within the perspective of being and experience invested and formed by power, the aphesis that characterizes nonpower does not register at all as "existent" or "practical"; at best, it comes to be tolerated and neutralized under the rubric of the theoretical (thus, in accordance with the binary logic of power, as im-practical, in-active, un-real, and so on). If being is constituted in and into the terms of power, then nonpower does not enter the zone of existence; it is, strictly speaking, the nonexistent par excellence. The nonexistent is not a plenipotentiary of a possible, better future, thus signified (as is often the case in Adorno) as the negative of what is absent or repressed in society. Instead, it indicates here the inability of power to register aphesis as a different, power-free modality of relating. As it reworks and transforms the very momentum of power, aphesis is, strictly speaking, neither making nor not making, neither action nor inaction, neither activity nor passivity; and, as such, it does not properly signify within the practices of power. Its valence of letting be, of release from power, indicates that aphesis accomplishes or brings into being without an act of making, thus exposing the limit intrinsic to the understanding of being within the metaphysics of production (this metaphysics is at the same time also the metaphysics of action and power) and manifesting its inadequacy for recognizing the nonproductionist, power-free modality of yielding—a yielding that grants and bestows without fabricating or fashioning.

Though aphesis is not equivalent to production, making, or action, it becomes misinterpreted, in accordance with the logic of power, as inaction or passivity, as not doing anything, since this is the only alternative made possible (and dictated) by the economy of power. In other words, power (mis)reads aphesis as powerlessness, for, as Blanchot explains, power can do anything except "dispower" itself, that is, power cannot mark its own limit or "conceive" of an "otherwise" to itself. As an alternative to the paradigm of production, nonpower becomes mis-signified as the absence of power or powerlessness. And this deliberate and inevitable misrepresentation testifies to power's ability to perpetuate itself by disallowing anything that does not abide by the terms of power, and by reinscribing it immediately within the terms of its own operation, namely, as powerlessness. Nonpower, signified as powerlessness, is re-presented as part and parcel of the economy of power, not as a radical challenge to it. It is thus said to be a simple absence of power, to be inefficiency, inaction, and so on. Anything and everything that does not present power is cast as it opposite and thus effectively made part of the same economy, part of power, for absence of power is as much power as inaction remains, in a way, action; that is, powerlessness is conceivable only in terms of power—namely, as its absence—just as inaction is understood as, in essence, action in its "deficient" mode, as lack of action. By contrast with inaction or passivity, the "transformative" force of nonpower is precisely a refusal to remain within the optics of power as either another power or as a counterpower, which exposes the "narrowness" or "falseness" of power as the global matrix of being. The importance of forcework in art lies precisely in this transformative force with which it "declines" to participate in power, without forcework's ever being reducible to powerlessness or inaction. It is in this sense that forcework can be conceived as an alternative to practice: conceived, that is, not just as another form of practice (for even practice free of inequality and injustice would still be a form of domination by and into power, as Adorno's writings intimate), not as a better, domination-free instantiation of practice, but as a radical (non)practice, inconceivable within the very horizon of praxis/power. As Adorno puts it, "Abstaining from praxis, art becomes the schema of social praxis. . . "[55] It is precisely to the extent that art refrains from the praxis of power that it becomes the graph of social practice, which allows us to understand its operations and limits. As Heidegger remarks in "The Question Concerning Technology," the essence of modern technology, *Technik* or technicity, which determines the shape of social praxis, can become visible in the extent and the fluidity of its "revealing" in art:[56] in other words, technicity and social praxis cannot be their own mirrors because they do not know of any determination of being other than power. Art's forcework, as power-free, reveals power in the global range and flexibility of its operations, in the same gesture by which it opens up a modality of relating that is alternative to power. Forcework, as alternative to production and power, enacts the enigmatic praxis of letting be, a way of enabling without action or making.

In "Letter on Humanism" Heidegger explains such an enabling as an act that exceeds all praxis: "Thus thinking is a deed. But a deed that also surpasses all *praxis*. Thinking towers above action and production, not through the grandeur of its achievement and not as a consequence of its effect, but through the humbleness of its inconsequential accomplishment."[57] The thinking Heidegger refers to is the thinking that is also "worked" within the work of art, that is, the thinking that displaces, in an artistic rupture discussed by Heidegger in "The Origin of the Work of

Art,"[58] all the usual forms of acting, knowing, doing, valuing, and so on. This thinking is a deed, but not in the sense of action or production: thinking and forcework, according to the parameters of acting and making, accomplish nothing of consequence, and yet because forcework inverts the paradigm of action and making, it exceeds the productionist metaphysics of being—it "towers" above and exceeds all production and power. It is "more"—because it is, in fact, "otherwise"—than praxis can ever be, while being "less" (as an inconsequential accomplishment) than any tangible practical action. Forcework is more than praxis can ever be because it exceeds the very parameters of action and inaction, of making and production. Simultaneously, it is "less" than praxis because it does not register as an act or an effect, since it does not operate in accordance with the paradigm of production: letting be is so radically different from manipulation, making, and power that it does not mark or explain itself in terms of praxis. As a form of enabling that is "nonproductive," forcework remains "invisible," unmarked, to production and praxis, constituting their "otherwise." Art's most radical deed is this not-doing, or not-producing, which exceeds the technometaphysical determination of doing as making and power. This artistic deed, by desisting from power, "accomplishes" without making, and in this accomplishment it releases forces from power, undermining power's hold on being. It is in this difficult and enigmatic distinction of enabling and aphesis from doing and making that the radical nature of art's forcework manifests itself. This release is the most radical (non)act of disabling power.

Adorno's discussions of art's radical critique in *Aesthetic Theory* have an uncannily similar tenor. "Artworks have the immanent character of being an act, even if they are carved in stone, and this endows them with the quality of being something momentary and sudden."[59] In its momentary suddenness, even the apparently most static and frozen artworks exercise their critical force:

> Art recapitulates praxis in itself, modified and in a sense neutralized, and by doing so it takes up positions toward reality. . . . [Artworks] are less than praxis and more: less because, as was codified once and for all in Tolstoy's *Kreutzer Sonata*, they recoil before what must be done, perhaps even thwart it. . . . Art, however, is more than praxis because by its aversion to praxis it simultaneously denounces the narrow untruth of the practical world. Immediate praxis wants to know nothing of this as long as the practical organization of the world has yet to succeed.

The critique exercised a priori by art is that of action as a cryptogram of domination.[60]

Art is both more and less than praxis: less because its action seems ineffective from the point of view of pragmatic action, more because it denounces the narrow conception of action on which social praxis relies. "Art is not only the plenipotentiary of a better praxis than that which has to date predominated, but is equally the critique of praxis as the rule of brutal self-preservation at the heart of the status quo and in its service."[61] In this narrow sense, action is "a cryptogram of domination." What Adorno identifies here, without spelling it out completely, is the intrinsic complicity between any form of action—whether that of domination or of resistance—and power. Such complicity of the very paradigm of acting with power makes "radical" resistance difficult, since any form of resistance or counterdeployment of power—its importance, critique, and accomplishments notwithstanding—remains part of the overall operations of power. In other words, it does not challenge or disable power as such, "only" (but often how significantly!) reformulates and changes its flows. Action knows no other ways of acting but those of producing and effecting, that is, the ways of domination, control, and power. It is thus action and praxis that become "neutralized" in art, and it is through this particular gesture that art positions itself in relation to reality and praxis. The position that art takes "thwarts" action, "recoils before what must be done," but not in the sense of inaction or not doing anything.

Heidegger appears to go further on this point than Adorno, suggesting that art's recoil from doing and power "towers" over any form of action or critique that might be taken, in just this specific sense: that art's refusal to participate in power shows power's limit and undermines it. In recoiling from action, artworks not only negate reality but also instantiate, as demonstrated by Dada art, Gertrude Stein's works, or Wodiczko's vehicles and instruments, forcework as an alternative to praxis. If praxis is always already a cryptogram of domination, an element in the intensification of power, then no action, no matter how politically and socially important and laudable, escapes this association with and co-optation by power. While it is not, strictly speaking, the business of art to explicitly intervene or comment on such actions within the social sphere (which would reduce art to social commentary), what makes artworks art is precisely their radical stance toward action as such: what I mean by "radical stance" here is art's desisting from participation in action, since action constitutes, always and already, a form of domination/power. Art makes visible the fact that what is required for a "true" radicalism is something other than praxis, namely, forcework: a redistribution of forces beyond production, as Duchamp's ready-mades make evident. The radical nature of art's forcework is in inverse proportion to the perceived lack of "action" on its part, the lack that is already proclaimed within the optics of practice. It is because art is so radically a nonpraxis that the more practically oriented society becomes, the less visible or tolerated art's forcework can be. Forcework, misrepresented as inaction, remains the "pariah" in the contemporary world of optimally efficient technologies of information and communication. Shunned, misunderstood, or ridiculed, it recoils from social praxis, thus revealing society's power-gripped face: the degree to which "powerful" forms of action, production, and resistance keep feeding into the intensifying momentum of power.

Forcework could be called a power-free praxis if this were not an oxymoron. Among avant-garde artworks, Stein's texts, in particular *How to Write* and *Stanzas in Meditation*, as well as works by such later poets as Lyn Hejinian and Susan Howe, elicit this kind of "praxis," where textuality, working against linguistic, literary, and cultural conventions, reformulates the mode of relationality so as to give a different texture to "experience," one fundamentally at odds with the constitution of reality within the parameters dictated by the power-oriented social sphere. Hejinian's *My Life* proffers experience as a nonnarrative, fragmentary, and language-formed texture of the "present," where the past unfolds (is written) as fragments existing in and through the moment of writing. Claiming that only "fragments are accurate,"[62] Hejinian avoids the strictures of identity, narration, and representation, thus allowing "life" to manifest itself in the spaces of the between: between the various fragments of past sensations and events, present reflections, and general remarks; between the present and the past; between the "me" and the "she"; between colors and sounds; between the forty-five sections of *My Life*; and, literally, between its sentences, whose sequences eschew the logic of (re)presentation, story, and image. These intervals are what begins more and more to draw our attention, precisely because the text releases such spaces from the various forms of power operative on the levels of representation, narrative, identity, composition, and, occasionally, even grammar. The network of spaces and relations that animates Hejinian's text is "hers," not so much by virtue of possession or identity but rather through the sense of placement within a relationality that is irreducible to the meaning or position of subjectivity. Nor is this relationality simply a space of intersubjective relations, since it also involves—just as much, if not more—things and events in their sensory-linguistic texture: their feel, smell, language; their taste, so to speak; their color. The book begins with the memorable phrase "A moment yellow, just as four years later, when my father returned home from the war."[63] The sensory-linguistic texture of relations comes to unfold through the always fleeting moment of writing, and it is to the textual "possession" of such a moment, and such a "life," that the title *My Life* refers. Hejinian, a subtle and creative inheritor of Stein, presents a version of "my" that, playing with the book's title, is often interestingly and appealingly free of possession, identity, or biographical narrative and yet speaks with a force that owes its unusual fluency and intensity to the evacuation of power from *My Life*, that is, to the power-free spaces whose web makes up the texture of the book.

For Adorno, "art is modern when, by its mode of experience and as the expression of the crisis of experience, it absorbs what industrialization has developed under the given relations of production. This involves a negative canon, a set of prohibitions against what the modern has disavowed in experience and technique; and such determinate negation is virtually the canon of what is to be done."[64] What is disavowed above all in modern technicity is the declining or letting go of power, which becomes misrepresented and concealed under the rubric of powerlessness. To the extent that modern reality understands and represents itself in terms of the fluid operations of power, what does not enter the territory of power and refuses its jurisdiction is denied the status of the real, for to be real means to be efficacious and active, to be representable and appropriable in terms of power. In other words, praxis in the contemporary world is always already technical, for what practice itself *is* comes to be defined in the language of technopower: the language of measure, calculation, information, and so on. If the very scheme of action is domination—not understood as an overpowering and subjugating, but rather as an inducting into the operations of power—then forcework must revise the very optics of action and inaction, to "act" "otherwise" than acting. What is signified here by such terms as "letting be" and "enabling" is art's ability to "act" or "enact" without this event's becoming conscripted into the workings of power. This enabling or aphesis is therefore not a negation of the social, nor is it a positive, new form of praxis. Art's forcework is beyond negation and positivity, occurring in a mode that revises the very momentum of relating: away from making and producing, positing and negation, and toward the letting be that is indicative of nonpower.

The enabling at issue in forcework exceeds the notions of subjectivity and action. Art's force field becomes the nonsubjective field of "action" that is both more and less than praxis and, as such, "otherwise" than power—a new modality of relating, beyond the notion of agency. This is why forcework is not just a critique or a dispersal of the subject but a redisposing of relations prior to the sphere of subjectivity and to the parameters of agency, which opens up a dimension of force relations closed to the operations of power.

The undermining of the subject is obviously nothing new in twentieth-century art; in fact, one way to understand the radical nature of twentieth-century avant-garde art is in terms of how it undoes the subject and what different parameters it deploys beyond the subject-object dialectic. Already Futurism had called for the abolishing of the I and the replacement of all psychology by lyric obsession with matter: a field of forces not only irreducible to the human but, more important, unpresentable and unformed with regard to subjectivity. In Dada, the singularity or individuality that the manifestos extol and celebrate is, interestingly enough, not simply that of a constituted particular individual but rather that of the singular instant or the event—the event irreducible to the configuration of subjectivity. This instant or event is not a matter of an "individual" experience but of a whole, "transsubjective" web of relations in which one always already finds oneself, prior to becoming constituted as a subject and as an individual. The simultaneist Dada poems and performances, their invocations of spontaneity and their emphasis on the temporality of experience, register this level of the occurrence of forces beyond the format of subjectivity. Viola's 1996 video installation *The Crossing* visually crosses the bounds of the dialectic of subjectivity, incorporating/effacing the subject into the "stillness" that bespeaks force relations in a nonsubjective dimension.

Nevertheless, this kind of attack and undoing of the subject has often been described, especially in socially and politically minded criticism, as resulting in a loss of agency, with a corollary forfeiture of the ability to act and of the power to critique. Especially in the context of disenfranchised voices, in discussions of domination and inequality, these calls for an undoing of the subject appear disingenuous and often meet with resistance. The criticism raised in response to the undoing of the subject claims that such strategies eviscerate any attempt to reclaim dominated, raced, subaltern, or gendered forms of subjectivity and agency. But such an interpretation of the "undoing of the subject" is a reading of "who comes after the subject" in terms already prescribed and delimited by power: simply put, the undermining of the subject means, in this context, the lack or absence of the subject, that is, the absence of power. This presumed powerlessness of the decomposed or dispersed subject is then understood as a way of prolonging, if unintentionally, the disempowerment of the dominated and subaltern subjects that such critiques are supposed to liberate and empower in the first place. The key question in this context is therefore how to understand force and resistance to power beyond the optics of the powerful and powerless subjectivity/agency. The answer indicated by art's forcework is a nonsubjective and power-free redisposition of forces that releases from, and thus radically critiques, the determinations of relations, subjectivity, and practice within the idiom of power. The notion of the power-free mode of relationality evinced in art, in which one is neither subject nor object, neither powerful nor powerless, but instead comes to be understood in terms of release and aphesis, is what makes it easier to understand the implications and, more important, the possibilities that such a radical transformation of the subject, beyond power, implies for various instances of dominated "subjectivities." What is disclosed by the undoing of the subject, an undoing characteristic of avant-garde forcework, is the extent to which subject, agency, and identity are not just "products" but also elements of power. They are part and parcel of the economy of production and thus instantiate "domination" and power beyond the immediately recognizable multiple forms of inequality, subjugation, and exploitation. In other words, in order to call power into question, it is not enough to empower a heretofore disempowered subject as a liberated agent, to give such a new subject an empowered identity. This kind of reversal or undoing of the relation of domination, while it is certainly important, and while it often results in a change in the balance of power, and thus in significant political and ethical transformations, will still produce itself in terms of power, thus perpetuating the technicist momentum of relations. In other words, it will effect a shift in power without affecting or calling into question the determination of being and relation *in terms of* power. Within the optics of power, the only way domination, inequality, or suppression can be undone is through empowerment, that is, through a channeling of power into sites that heretofore have been deprived of it. Empowerment replaces (the absence of) power with (the presence of) power, but it leaves the organization of being intact, in terms of power: certainly altered, and sometimes profoundly and importantly, yet still governed by the economy of power. To the extent that art's power-free forcework does not just change the balance or distribution of power but also undoes power as such, it is, in this very specific sense, more radical than empowerment. Empowerment still relies on and thus contributes to the intensification of power, whereas forcework relinquishes power and thus allows us to radically reformulate the problematic of subjectivity beyond the conjoined optics of power, production, and action.

Obviously, this complex problematic of the transsubjective and nondialectical forms of relating and mediation instantiated by forcework, as well as of their bearing on the notions of subjectivity and practice, would merit a book-length study in its own right. Since that level of study is impossible within the scope of this project, what I want to do instead, as an indication of how the implications of radical art and its forcework can be extended into discussion of subjectivity, is to focus in the remainder of this chapter on understanding the possible implications of forcework for the problems of race and sexual difference. This specific delimitation of the issues is motivated first of all by the fact that gender and race are the sites of probably the most intense discussions and contestations of power, the places where heated debates about revising subjectivity, agency, and practice continuously take place. There is another compelling reason, however, for this choice: there exists a trail of theoretical and literary texts about the problems of race and sexual difference that have explicitly tried to approach these questions in terms of a poiēsis understood as a transformative redisposition of forces. Such directions for rethinking the problem of sexual difference come from the work of Luce Irigaray, who explicitly conceives of the ethics of sexual difference as a poetics. They also animate, as I have shown in *The Historicity of Experience*, the poetry of

Gertrude Stein and Susan Howe.[65] Within the problematic of race, Dubois, Gilroy, and Fanon (especially in his first book, *Black Skin, White Masks*) point to the inadequacy of explaining the "transformation" involved in the liberation from slavery in terms of the master/slave dialectic or the paradigm of production. It is significant that all three thinkers point to aesthetics and poiēsis as the transformative dimension that allows for a radical questioning of the distribution of power. As different as their texts ultimately are, what they all more or less explicitly have in common is the notion of poiēsis as a critical and transformative reformulation of the very dynamic of relating. Therefore, my interest here lies not in exhaustively answering questions about the problem of raced and sexed subjects but in indicating the importance and transformative potential of art's forcework for reconceiving subjectivity and action in their bearing on racial and sexual differences.

The Subject of Sexual Difference

In one way or another, all of Irigaray's work is concerned with (re)thinking the subject of sexual difference; more specifically, it is aimed at elaborating a postsubjective manner of understanding the "neither one nor two" that is both involved in and evolves as a result of reconceiving the subject through the optics of sexual difference. Three vectors of Irigaray's thought are most relevant in this respect: the notion of the between, or interval; the rethinking of the conception of the negative; and the idea of "being two," in terms of which Irigaray revises the concept of the universal in her later writings. Already in her first book, *The Speculum,* and, most important, in her second study, *This Sex Which Is Not One,* Irigaray had focused her work on radically revising the parameters of mediation, reworking the dialectical notion of mediation as negation, together with the forms of subjectivity and objectivity associated with it, in terms of the between and the interval irreducible to dialectical exchanges and progressions. In her early work, the between or interval characteristic of the "two lips," as the cipher of femininity and feminine difference, begins also to take on the characteristics of a paradigm shift in thinking about difference and relation.[66] "We are luminous. Neither one nor two. I've never known how to count. Up to you. In their calculations, we make two. Really, two? Doesn't that make you laugh? An odd sort of

two. And yet not one. Especially not one. Let's leave *one* to them: their oneness, with its prerogatives, its domination, its solipsism: like the sun's. . . . Dedicated to reproducing—that sameness in which we have remained for centuries, as the other."[67] Though Irigaray does not flesh out her fluid, "poetic" writings into an argumentative progression, she clearly indicates ways in which the economy of difference that she is elaborating breaches the confines of dialectical and monosexual forms of relating. She calls this alternative economy "proximity": an economy of intervals, betweens, interludes, and distances that elude calculative logic and linear progression. The two lips—of the female sexual organs and the human mouth—figure the "specificity" of the feminine without being somehow confined to the sphere of femininity, for in the figure of the mouth and language, the lips not only become discursively charged but also begin to describe the very economy of difference that is constitutive of sexuality. In other words, the two lips are both specifically feminine and "sexually differentiated": neither simply one nor two, neither reserved exclusively for the feminine (at the same time as they inescapably indicate something singularly feminine) nor allowed to figure an empty, sexually neutral "generality" of language and humankind: the solipsistic cipher of difference all too easily collapsible, in fact always already sublated, into *one.* Proximity signifies neither one nor two: it is neither the positing of the one (and thus always already of the two), nor the negation of the one by the other, and certainly not their resolution into a higher "one." Simply put, proximity offers a nondialectical understanding of relationality. Again, by "relationality" I do not mean here a link between two or more already constituted entities that come into reciprocal exchange but rather the very spanning or dimension that opens up and disposes the relating as such and thus participates in the constitution of what exists precisely by virtue of the manner of relating that it establishes. In other words, what exists, exists as it does to the extent that it continuously comes to be constituted through and as part of relating: its identity is relational and becomes shaped (and reshaped) through the very event of relating. Above all, in Irigaray this relationality emphasizes the spatial-temporal play of the interval: the active occurrence of the between, the proximity, whose event cannot be translated into identity positions, into a "one," either solitary or in relation to an "other" (one). To the extent that proximity is "neither one nor two," it does not involve, strictly speaking, either positing or negating, in the dialectical sense. In other words, there is no "one" to be negated or to perform the negating, for the "subject in sexual difference" is neither one nor two. It is possible to say here that in Irigaray the subject is not so much in difference as in/of proximity, where "proximity" is to be understood as denoting an alternative economy of relating to the phallic and logocentric economies of power. Proximity, as the economy of "neither one nor two," is not about identity and difference in their traditional transactions and exchanges but is instead about an "otherwise" to identity, an "otherwise" to the economy of the one and the two, that is, the economy of difference *and* negation and of difference *as* negation. For Irigaray, the rethinking of the subject of sexual difference involves the thought of the subject *as* proximity, as otherwise than identity (one) and difference (two, always already conceived on the model of, and calculable as, *one*).

Sexual difference, in order to be marked in the monological and monosexual economy of language, therefore requires an alternative paradigm of relationality. The excerpt, above, from *This Sex Which Is Not One* makes clear that the relationality Irigaray has in mind is explicitly not based on calculation, for the "calculative" idea of difference is based on the economy of the one and the two: either the subject is one or there are two subjects. Calculative relationality is also what, in Irigaray's texts, underlies the market economy of Western societies: societies whose economies make trading in general, and trade in women, possible. Such economies are predicated on the possibility of positing, fixing, and calculating the one as one; in other words, they are dependent on the very positing of identity (as either one or two, as self-sameness or difference). Within such economies, the different or the other functions also as, in principle, a one, that is, (an)other one. An other one, the other is as such also a one and thus instantiates a repetition of sameness as difference. This is why all of Irigaray's texts insist on the idea that the notion of otherness, which is based on difference and negation, is part and parcel of the "same" economy of sameness. In other words, difference conceived in terms of negation—of one by (an)other one—fails to truly register difference, to mark what might be called here "radical difference," that is, the kind of difference that, for Irigaray, marks humans as sexed subjects. Dialectical difference, as difference signified by the movement of negation, amounts to the repetition of the same in this specific sense: that each difference remains in principle still calculable in terms of the one—as oneness, sameness, identity. Difference is the obverse of identity and, as such, is supported by the same logic of sameness and oneness.

This logic of oneness is calculative, based on the mechanism of one plus one plus one plus one. . . . As some of Irigaray's texts in *Sexes and Genealogies* indicate, this calculative relationality, on which the edifice of Western civilization and commerce is predicated, is a technicist one: it is, in principle, the technologic that governs modern social praxis, markets, and exchanges. One of the most important aspects of the calculative economy is the extent to which it makes exchange possible in the first place. What Irigaray does not develop is the way in which this economy is an instance of the technicist relationality that forms relations in terms of power. That much is indicated, though, by Irigaray's insistence on the fact that her thinking about the new culture of sexual difference is intrinsically an ethics, not only in the sense of new norms or prescriptions for a practice reflective and respectful of sexual difference—as proximity, not as a logic of identity and difference—but also as an alternative paradigm of relationality that points beyond the instantiations of power. In this context, proximity focuses attention on the between, the interval, as the constitutive and dispositive element of relations between forces. Proximity becomes an alternative manner of disposing and constellating forces into relations that do not follow the principle of identity and difference. The principle of identity and difference is instrumental in forming forces into relations of power; proximity, by contrast, bears the trace of a certain relationality of nonpower. Irigaray's rethinking of Nietzsche in *Marine Lover of Friedrich Nietzsche* suggests that her thought, developed as it is through constant exchanges with Nietzsche, Heidegger, Hegel, and psychoanalysis, aims at a critical redisposing and recoding of the valence of force relations.

One base of power's operations, perhaps the most critical one, is the intrinsic calculability of what *is*, the reducibility and representation of beings as graspable, identified, known "quantities"—in other words, the instantiation of the calculative logic of identity. In the age of information technology, there is no doubt that this "calculative" momentum constitutes the very logic of being: the plasticity with which what is can become identified in its informational "essence," translated into the binary alphabet of computer calculations, stored, transmitted, and (re)programmed. Thus the revised notion of relationality as proximity touches on the very core of the operations of power precisely to the extent that it concerns itself with the "potency" of power to disclose forces as intrinsically calculable, and then to form them into relations, exchanges, and transactions that expand and render the calculative "power" principles of relationality infinitely flexible and globally applicable. Even though Irigaray does not push her reflections sufficiently in this direction, some of her remarks in *Sexes and Genealogies* point toward this "central" position of the problematic of sexual difference in relation to power. It is not just that sexual difference, like everything else, appears to be a question of power but that, much more important, what is at stake in rethinking sexual difference as proximity is the power momentum of relations. In all of Irigaray's work, sexuality and sexual difference become the locus for reinventing or reimagining the notion of relation. Proximity, inflecting and altering the dynamic and vectors of relation toward an "economy" of neither one nor two, discloses and revises the power logic of forces. If power operates on the principle of either one or two (almost literally reenacted in the language of informational computation and transmissibility), then proximity, working on the "antiprinciple" of "neither one nor two," becomes the alternative to the power economy of being: nonpower, or the power-free. Irigaray's work prompts the understanding of how power requires the economy of identity and difference, its seemingly infinite extensions and playfulness, to implement its operational principle of increasing reach and flexibility. What makes it possible to let go of this logic of power is thus not a multiplicity of differences but proximity taken as an "otherwise" to the mechanic of differentiation. As the index of differentiation, proximity indicates that the momentum of differentiation is neither difference nor identity, neither one nor two, neither power nor powerlessness. In this strange nonequation of neither one nor two, proximity is beyond calculation and thus beyond programming, information, transmission, and so on—that is, beyond the flexible operations of modern power. The importance of Irigaray's insight, which proves "right" her claims about sexual difference being the issue of our age, one that could change its intensifying momentum of power, cannot be understood in any naive way but must be correlated with the infotechnical modalities in which contemporary power operates and disseminates its potency of forming all that is into the expanding conduits of power.

Proximity in this context serves as the index of the revision of sexual difference and of difference as such, as both a further development and a radical revision of what Nietzsche understood as the aesthetic state. The aesthetic state, briefly, was a state of the enhancement of forces, which Heidegger, in his reading of Nietzsche, juxtaposed with the technological increase of force, both elemental and instrumental to the operations of modern technologic. Nietzsche clearly codes this state of the enhancement of force as "masculine," and Heidegger does not explicitly inscribe the problematic of sexual difference into his rethinking of technology, but Irigaray makes clear that the proximity characteristic of sexual difference is what revises the intensifying momentum of power and points to an alternative relationality. I would suggest that we can think of Irigaray's proximity as the instantiation of a power-free relationality: a relationality simultaneously, though on different levels, emblematic of the feminine, the revision of sexual difference, and the recoding of the very momentum of differentiation as such. Proximity, inflecting and revising the paradigms of identity and difference, extracts the feminine, sexual difference, and, ultimately, difference as such from the power logic of calculation and technicity. In this context of power and the aesthetic state, Irigaray's claim that her ethics of sexual difference is also a poetics makes a new and radical sense. Proximity is a new, poietic dynamic of relations: beyond markets, exchange, and calculation but also, and most important, beyond power.

Irigaray's notion of proximity can be interpreted as an alternative modality of relation, as a kind of forcework, one intrinsically tied to a poietic unfolding of being. Seen in this perspective, Irigaray's multiple conversations with Hegel, Nietzsche, and Heidegger acquire their critical force in relation to modern technicity. What is at stake in rethinking sexual difference as proximity is the crux of modern relationality: power in its flexible deployments that affect, at the very core of "identification," all that exists, including, in the first place, sexual difference, for it is only through fixing, calculating, and erasing the incalculable "proximities" that mark and continuously reincarnate sexual difference in embodied being and bodily encounters that power can emerge in the first place. Irigaray's analyses of Platonic discourse are most evocative in this respect, suggesting the foundational importance, for the modern economy of power, of the Platonic gesture of sexualizing the divide between matter and spirit and the simultaneous erasure and devaluation of matter as inferior and sublatable into spirit: the establishment of the very economy of the one and the other (one) guaranteeing the reproduction of sameness, that is, the intensifying mirroring and (re)production of power.[68] Proximity, understood as a critique of power, also becomes the instantiation of a different praxis: it is the praxis of "neither one nor two," of incalculable exchanges, of "unmarketable," information-free surges of force that divest themselves of the power momentum regulative of contemporary being. Such practices occur in the middle voice, with the "agency" being neither one nor two, eschewing the optics of subjectivity, and exposing the ways in which identity and agency are intrinsically and, in a way, irremediably interlaced with the operations and extensions of power. It is only when the relation has the momentum of proximity, the calculative nonvalue of neither one nor two, that the relations, exchanges, or touching figured in Irigaray's two lips unfold, as it were, free of power.

This is also the practice of the different universality of "to be two," as Irigaray's more recent writings make clear. Because proximity means 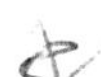 that being two is irreducible to either one or two (ones), it indicates a different momentum of relating, which, in Irigaray's eyes, necessitates the reformulation of the notion of the universal. The calculable universal of the one is nothing else than the infinitely flexible instantiation of power, which, while capable of entertaining a multiplicity of differences, works on the principle which asserts that, in the last instance, all differences are intrinsically calculable and reducible to their informational content. It is as information that all differences become the same: the multiple repetition of the sameness of power infiltrating and regulating all forms of relations. This is why the dialectical universal is not only based on but also reflects and perpetuates power. To counter this tendency, the universal needs to be based on proximity: on the power-free vector of relating, in which the "subject" is neither one nor two but intrinsically opened to, inscribed with, and *enhanced by* the other. Taking the negative upon oneself, as Irigaray refers to it,[69] changes the very momentum of negation from power to the "otherwise" than power, from difference (between "ones") to proximity. What changes in proximity is thus the vector or the momentum of relating. In proximity, there is no "one" and no "subject," only "being two," and "to be two" means neither being one nor being a subject but instead delineates a relationality of forces beyond identity and power-oriented praxis. Reformulating the universal, Irigaray not only makes clear the critical importance of sexual difference (as proximity) for the critique of power but also revises the notion of the sexed "subject": for the human "one" to be sexed means always already "to be two"—to be singular and yet, at the same time, representative of one's gender, a "one" always already inscribed with and inflected by the "other," where both are "neither one nor two."[70] "To be two" signifies singularity beyond particularity, and universality beyond the universal of the one, beyond (the) one universal, and beyond the universal of oneness. If the universal inscribes the very dynamic of relations, between the one and the other (one), then Irigaray's universal of "being two" revises this dynamic, changes the valence of relating, and makes the new, sexed "subject" neither one nor the other. The Irigarayan subject conceived as proximity no longer submits to the plays and profits of the games of power: underneath the calculability and informational exchanges in the service of intensifying power, "to be two" marks an alternative space of relating, free from power and irreducible to the technical calculus of being. Most important for our discussion of forcework, Irigaray's thought indicates the way in which the "subject" reconceived in the context of forcework can be understood to inscribe sexual difference: if sexual difference undermines the calculative momentum of power, to think sexed "subjectivity" means to think an "otherwise" to power: a power-free relationality in which what exists is "neither one nor the other."

L'homme actionnel: Race and the Poiēsis of Invention

Forcework, the transformative, power-free "praxis" of aphesis, carries similar implications for the problematic of race and raced subjectivity. Already Du Bois, in his rethinking of Hegel and the master/slave dialectic, had implied the importance of supplementing the idea of production with art.[71] Picking up on this possibility, Gilroy, in *The Black Atlantic,* claims that the paradigm of production is unable to provide and explain liberation from slavery because it is the underlying principle of enslavement itself. Gilroy points toward poiēsis and especially the transforming influence of African music as the necessary aspects of liberation from slavery and establishment of a different, post–master/slave identity.[72] What Du Bois and Gilroy point to but do not develop as such is the intrinsic connection between slavery and the operations of power as production, for slavery is not simply a paradigm of domination and exploitation intrinsic to and constitutive of the Enlightenment but also an extension of the very notion of production. Production works on the principle of making and manipulation and thus is the very conduit for the instantiation and production of power. What is suggested in Gilroy is the idea that liberation from slavery is never simply understandable as a reclaiming of power, as a new form of empowerment for the disenfranchised and subjugated, that is, for a newly born subjectivity or agency. Rather, emancipation needs to go further and embrace another mode of being or relating, and thus to question the logic of production, and with it the formative influence of power, both in its subjugating and productive or liberatory effects. Liberation and the contestation of slavery imply a more radical questioning of the subject as the site of the instantiation of power and its progressive grasp of being.

Gilroy gestures toward art and poiēsis as this alternative *modus,* which goes beyond the logic of production and redescribes liberation from slavery as a revision of the paradigm, and metaphysic, of production. Referring to Heidegger, I have explained the difference that poiēsis introduces into the Western metaphysics of production in terms of a shift from making, manipulation, and power (the correlation between *Macht* and *machen*) to letting be (*lassen*), that is, to aphesis as the alternative form of relationality. What is necessary for such a critique, however, is a radical questioning of the modern, technicist operations of power, a questioning that takes us beyond the ideas of subjectivity and domination, with their inherent entwinement with the logic of production. In the remainder of this chapter, I want to suggest briefly the possibility of such a (re)thinking of the raced "subject"—irreducible, like the sexed "subject" in Irigaray, to either "one" or the "other" (one)—through the redisposition of force relations on the basis of Fanon's ideas as expounded in *Black Skin, White Masks*.

Early on in that work, Fanon announces his intention of liberating the black man from his own color, "à libérer l'homme de couleur de lui-même,"[73] from the epidermal racial schema that comes to define the black man both in society and in his own psyche. Fanon proposes, as the critical agent of such liberation, his idea of the *l'homme actionnel,* "the actional man"—an answer to the psychoexistential complex—which blends elements of dialectic, psychoanalysis, and the invention of poetic language into a new form of relating. In proposing the notion of *l'homme actionnel,* Fanon refuses to be the prisoner of history, of the past events and former figurations of "the Negro," as he becomes adamant about refusing to lock himself into the dialectic of hatred, reparations, or guilt, for, as Fanon explains, to lock oneself into these forms of the dialectic of history means to relinquish oneself to abstractions and concepts, to allow one's singularity to become subsumed into the abstract "universal" of blackness, and into the power struggle between "blacks" and "whites." I would add that such entwinement also means a necessary inscription into the operations of power, within which the unrepeatable singularity of the event becomes formed into the image of a particularity, referable, through a logic internal to power, to a universality. Both the particular and the universal are aspects of the same logic of power. Even though Fanon does not address the problematic of power in these terms, it becomes clear that what is at stake in his insistence on singularity beyond the particular, both historical and bodily, is the understanding of the insufficiency of the dialectic to account for the liberation from one's "color." The refusal to submit one's singularity to the abstract logic of history manifests itself in the dissolution of concepts: "The Negro is not. Any more than the white man."[74] The dialectic proceeds from the particular to the universal, from a particular black man or Martinican to blacks or Martinicans as such. It is this movement that Fanon interrupts and attempts to radically reinvent, for, as he repeatedly asserts, his being a black Martinican makes him neither an exemplar nor a particular of the universals "blacks" or "Martinicans."

Conceiving of himself not as a subject but as an actional human being, Fanon underscores the fact that the "event" of being human cannot be foreclosed or circumscribed in any kind of identificatory logic, to which social praxis constantly submits all humans as "subjects": "Je me définis comme tension absolue d'ouverture"/ "I defined myself as an absolute intensity of beginning"[75]: the actional human being comes to be defined as the absolute tension of opening, a definition that, by keeping differences in play, allows for inventing oneself through difference. Yet what, exactly, is the "action," the invention, that constitutes a human as an actional man? It is significant that this action is not a form of production, a making or a remaking of sorts, but instead a constant questioning: "My final prayer: / O my body, make of me always a man who questions!"[76] Action becomes reconceived in terms of a relationality of questioning, which, rather than producing what is (the other) as an object for a comprehending and representing subject, allows one to build the world of the you—the singular, concrete you, not the abstract, "dialectical" you—for it is only as a questioning, actional human being that one can touch the other, feel the other, explain the other (as other) to oneself.[77] Thus the condition of one's liberation into an actional human being is the constant questioning in which one comes to relate to another beyond the subject-object dialectic. One's freedom is allowing the other his or her freedom as a singular being: not as an object or, at best, an other subject but as a singularly embodied and historically existing being. Such a singularly embodied and existing being desists from abstractions and concepts: while repeatedly defined within the social praxis as black, white, male, female, and so on, with all that those definitions come to bear with them, such a singular being escapes those classifications to the extent that he or she remains an actional human being.

The "actional man" also intimates the parameters of Fanon's definition of revolt/revolution in *Black Skin, White Mask*. The entire discussion of questioning, and of its "revolutionary" and transformative effect on being and history, comes in the concluding section of the book, prefaced by an epigraph from Marx's "The Eighteenth Brumaire," about the social revolution drawing its poetry not from the past but from the future.[78] For Fanon, the poetry of the revolution is indeed not simply of the future but rather is itself *futural*: that is, it involves a leap, a leaping over oneself, so to speak, which reinvents one's bodily and social existence: "the real *leap* consists in introducing invention into existence"; "I am endlessly creating myself."[79] There are echoes here of Nietzsche's aesthetic state, for in order to reinvent, one needs the power of art, the force of language. It is in this artistic, "poietic" state of the (re)disposition of forces that one invents oneself in a leap of questioning. The "praxis" that Fanon implies here is "revolutionary" poiēsis understood as a key redisposition of forces in terms of one's bodily existence, in relation to others and beyond the parameters imposed by historical conditions and existing social practices. The revolutionary character of such poiēsis—as Fanon makes clear in the conclusion but emphasizes throughout the book, through numerous references to the poetry and art of the Negritude movement—has been sorely neglected by the criticism of Fanon's work, in favor of the more explicitly "political" conception of violence and anticolonialism in *The Wretched of the Earth*.[80] Yet I would argue that the notion of the "actional man," whose "action" is revolutionary poiēsis, persists in Fanon's writings as his most radical contribution to the critique of power. Even as he embraces and endorses the necessity of violence and the overthrow of colonizing power, Fanon is well aware that liberation from slavery necessitates a further and even more radical liberation from power. "Actional man" is not a subject who claims power for himself but rather is a questioning force that allows forces to exist otherwise than as power: as, indeed, other and singular in their character as event. Fanon's ample quotations from Aimé Césaire and Léopold Senghor relate this conception of invention to the problem of art and language, that is, to the question of poiēsis. One of the quotations from Césaire describes African sculpture in terms of a gathering and disposition of the most fundamental forces in the universe:

> They had their magnificent sculpture, in which human feeling erupted so unrestrained yet always followed the obsessive laws of rhythm in its organization of the major elements of a material called upon to capture, in order to redistribute, the most secret forces of the universe.[81]

The rhythm that pervades African cultures and African art, from music to sculpture, redistributes, as Césaire indicates, the most secret forces of the universe, forces drawn out into specific and alternative configurations in works of art. Senghor, too, in "Negritude and Modernity," focuses his discussion of art on the question of the composition of force relations into a rhythm: "It is a matter of rendering the ultimate reality of the universe, which is the *inter-action* of vital forces: *rhythm*."[82] Discussing Black African ontology, Senghor underscores the importance in it of force, understood as the very essence of beings, and expressed by the root *ntu* in Bantu.[83] Developing his initial remarks, Senghor draws a parallel between this African ontology of force and Heidegger's critical rethinking of logos in terms of a gathering and a laying out. In Black African ontology, "to speak is to gather the vital force, the Being of the being in the shape of a rough sketch, in order to lay it there by giving it a form, that is to say, existence."[84] In this context, the role of human beings is not to "act," in the sense of autonomous, active subjects or agents, but to make "BEING more-being in more and more numerous and diverse forms."[85] As a result, "*Negro art is a technique of essentialization toward being-more.*"[86] Senghor's observations strike a very similar note to Heidegger's comments, in his own texts on Nietzsche and in his "Letter on Humanism," about thinking as a form of enabling, that is, as an "act" of letting be "more-being" (*seien-*

der). Poiēsis comes to designate this different rhythm of force relations, a rhythm that lets forces be "more-being" rather than channeling them into technical flows of power. As Senghor suggests, art is a technique that produces a turn in technē, a pivot into a poietic rhythm of interaction between forces. Without making fully explicit this question of "more-being" or its link with Césaire's and Senghor's claims about African art, Fanon tries to think of an actional human being in terms of such a poiēsis, which would consist in a redistribution of forces in a specific situation, without reference to concepts and without generalization.

Fanon's work implies a radical reconceptualization of the notion of the raced bodily being beyond the parameters of subjectivity: no longer or not simply a subject, for being a subject means having already been inscribed into and under the dominion of power. Furthermore, this novel understanding of bodily being, of an actional human, can be thought of in terms of a certain forcework, that is, as a redisposition or redistribution—to recall Césaire, in a leap of invention—of forces beyond their assignation to power. Thus one *is* as a black body without being black, that is, without embodying a particular instance of the concept of blackness, and the poetry of such a "revolution" extends beyond the technicist organization of being into power. In his critique of race, that is, of the designation of singular beings into the abstractions of blackness and whiteness, Fanon retains the singularly embodied being, colored yet without color, "universally" singular, who, however, in his or her defining leap(s) of invention, remains irreducible to a subject of/to power. The project of the liberation of the "actional man" in *Black Skin, White Masks* is thus poietic in just this sense: that Fanon's notion of invention involves a redistribution of forces, beyond subject/object, master/slave, superiority/inferiority.[87] Fanon therefore makes it possible to extend the questioning of the master/slave dialectic inaugurated by Du Bois, and to revise the paradigm of production constitutive of Western being, by moving the conception of human being and action toward poiēsis understood as an alternative, non-productionist mode of relationality.

In Baraka's recent poetry, it is the image of the black snake from "Art Against Art Not" that figures this alternative relationality: the rhythm of being in which only degrees of "the swinging" exist instead of posited identities. The snakelike jazz rhythm of the universe becomes the new "universality" of the degrees of swinging, the nexus of intervals and betweens, which figures a praxis—a beat of events—beyond the notions of subjectivity, opposition, and dialectic. What Baraka's poetry opens up is the possibility of and need for thinking of the raced "subject" in a rhythm alternative to power, which also means understanding bodily existence as a leaping movement of reinvention in which openness to otherness, the concrete event of being in one's body, shatters and rewrites the very schema continuously imprinted on that body by social practice. After Fanon, the raced subject can exist as embodied and colored and yet continuously "leaping" beyond color and concept, beyond the duality and negation intrinsic to power. The movement of liberation that Fanon's thought catalyzes understands the actional man not as self-produced but as freed from the very paradigm of production, which generates slavery but also subtends a broader "enslavement" to power, one that pervades and regulates praxis as such. This is why emancipation in Fanon's works is twofold: liberation from colonialism and slavery, and freeing of the human mode of being from its "enslavement" to the metaphysics, and thus to the culture, of power and production. Liberation from slavery, then, necessarily contains and yet is not limited to the question of empowering the disenfranchised, because it entails a parallel and, in a way, more comprehensive reworking of relations, a redirection of relations away from power. To liberate from slavery, it is not enough to free society from the injustices of the colonial past on the political, economic, and cultural levels, or to emancipate the postcolonial psyche—both that of the colonized and that of the colonizers—from the ghosts and complexes haunting it. What is also necessary is to call into question the very operations of power that produce what exists as political and economic relations. Power, resistance, and empowerment no doubt can and in fact often do come to serve critical liberating functions. Fanon, however, goes even further than this sense of political, economic, and psychic liberation, asking for a leap of invention that would emancipate not only from inequality, domination, and prejudice but even from the flexible, seductive, and empowering sense of power. To use Heidegger's terminology here for a moment, what I see in Fanon is a call not only for an "ontic" liberation from forms of political and economic slavery or injustice but also an "ontological" emancipation from the generative flows and operations of power, the flows and operations constitutive of the very formation of experience into subjectivities, identities, and differences. Such liberation would open existence toward an "actional" being, where action is no longer an instance of power but instead signifies the invention of relations beyond power. To that effect, the undermining of slavery and power takes on the forms of the transsubjective "rhythm" of relating, beyond subject and object, beyond the operations of power that abstract and code the singularities of experience. In Fanon, liberation from the specter of slavery involves emancipation of the very site of relationality, emancipation not only from the past but, more important, *into* the future, in the specific sense in which power as such has to be called into question, as though "leapt" over into nonpower, so that the very modalities of force relations that produce not only enslavement or domination but also subjectivity and identity, without which enslavement would not be possible, would come to be changed in their momentum. His critique of the historical forms of slavery and its effects takes Fanon into an even more comprehensive critique of power *qua* power: Fanon calls into question not just the operations of power that bring about inequality and injustice but also the very "submission" of being and experience to power, that is, to the operations of production and manipulation that shape the event into the various forms of power relations. This is why the momentum that Fanon gives to "free" relations is not empowerment or production but, as the concluding sentence of *Black Skin, White Masks* announces, questioning.

Conclusion: Revolt in Art

Art and the Re-volt in Technology

In the context of my overall argument about rethinking the force of contemporary art, the term "revolt" takes on a specific, "technological" meaning, indicating a turn within technicity, that is, within the power-motivated modality of relations dominant in, and as, modernity, a turn that redirects relations toward aphesis, that is, toward "letting be" and nonpower. This change in the vector of relating signifies also a "re-volt" in aesthetics—specifically a reformulation of the artwork as *forcework,* beyond the optics of the modern technoaesthetic categorizations of art—and, with it, a corollary rethinking of art's "aesthetic" role in society. This reformulated optics for understanding revolt in art, or, in other words, art's "revolutionary" force, makes it possible to discern more sharply where, exactly, art's critical impetus lies in the age when the global yet decentralized operations of power significantly change the parameters and strategies of resistance. This new optics is also important because it makes clear that art can retain a revolutionary momentum at a time when the avant-garde seems to have all but disappeared, and when art increasingly submits to the pressures and operations of the accelerating global market.

At present, the avant-garde movements have disappeared, and their radical proclamations, provocations, and rebellious performances no longer fracture the fabric of the modern technologic regulating contemporary social commerce. If an artistic work or event with a revoltlike force appears or takes place, it has only isolated, "local" significance; it no longer makes headlines in newspaper articles or chronicles of current events. As Julia Kristeva remarks in *Sens et Non-sens de la Révolte* and *La Révolte Intime*, the conditions for revolution and revolt have changed significantly in the contemporary world of global capital and commerce because with the global economy, multiculturalism, and the culture of difference(s), old instantiations of hegemonic authorities, discourses, and values have given way to decentralized operations of power. There are now no obvious centers of power, cultural hegemonies, or hierarchies of values to be challenged, critiqued, and revolutionized. Kristeva responds to this situation by reformulating the sense (and "non-sense," that is, resistance to sense) of revolt in terms of a (psychoanalytic) sense of subjectivity, operating on the principle of anamnesis or rememoration, that is, of a re-turn of the archaic, or of the beyond-time (*hors-temps*) of the drive, which recovers a sense of experience foreclosed by contemporary culture.[1] While I would agree that revolt in its contemporary manifestations has indeed to do importantly with temporality, it is the temporality of the event and its transformative relation to the technicity of modern power that comes to define the (non)sense of the revolt, its refusal to participate not only in the existing regimes of signification but, more important, in the prevailing and intensifying technopower. Globalization, multi- and transnational capital, and the general fluidity of power are all markers of the rapidly expanding reach and intensity of modern technicist forms of relations and their determining, albeit sometimes unnoticed, influence on all areas of everyday life. This is why revolt, in the sense mentioned above, only increases in its importance and significance, even if it is much harder to recognize, since the target of critique is no longer easily discernible and identifiable: it is not bourgeois culture and morality, aesthetic conventions, national politics, class domination, and so on—all ostensible targets of the avant-garde rebellion in its explicitly social aspects—but rather the much more flexible, agile, and power-ful dispositions of modern technicity, which have penetrated and come to regulate reality simultaneously on the microscopic and global levels. This revolt in art takes place not against an ideology (for example, against the almost unquestionably socially dominant ideology of technoscience), morality, practices of domination, or inequality, but against technological rationality and its contemporary, infotechnical forms of power. Revolt in this context is not resistance or opposition, not a revolutionary overthrow of power (and eventual instantiation of another power, with both gestures constituting essential parts of the logic of power), and so this revolt should be thought of as beyond resistance and conformity, beyond critique and complicity.

This need to rethink the very conditions of resistance and revolt in the age of global power is persuasively argued by Michael Hardt and Antonio Negri in *Empire*. As Hardt and Negri diagnose and, often, critique the workings of today's global sovereignty, which they call "Empire," they draw attention to the important fact that this global configuration of power is not totally repressive or constrictive but opens new sites for resistance and multiple paths for emancipation; they claim that "against all moralisms and all positions of resentment and nostalgia, . . . this new imperial terrain provides greater possibilities for creation and liberation. The multitude, in its will to be-against and its desire for liberation, must push through Empire to come out the other side."[2] This reconceptualization of contemporary operations of capital and power as the idea of a "postmodern" Empire mandates a crucial reformulation of the strategies of resistance and transformation. Empire, having no central site of power or stable boundaries, operates instead as multiple and shifting flows of power, which means that no revolutionary overthrow of its "apparatus" is possible. In the face of such changed circumstances, Hardt and Negri call for a different idea of action, one that operates "beyond measure": "Beyond measure refers to *the new place in the non-place*, the place defined by the productive activity that is autonomous from any external regime of measure."[3] Relying on Foucault and Deleuze, the authors reformulate resistance in the age of Empire as practices that remain contingent, local, and nonrevolutionary. Interestingly enough for our discussion here, the idea of action "beyond measure" appears still to be formulated as a power, here understood as a power to transform and magnify: "This ontological apparatus beyond measure is an *expansive power*, a power of freedom, ontological construction, and omnilateral dissemination."[4]

Because of the "postmodern," diffused, and decentralized character of imperial power, resistance to Empire needs to take a new form of the multitude, defined in relation to its characteristic activity beyond measure. To encourage such "experimentation," Hardt and Negri reformulate the notion of contemporary democracy not as the idea of a res publica but as 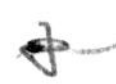
the contingent, local, and metamorphosing action of a posse.[5] In such sig-

nificantly altered circumstances, a political party, a labor movement, or even a class is no longer a sufficient agent of opposition. Instead, Hardt and Negri point to Saint Francis of Assisi, who, standing for "the irrepressible lightness and joy of being communist,"[6] testifies to the possibility of an action "beyond measure," directed against the misery of power.

Even as they rethink resistance after Foucault and Deleuze, Hardt and Negri follow Marx in seeing labor as the driving force of history,[7] and, more important for our discussion of forcework, they grant labor and production an intrinsically emancipatory force. As a result, the alternative they propose to Empire is based on the notion of labor as transformation, where labor comes to signify a creative power beyond the measure of the operations of imperial power. Hardt and Negri therefore insist on the need to liberate what they call "the ontological fabric" of Empire, namely, the flexible and contingent activity of the multitude. The assumption here is that, in the absence of Empire's regulatory powers, its ontological fabric, especially its forms of activity and production, as well as its virtual powers, are in principle free and unbound. In other words, the organizing powers of Empire are what constrains and limits the multitude. What does not come into question in *Empire* is technopower as such, that is, the technicist organization of the ontological fabric of modern being. One of the cornerstones of the critical conception of Empire put forth by Hardt and Negri, although it is not explicitly articulated, is the premise of the progressive and emancipatory character of the technological forms of relations. As I have argued in the context of Heidegger's and Adorno's reflections on technology, however, what constrains freedom from within the contemporary fluid and expansive operations of power is the essentially technicist constitution of relations and, by extension, of the ontological fabric of Empire. For Hardt and Negri, desire and creativity as such are unconstrained in their activity. For me, however, the multitude's array of virtual powers is not necessarily free in and of itself but has to be examined in relation to the technicist disposition of being in modernity. What needs to be questioned in the contemporary context is not only the operations of Empire but also the notion of production itself in its modern technicist determination.

If we look at these issues through the prism of "the question of technology," then production, creation, and virtuality appear as always already formed and regulated by technicity. The freedom in question here is not simply freedom from the pervasive and shifting operations of Empire's powers but also from the intensifying technic disposition of relations. This is why the problem of freedom cannot be delimited to the question of the extent to which capital, in its global and yet diffuse operations within Empire, has power over production, creativity, and technology. Instead, this problem has to be rethought in the context of the technicity of power relations. A much desired freedom from Empire does not, unfortunately, guarantee liberation from "domination by power," that is, from the pervasive influence of technicity on modern relations. As I have shown by drawing out the critical tension between making (*machen*) and letting/releasing (*lassen*), the question of freedom and resistance can no longer be circumscribed within the problematic of free, creative, and empowering production but instead has to call into question the very paradigm of production, which remains implicated within the overall productionist momentum of power. To put the point differently, another vector of freedom is involved here: not simply freedom from restrictions and control but release from the mobilizing pull intrinsic to production, even if production take places free of repressive and regulative power. All forms of production and making, free or not, are calibrated and regulated—determined, in short, by the drive toward power intrinsic to the technicity that is characteristic of modern relations. Producing and creating are inherently propelled toward power, which means that power becomes the "language" of relating, the direction with respect to which relations and forces come to be disposed in production. In this context, resistance and revolt can no longer be limited to freedom from the powers regulating broadly understood practices of production but must involve a more "radical" release from the productionist paradigm of being.

This is why it is in the notion of aphesis, understood as an alternative to production and power, that I see the key to understanding art's potential today for revolt and critique. From the perspective of ideology or power relations, the issues of resistance and complicity are of critical importance and need continuous (re)negotiation, but the revolt I am interested in here occurs on another level and touches on the very disposition of relations toward power, a disposition that remains anterior to various forms of power or practices of domination. To call this disposition "anterior" is not to say that it is separate or disconnected; rather, it is to indicate the way in which technicity underlies and orchestrates forms of power. The discussion of forcework as revolt bears directly on such cultural, social, and political considerations, precisely to the extent to which it indicates the way in which these phenomena are subtended and informed by technicity.

Even today, no doubt, art sometimes succeeds in claiming the media's attention, but mostly in the context of moral, religious, or political "scandals," and such incidents have no explicit or critical bearing on power or capital. The conservative attacks on the National Endowment for the Arts some years ago, and former New York Mayor Rudy Giuliani's threats against the Brooklyn Museum of Art for exhibiting artwork that was ostensibly offensive in a religious sense, are just two recent examples of how art can still provoke social controversy—or, to take a more cynical view, be used as a pawn in larger political games. But even if its critical force has been weakened, art clearly preserves the ability to incite polemics, to critique existing or dominant ideologies, or to resist prevailing power relations, and this critical capacity remains culturally important, no doubt, if on an increasingly localized scale. Yet there is also a sense that these kinds of critiques and resistances ultimately continue to play into the hands of power, since they tend to obey the rules (of critique, resistance, polemic) that preserve the status quo. As Adorno would say, the means of critique recognized and "legitimated" within the social sphere (that is, made possible within the discourses and regimes of power extant in specific historical contexts), and which clearly include forms of aesthetic resistance and subversion, are not really critical, for they become neutralized, in a sense, within the overall optics of the modern global exercise of power. What art needs is not so much to be critical as to develop the "negative" of the forms of critique and resistance attainable within the social domain. In its "critique," art has to revolt even "against" the practices of critique and contestation, to turn and transform critique into a "re-volt," that is, into a turn within power, *beyond* forms of power. In the same vein, Dadaism was never simply a revolt against bourgeois culture and morality but rather a turn within the logic of Enlightenment rationality—which Tzara identified as the organic disease of modern life—and toward an eventlike rupture of experience free from investments of power: "Dada is a virgin microbe that penetrates with the insistence of air into all the spaces that reason has not been able to fill with words or conventions."[8] As an antidote to technical rationality, Dada insinuates itself into any tiny space left unmapped or unregulated by reason. It is agile like air, liberating like a breath of fresh air. It presses from within on forms of knowledge and power, destroying them and disclosing a different mode of being. "Dada is a state of mind. . . . Dada applies itself to everything, and yet it is nothing, it is the point where the yes and the no and all the opposites meet, not solemnly in the castles of human philosophies, but very simply at street corners, like dogs and grasshoppers."[9] A "state of mind," Dada is a state of relations, a disposition, a mood or a *Stimmung*, that is, the key in which relations, beyond affirmation and negation, beyond oppositional structures and values, unfold and come to be formed in their everyday occurrence. To claim that the key to relationality is "Dada" does not mean that it is nonsensical or nihilistic but that it operates beyond the boundaries of meaning (and thus meaninglessness as well). Beyond sense and nonsense, "Dada" signifies the "non-sense" of the revolt: the "beyond" of sense, which marks not simply a linguistic play but also a turn in relationality, activated as well in *zaum*, that is, in the "beyonsense" language of Russian Cubo-Futurists like Khlebnikov, Kruchenykh, and Iliazd. Dada is not only an attack on power but, most important, also the disclosure of a beyond to power and powerlessness, that is, the power-free, whose different language of relations becomes "Dada" when (non)sensed or (non)signified within language that is already saturated with power on the levels of grammar and signification. Dada thus constitutes perhaps the most radical instantiation of revolt in avant-garde art: not nihilism but the radically nihilating force of temporality, beyond negation and critique.

This (non)sense of revolt in art is, strictly speaking, containable neither within the problematic of sociopolitical critique nor within the notion of aesthetic rebellion against conventions, rules, or values. It cannot be properly explained in terms of art's social relations and functions, cultural expectations and resistance, or aesthetic fashions and revolutions. They all form part of the cultural/aesthetic spectrum of art's existence, and the understanding of how art operates within these strictures constitutes an indispensable element of our "sense" of art and its social role. Yet this knowledge is not enough to explain the specific artistic sense of revolt as the turn that art initiates in the technorationality of modern social praxis, for this revolt has a distinctive meaning: the "non-sense" associated with the instantiation of a different relationality, where forces occur "otherwise" than does power, that is, as power-free forcework. With intensification of 

the practices and proliferation of the channels through which modern technopower (re)produces and regulates social praxis, the importance of revolt in art, and the possibility of the alternative disposition of forces associated with it, seems only to increase, in a kind of inverse ratio with respect to the way in which contemporary culture accelerates the marginalization ("elitism," "esoterism") and insignificance of art. As the technicism of being amplifies, recognizing and appreciating the revolt inscribed in art becomes more and more difficult because technicist deployments of modern power tend to strengthen their determination of being to such an extent that no other disposition appears possible or real. It is thus in the "interest" of power to progressively marginalize art, to ascribe to it specific social and aesthetic functions, in order to conceal art's force and preclude the possibility of the turn or revolt in technicity that art still harbors.

The Avant-Garde Turn of Art

In the larger historical context of artistic developments that took place over the course of the last century, this revolt in art can be identified with the avant-garde and its various later manifestations, which extend beyond the aesthetic upheaval of the 1910's and the 1920's. Competing interpretations of the avant-garde(s) exist, but the enduring, and re-turning, significance of the avant-garde aesthetic lies in its critique of the aesthetic formation of art and in its instantiation of the artwork as a reworking of forces. This critique happens not merely in the name of praxis, or of the reintegration of art into life, but for the sake of a turn in the increasingly technic formation of relations in modernity. After the demise of the historical avant-gardes, what "re-turns" in twentieth-century art, whether one thinks of Pop Art, the Darmstadt school of music, or language poetry, is the turn in technē, the revolt in the practices of power, that "enables" the power-free form of relationality. As I showed in chapter 2, Futurism, especially in its Italian incarnation, remained inherently ambiguous about technology, both exalting its promise of an alluring future and seeing its technoaesthetic as a venue for a new radical "lyricism" of matter and existence. Surrealism, in its flight into the marvelous, often tended to cover the radical nature of its questioning of experience, and Wyndham Lewis's Vorticism gravitated toward the exaltation of the masculine and of nature. It was in Dada that, in Tzara's words, the "virgin microbe" of nonpower was released into the everyday, not only attacking the sclerotic morality and cultural traditionalism of the bourgeoisie but also, above all, transforming the technicity that underpins and shapes the manipulative relationality constitutive of the modern manifestations of power. The radical force of Dada, too often muffled and misrepresented by such notions as anarchism, nihilism, and nonsense, reveals itself precisely in relation to technicity, in radical forcework that, underneath the images, aesthetic forms, and ideological inscriptions constitutive of the aesthetic dimension of art, reconfigures the field of forces, freeing their momentum from the ordination of power.

In the historical rupture of the 1910's avant-garde movements, the nontechnicist impetus of the avant-garde art remains often confusing and difficult to read, given the explicit and ostensibly unequivocal and enthusiastic endorsement of technology represented by Futurism, often regarded, because of the publication by F. T. Marinetti of the "Manifesto of Futurism" in 1909, as the originating moment of the avant-garde. What further complicates the reception of the avant-garde, and the formulation of its theory, is the fact that, unlike in today's reality of postindustrial global capitalism thriving on (in spite of?) the new ideologies of multiculturalism and difference, the historical avant-gardes still had clearly identifiable targets of attack and resistance: bourgeois culture, Enlightenment rationality, imperialism, aesthetic conventions, and so on. Those aims are often perceived as the motivating factors of the avant-garde rupture, as the cornerstones of the avant-garde rebellion, which is remarked in aesthetic and social terms but not really explicated with regard to technopower as the key determinant of modern relations. Indeed, such forms of aesthetic, social, and cultural critique constitute some of the most pronounced and well-known tenets of avant-garde manifestos and artworks, but my approach to the avant-garde contextualizes them in reference to what I take to be the abiding force of the avant-garde: its turn of technicity against itself—a kind of a disinvestiture of power. Even the Futurist intoxication with speed and technology is entwined with a rethinking of technology, a reformulation of the increasing technicity of relations through the poetic rupture of the event. The embrace of the future in "The Trumpet of the Martians," one of the Russian Futurist proclamations, cosigned by, among others, Khlebnikov, evinces a complicated reconceptualization of time, and thus of futurity, beyond the linear notions of temporality that are customarily associated with avant-gardist notions of technology and progress. "The human brain until now has been hopping around on three legs (the three axes of location)! We intend to refurrow the human brain and to give this puppy dog a fourth leg—namely, the axis of TIME."[10] The manifesto calls for replacing space with time, but this proclamation is not about exalting the future or pushing the familiar ideology of progress; rather, it is a radical opposition to and displacement of the spatialization of time, which deforms temporality into sequentiality and linear progression, covering over the event and making possible the calculative representation and manipulation of being. "Refurrowing" the human brain refers to a fundamental transformation in the mode of being, an iconoclastic "temporalization" of relations. The dramatic distinction between inventors/explorers and investors/exploiters introduced in "The Trumpet of the Martians" reflects the familiar revolutionary critique of capital and exploitation, but at the same time it extends beyond political rhetoric, into a new conception of power. "That is why the inventor/explorers, in full consciousness of their particular nature, their different way of life and their special mission, separate themselves from the in-vestor/exploiters in order to form an independent government of *time*. . . ."[11] The idea of inventors/explorers outlined in "The Trumpet of the Martians," though clearly sympathetic toward socialist critiques of capitalist society, is not a political call for class revolution. Rather, it suggests an even more radical "revolt" in the forms of relations: an establishment of the government of time as an alternative to the government of power. The inventors/explorers, scientists and artists, are "organized" by Khlebnikov into the Martian Council, or, in other texts, into the Government of the Presidents of Planet Earth.[12] This new government of artists is not a parody of political parties and ideologies but implies a stunningly radical transformation of the notion of power in Khlebnikov. Though Khlebnikov himself does not make it explicit, his radically pacifist renunciation of power in "Refusal,"[13] where the lyrical subject opts to be shot rather than use violence, implies, within the perspective of the Russian Futurists' evident sympathies for revolutionary social change in Russia, a novel stance with regard to power.

The new government of artists that Khlebnikov envisions in his writings about the future obviously has no actual political or military power and thus appears preposterous and laughable from the point of view of the power-oriented forms of government and social organization. Yet this government lays no claim to a new form of power, that is, to a different configuration of society, where power would come to be redistributed without essentially changing its valence or momentum. Khlebnikov's Martian Council, as a government of artists, instantiates the future in terms of the possible disordination of power. The "power" that the artists—the Presidents of Planet Earth—exercise is that of the transformation of relations into the power-free temporality of the event. What is astonishing about Khlebnikov's idea of the artist/presidents is not just the supranational, global conception of government but also the implicit notion of an alternative artistic form of "governing." The government that Khlebnikov proposes is the government of time, of the nihilating force of temporality manifested in the "non-sense" of *zaum*. Perhaps in an echo of Shelley, what the artist "legislates" in Khlebnikov, through a radical transformation of language into *zaum*, is not new norms, conventions, or laws but nihilating temporality as the very moment of the disarticulation of power. The artist "governs," not in terms of power, but by reworking the dynamic of relationality, by enacting and "authorizing" a new way of relating. This mode of "governing" and "legislating," by disposing relations in terms of the temporality of the event, as Khlebnikov's poem "Russia and Me" makes explicit, extends and radicalizes revolutionary social transformation beyond the introduction of political and economic freedoms, and it does so by "shedding" power, so to speak, as imaged by the poet in the gesture of taking off his shirt: "Russia has granted freedom to thousands and thousands. / It was really a terrific thing to do, / people will never forget it. / But what I did was to take off my shirt. . . . that's how I gave freedom to my people."[14] The Government of Planet Earth is not the naive, depoliticized dream of a poet incapable of understanding the operations of power but instead is a radical call to disinvesting modern reality of power, to a poetic "government" of nonpower. The prophetic vision of history in *Zangezi* aims at breaking the chains of power and freeing beings and their relations—"the building blocks of space"—not just from political forms of oppression but from a "general" constraint of being within the terms and operations of power.[15]

Here, it is important to distinguish Khlebnikov's revolutionary vision of "poetic governance" from the idea of social engineering, which took over Soviet society under Stalin, and the machinist aesthetics at work, for instance, in the texts of Gastev, which aligned art with the technosocial manipulation of relations. Social engineering and the machinist aesthetic, with its unmistakable echoes of Marinetti's machinocentrism, aims at a thorough saturation of the social domain—its bodily, material, psychic, and even incorporeal dimensions—with power, toward the end of maximizing the technicist potential of being. Khlebnikov's artist/presidents, by contrast, aspire to free the private and public spheres from power by "governing time." The "Martians" are not just prophets of a better, technologically engineered future but are also, I would argue, the "revolutionaries" of time as an event.[16] The Futurist revolt in art takes place against the manipulation of the event into calculable and representable "experience," against both the political/totalitarian engineering of society and the inconspicuous formation of forces into power relations. The Futurist revolt, though fascinated and inspired by technological development, nevertheless may be seen as calling into question the "rising" technicist pitch of modern experience, the manner in which relations, occurrences, and things come to be keyed to the dispositions of power, distributed and mobilized in the general manipulative schema of being, where the nihilating force of time is covered over, deprived of its "negating" force, and subsumed into the axes of space.

Another important example of such a double revolt is Dziga Vertov's 1929 film *Man with the Movie Camera*, where revolt takes place not only in terms of the new cinematic aesthetic of seeing but also, and quite explicitly, with respect to the technorhythm of modern life that the film so inventively depicts. Vertov's work is not merely a revolutionary film of the early cinema but is also a complicated statement on the technoaesthetic of modern art. Through its elaborate architectonic of montage, Vertov's artistic documentary celebrates technologically facilitated changes in perception and representation, explicitly drawing attention, in its repeated inscriptions of the cameraman into the narrative, to the fact that the film marks the instantiation of a new, filmic vision, a modern cinematic way of seeing. The technology "represented" in the film—modern factories, city traffic, trams and cars, the rhythmic movement of industrial machinery—is itself formed into a technological image, into the technologically registered and composed constellation of rhythmically unfolding scenes. Beyond the literal senses of technology portrayed by Vertov—beyond, that is, technological processes and technologically produced objects, which in many scenes constitute, together with people, the "heroes" of this modern filmic text—*Man with the Movie Camera* self-consciously constructs the weave of its textuality as technic; for instance, the movement of the weaving machines is not only literally depicted by the film's images but is also taken up and reworked into the textual rhythm of the film. Many scenes in the film—those containing repeated shots of tram crossings, or depicting the action of various machines, and so on—play with this twofold instantiation of technology and technicity in modern reality. In Vertov's film, not only is this reality filled with and facilitated and regulated by technological products and processes, it is also structured technically; that is, the rhythm of being in the modern city is presented as technic. The cinematic weave in *Man with the Movie Camera* instantiates technicity as the operational center of social life, as the regulator of daily experience not only within the realm of the visible, as illustrated by shots of factories and panoramas of city streets, but also within the realm of the "invisible" but cinematically foregrounded technical pulse of modern life. What is indeed radical about Vertov's film is its montage, not when it is understood in limited fashion, as a new aesthetic principle or technique, but when it is approached as an artistic disclosure of the technicity of modern experience. From the contemporary perspective, Vertov's importance lies precisely in his ability to employ new technology as an artistic means of highlighting the ways in which the very composition of modern relations, the relationality constitutive of modern being, has itself become a matter of technicity. Yet it is precisely in its disclosure of what I would call the technic modality of relating, which underpins the increasing technologization of everyday life, that *Man with the Movie Camera* becomes both celebratory and ambiguous.

Vertov, a trained musician, structures his montage as a highly elaborate musical sequence of rhythmically timed and composed shots. In short, the film is a musical-cinematic composition, an artistic creation that introduces musical rhythm into the modern technologic of seeing. Thus the rhythmic weave of *Man with the Movie Camera* is both technic and musical/poieitc, and this ambiguity, so obvious in the early shots in the film, constitutes the organizing principle of Vertov's work. This is the principle of revolt, understood in the specific sense given above. Vertov's film, inscribing technology into modern ways of seeing and living, into the composition of shots and montage, points to technicity as the organiza-

tional center of modern reality and, in the same gesture, turns this technicity into "music," suggesting the possibility and the need for a transformation within technē. For Vertov, film—in his day the most technologically advanced form of art—becomes invested with the double task of disclosing and recomposing technicity. Film is not only a technological revolution in perception, artmaking, and distribution, as Benjamin argues 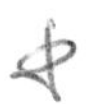 in "The Work of Art in the Age of Its Technical Reproducibility," but also the possibility of a "revolt" within technicity. It is clearly a revolution in aesthetics, one undoubtedly (and Vertov himself overemphasizes this point) prompted by technology, but in Vertov's hands it also becomes a revolt in art, that is, an artistic turn or transformation in technicity. It anticipates, for instance, Stockhausen's *Helikopter-Streichquartett,* in which technological noise frames the musical (re)composition and yet, in the course of the work, comes to be transformed into artistic forcework. In *Man with the Movie Camera*, modern forces, means, and relations of production, with the inclusion of the necessary periods for relaxation, rest, and entertainment (as in the sport and beach scenes), all come to constitute elements in the overall musical montage of the film. They are mobilized technologically—even sporting activities and relaxation from work become technologically organized, both on a mass scale and in terms of competitive excellence—for the global increase of productivity, machination, and power (in Vertov's case, the power of the newly build Soviet society). Yet this mobilization of all forces into an organizing technicity, as reflected in the elaborate montage of the film, becomes in the same gesture rendered into an artistic composition.

Vertov consistently shows that the musical/poetic composition of the film is not to be subordinated to praxis or politics. He deliberately eschews propaganda gestures and in fact overtly displaces politics with art: in the scene showing Lenin's club, there is no allusion to politics, propaganda, or governmental structures; instead, the club becomes the place where Vertov's film-within-a-film is shown. It could be argued that this scene indicates a seamless merging of film and art *into* propaganda, as desired and often forced by the Soviet state, but such an explanation would not be convincing within the overall structure and "poetics" of Vertov's film. Rather, Vertov points to the fact that politics and praxis, just like his art, are underpinned and regulated by technology; like the trams crossing and recrossing in Vertov's magnificent vertical montage, they all participate in the diverse, technologically motivated relations constitutive of modern social life. Yet art, thanks in part to the self-reflective structure so abundantly illustrated in the film, can also place in question the very relations that come to determine art as part of modern technological society. Thus the scenes of the film-within-a-film are not only self-conscious comments on the emergent art of filmmaking but also indexes of an artistic transformation in the momentum given to forces by modern technology. In Vertov's images, forces are shown to be mobilized into technological patterns of relation: a highly organized day, from the moment of waking and morning ablutions through work, city life, and evening entertainment, seems a picture-perfect illustration of the new society's social engineering as dreamt up by Soviet ideology. Yet, through the cinematic technique of montage, Vertov "celebrates" this technicity of relations in a way that permits him to transform these relations into a musical rhythm: montage allows the technologically mobilized forces—the humans, the machines, the pulse of modern city life—to be disclosed in a different, artistic manner. Shots of human faces overlaid with the rapid movements of weaving machines become emblematic in this context: the technical beat of relations becomes musicalized, the machine rhythm comes to be dissolved and transformed into musical, though silent, poietic rhythm. Even though Vertov himself supplied directions for the composition of background music, his is a silent film, and perhaps this fact indicates that the cinematic "music" Vertov was after does indeed concern the silent disposition of forces underlying modern reality, rendered "visible" by the film, and that this disposition turns on the difference marked by art. *Man with the Movie Camera* draws out and captures the technologic that saturates and intensifies modern life. But what is truly fascinating and enduring in Vertov's film is that this pioneering artistic disclosure of the power of technicity, and of the facility with which it subtends and motivates everyday existence, comes side by side with a "revolt" in technicity, with the creation of a cinematic forcework.

With the disappearance of avant-garde movements and their provocative statements and performances, the spectacularity of their revolt has also vanished from the public arena and, perhaps to a lesser extent, from aesthetic debates. This apparently negative consequence of what is sometimes called the "death" of the avant-garde nevertheless has a more interesting and complex obverse side: the marginalization of the avant-garde

and the calls for its abandonment, as critically analyzed by Jean-François Lyotard,[17] paradoxically make possible a different way of thinking about the revolt enacted by avant-garde works. The prevalent explanations of the avant-garde revolt tend to define its revolutionary force in terms of aesthetic forms, especially the aesthetic of shock—as a radical tide sweeping away ages of artistic conventions and rules, in the name of a new, contemporary aesthetic. Parallel to the aesthetic explanations of the avant-garde runs the notion of the revolutionary politics of some of the avant-garde "isms"—their critique of society, morality, and capitalist praxis. These two dominant notions of revolution/rebellion in the avant-garde, as important as their resonance has been throughout twentieth-century art, tend to obscure the "other" meaning of the avant-garde "re-volt": as a turn in the technicist dispositions of modern power. Historically, when debates about the political and aesthetic rebellion of the avant-garde subside in the wake of declarations of its demise, room is made for a different perspective on the avant-garde revolution in art and culture, one that can perhaps finally begin to appreciate the "non-sense" of art's revolt in terms of its disarticulation of power and technicity.

The fact that the social meaning of the revolt in art is not reducible to politics or to cultural critique instigates a revision in the understanding of art's "revolutionizing" force, beyond the province of aesthetics and its corollary social institutions. The post- or nonaesthetic idea of art's force gives a different valence to the problematic of revolt in the artwork: a change in the *modality* of relating, a transformative redisposition of forces into their power-free element, and thus a shift in the power momentum that characterizes contemporary social praxis. To the extent that social practice, together with the possibility for changes and modifications within it, is circumscribed by power, art's forcework represents neither a negation nor a critique of praxis but rather a release from the fashioning influence of power over the very manner in which relations take place. Revolt in art thus brings into the open the distinctions between art's dimensions as (a) sociopolitical critique, (b) aesthetic subversion, and (c) forcework. The explanation of the resistance and subversiveness of new aesthetic constructs with regard to political and economic determinations of social praxis diagnoses art's entwinement with the various forms and relations of power that are characteristic of the contemporary world. Yet the changing forces and relations of production, whose increasingly technicist momentum shapes modern life with more and more flexible and extensive operations of power, are best registered and revised in art's forcework. With the changes in the forces of production characteristic of life in the Information Age, of life as influenced by the Internet, and of biogenetic technologies, the problematic of revolt in art also comes to be concerned with the very nature of the operations that determine and shape being in its contemporary technoinformational manifestations: force, power, relationality.

It might be possible to produce the "history" of art's evolving revolt in the twentieth century—extending from Italian and Russian Futurism through Dada, the writings of Getrude Stein, serialism in music, language poetry in Poland and the United States, Pop Art, and the poetry of Amiri Baraka to Bill Viola's installations, the vehicles, projections, and "immigrant instruments" of Krzysztof Wodiczko, and Eduardo Kac's transgenic art—a history that in turn would make it possible to trace the complicated "non-sense" of revolt in art as it extends beyond and questions the problematic of aesthetic subversion and cultural critique. Some of the most poignant examples of how the dimensions of cultural/political critique, aesthetic invention, and the revision of power come to constitute the density of art's force field have already been discussed in the context of Wodiczko's "public events" and Baraka's poetic language. In *Funk Lore*, Baraka's vociferous, angry critique is sharply unequivocal in its attack on multinational corporations, cultural elites, and racism as well as historically and culturally specific in its invocation of events and phenomena that claimed public attention in the 1980's and 1990's—for instance, Anita Hill's testimony at the hearings on Clarence Thomas's appointment to the U.S. Supreme Court, O. J. Simpson's televised trial, and Spike Lee's film *X*. Through contemporary social and cultural events that have had implications for the issues of racism, class inequality, and African American identity, Baraka's criticisms take on a particular polemical poignancy and concreteness.[18] At the same time, however, Baraka consciously uses aesthetic innovation to inflect the critical message of his poetry, bringing together the heritage of the European and American avant-gardes, the radical musical idiom of such jazz musicians as Thelonious Monk, John Coltrane, and Sun Ra, and elements of African and African American heritage. This fusion of political message and avant-garde aesthetic has the double effect of nuancing Baraka's outspoken and often polarizing critique and, in the same gesture, adding a new force to its social and political

momentum. The radical aesthetic of his poetry both discloses his political and militant language as verging on the idiom of a political pamphlet and simultaneously reweaves it into an avant-garde textuality, into a critique of the operations of power, which discloses, in the snakelike meanderings of Baraka's texts, in their language of "is' story," an artistic dimension to force, beyond dualism, opposition, and negation. The central poem of *Funk Lore* calls this dimension "art against art not," indicative of an artistic forcework beyond negation and critique, of a nihilation of "Be," that is, of the temporality of being. The "against" in the title "Art Against Art Not" intimates the nihilating momentum of forcework, which undoes the power determinations of being and liberates the alternative rhythm of the universe. Beyond the dualism of negation and affirmation, the oppositions of classes and races, there are "the waves of is' story,"[19] the "be" of being, whose rhythm is that of the "degrees of the swinging," challenging and melting divides, dualities, and opposites. In "There Was Something I Wanted to Tell You," Baraka writes about "*Motion*, the beat, tender mind / . . . / is rise is new is / Changed, a glowing peaceful / Musical / World."[20] This motion, the beat of the musical world, is the continuous rising of the new, the temporality of change that flows through and "betrays," in a very specific sense, political and social revolutions: "What betrays revolution is the need / for revolution. It can not stop in life." Baraka points here to the double meaning of revolution: on the one hand, the much needed social and political revolutionary change, and, on the other, the transformation intrinsic to the temporal rhythm of being. This "second order" revolution engages us in the nihilating force of temporality, in the resistance to "order" and forms of power inherent in the "electricity" of being: "We are servants of life in upward / progressive motion. Fanners / of the flame. Resistance is electric." The funky motion and beat of being undermine and "betray" even the new orders that could be brought about by social and political revolutions, entwining those revolutionary changes, of which Baraka remains one of the outspoken and sometimes controversial advocates, in the serpentine "is' story." And it is this rhythm that encodes, in Baraka's poetry, the "electric" resistance to power on the level of infinitesimal forces of being, a resistance to the formation of force relations into the flow of power.

Beyond political meaning and ideology, beyond the fanfare of manifestos and aesthetic polemics, what makes art *work* is its forcework. This double character of the work performed by art—its explicit intervention in the public sphere, on the one hand, and its "invisible" forcework, on the other—constitutes the core of Krzysztof Wodiczko's artistic ventures. His vehicles, projections, and instruments come to exist for short intervals only as events or situations within the public sphere: in the streets or parks, on the sides of official buildings, in airports. Nevertheless, as disruptions and performances within urban landscapes, these events do not exhaust themselves in their capacity as cultural interventions or radical political gestures. Indeed, most of the time, as has been especially the case with Wodiczko's projections, his works feed off the social problems and political events of the day, yet they do so not only to make polemical statements or deliver social criticisms but also to bring into the open the hidden configurations of power and their parallel inscriptions in public spaces and in the social symbolic, in order to attempt a transformation within them. Wodiczko is less interested in making a political statement than in designing artworks that deploy technology to enable forms of relations that do not conform to or exhaust themselves within the dominant matrix of power. Continuing the tradition of "public art" in the vein of Dadaism and Situationism, Wodiczko sees the "public" dimension of art primarily in its ability to transform relations, and to enable different ways of acting toward the other. Describing his *Homeless Vehicle*, Wodiczko remarks that the project's goal is "twofold: to fulfill the need of homeless people for a means of transportation and shelter, and to aid in creating a legitimized status for its users in the community of the city."[21]

This rhetoric of facilitating and enabling pervades many of Wodiczko's works and writings, and his texts are always careful to articulate such enabling as pivotal to what he calls "public art."[22] He understands public art as "an engagement in strategic challenges to the city structures and mediums that mediate our everyday perception of the world; an engagement through aesthetic-critical interruptions, infiltrations, and appropriations that question the symbolic, psycho-political, and economic operations of the city."[23] *Xenology*, his project of designing instruments helpful in negotiating the alien status so pervasive in contemporary global culture(s), employs information technologies to stage events and situations that, interrupting the habitual and unseen flows of power in urban spaces, facilitate different patterns of relating between the migrant and his or her new culture. In these interruptions of power's inscription in public spaces, technology is always the "medium" in which Wodiczko works, and his artworks come into existence as industrial designs and technological innovations: from manufactured vehicles and video projection equipment to computer technology and engineering deployed in the various instruments developed for the project of "xenology." Yet the performative role of these artifacts and prosthetic devices is less technological than artistic, since they help unfold a situation or event in which the bearer of the instrument finds herself within a transformed nexus of relations with her surroundings. The technological workings of Wodiczko's projects become part of their artistic "forcework"; that is, are one element in a transformative capacity that enables alternative, power-free modalities of relating. In this sense, one could see Wodiczko's work as attempting a turn within technē, that is, within the technicity of relations in modernity, a turn in which technology becomes employed not to augment or intensify power but to "evacuate" power from the event that technology itself has helped bring into being. In Wodiczko's works, technology is thus both technical—industrial and productionist—and artistic, since it seems to regain the complex sense that the Greek term technē, at least according to Heidegger, implies. Clearly aware of the implications that his interrogative designs have for the paradigm of production, Wodiczko suggests that his use of technology leads to "'productivism' of a new kind."[24] His quotation marks around the word "productivism" imply an important change in the very meaning of the term, a change that opens onto the possibility of a different kind of work undertaken by art: not production, making, or creation, but forcework.

Art's forcework, undoing and reworking power, enacts a release of forces, an aphesis, that allows what *is* to emerge in its power-free valence. As in the title of Bill Viola's installation *The Crossing,* art performs a crossing into a different mode of relationality, into the zone of nonpower, whose critical force consists in a detechnicization of relations, that is, in a freeing of relations, occurrences, and beings from their calculative and informational momentum. This "crossing" is the silent revolt in art, the turn that art performs on the level of the technicist disposition of relations, freeing them from insistent and repeated deployment into the flexible array of the modern operations of power. The "re-volt" in modern art is therefore neither aesthetic nor political, strictly speaking, and its social force is the inverse of its incommensurability with power. The "dissonance" of modern art—with culture at large, technicity, social praxis—comes from the peculiar manner in which artworks contest power, from their discord with the technical determinateness of being. The force of artworks lies in their enigmatic ability to desist from power, and the "revolutionary" index of this force reflects a difficult freedom from the globally pervasive technicity of power.

Art in the Age of the Internet Revolution

The very terms "Internet revolution" and "e-revolution" indicate that the power of revolt and transformation, in contemporary culture, is assigned to technology. Internet and other electronic technologies, e-commerce and e-business, and the Information Superhighway appear to be reforming, almost daily, the way things get done, the way information becomes acquired and circulated, and the way commodities are produced, distributed, and sold. The fact that I can so easily buy books and CDs from Germany, France, or England—from anyone who has established a presence on the World Wide Web—constitutes, for myself at least, the most immediate testimony to the changing speed and mode of interaction in today's world. It remains to be seen where such changes will take contemporary cultures and societies, but the first indications are beginning to emerge about the impact of information technologies on art. Internet art has begun to proliferate, creating new possibilities for interactive art, unprecedented multimedia and hybrid aesthetic genres, and multiple modes and forms of artistic cooperation. No doubt a new e-aesthetics and e-sociology of art will be developed in the near future. Manifestos proclaiming new electronic, telematic, and transgenic artworks—manifestos of the twenty-first-century avant-garde—are appearing with increasing frequency on the Web, and, to judge from the vastness of the Internet and its inundation with informational noise, no comprehensive overview of Internet-related art and aesthetics is or will be possible. In some ways, the technological ferment created by the rapid commodification and spread of electronic and information technologies evokes anew the excitement that animated pre–World War I artistic communities. New e-based artistic communities and aesthetic orientations are already a reality—or should one say, a virtuality? New Web pages and centers interlinking cooperating artists and related aesthetic developments are easily found on the Internet, even if they may need to be updated rather frequently.

Yet, given the historical, technological, and social changes brought about by the computer industry and information technology, as well as their increasing relevance for future art, the preeminent question in the aesthetic domain is whether anything like the artistic ferment of the early-twentieth-century avant-gardes is again possible. The new media—in terms of aesthetic innovations, new artistic forms and genres, and perceptual and aesthetic hybridity—offer novel, numerous, and diverse possibilities. But in the fervor and enthusiasm that characterize the embrace of the new technologies, the deeper underlying question about technicity posed by the avant-garde often seems to disappear. New artforms related to computers, the Internet, and information or genetic technologies, echoing Marinetti's fascination with speed and the technologization of experience, evince intoxication with electronic speed, global networks of links, and universal interactivity (the latter phenomenon dependent, of course, on how universally accessible computers and Internet connections actually become). The chimney pots of Milan have been replaced by flickering computer screens; speeding automobiles, trains, and planes have been overtaken by fiberoptic velocity and DSL connections; and the cubes, planes, and forces that revolutionized the visual arts have given way to hyperlinks and interactive connections. The nonrepresentational space of avant-garde art and literature has found its e-analogue in virtual space and hypertext. For all those exciting and invigorating changes, however, the parameters of the question of revolt in art do not seem to have changed substantially over the last century; they remain evocative of the Futurist and Dadaist outburst. In a way, the new developments in art prompted by computer and genetic technology intensify one of the worries that I have already traced in connection with avant-garde art: is artistic "revolt" possible outside, or otherwise than in terms of, the prevailing technicity of being that is constitutive of modernity? Art today—celebrating the e-based and genetic-based possibilities for new aesthetic innovations and the sociocultural significance of contemporary art forms—appears to consign the powers of revolt to technology. The Internet art experiments of Seiko Mikami and Eduardo Kac, inventive and provocative in their own right, are nonetheless thoroughly determined by the same principle of interactivity that underlies e-commerce, Internet trading and banking, and so on, as well as other forms of Web interactivity (see, for instance, Mikami's *Molecular Clinic,* in which visitors to a Web site can become involved in reprogramming a virtual spider's DNA, an activity leading to the spider's continuing transformation (or e-volution). In a way, *Molecular Clinic* and Kac's *Genesis* are "revelatory" in just this sense: that they reveal the microlevel operations of power; they allow the average Internet user to taste the power of genetic engineering, to become part of the latest culmination of the various forms of manipulative power structuring present-day experience. It is a hands-on, even though distanced, experience of modern technopower. In this respect, interactive Web projects dramatize the disclosure of how power flows in the contemporary technological world, and they have the unprecedented advantage of interactivity, a new form of participation in the work of art, which goes beyond avant-garde performances, theater productions involving audience participation, and "happenings." Possibilities for interactivity change the very notion of participation, further blurring the boundary between creation and reception, turning the Web viewer/visitor into a quasi-artist/engineer. In the case of Mikami's *Molecular Clinic,* a visitor to the Web site, after downloading the appropriate program, can take part in the spider's evolution by manipulating its DNA molecules, thus becoming a cocreator of the evolving work of Internet art; or, in the case of Kac's *Genesis,* anyone can wait for a turn to illuminate a petri dish containing genetically altered *E. coli* and thus participate in the bacteria's ongoing mutation, as part of the artwork. The technological phenomenon of the Internet becomes the determinant of new kinds of mediations involved in blurring the boundaries between artist and audience—the "inter" of interactivity. Is interactivity, then, the palpable, technologically grounded realization of the notion of activity in the middle voice? Or is it rather the twenty-first-century instantiation, in the realm of technology and virtual reality, of the old paradigm of intersubjectivity?

It clearly allows more audience participation, leaving the interactive work to the interactions of the audience and the programming. The activity itself, however, even though new, because involving new technologies, programs, and links, does not appear to be changed to or inflected with the valence of enabling and letting be. Interactivity still appears to be based on the notion of activity, itself grounded in the paradigm of action as production, making, or manipulation (*machen*), even if the manipulation happens at a distance and becomes telemanipulation. In other words, interactivity still operates within the determination of relationality in terms of manipulative power. It obviously foregrounds, to an unprecedented degree, the between, the "inter" of activity, modifying the more traditional sense of action governed by the notion of a discrete, if not exactly integrated, subjectivity. Instead of a distinct authorial creation and control over the work of art, we have a multiply inflected, altered, and activated nexus of participatory links, which continue to evolve the essentially open-ended "Web work." The center of gravity thus shifts from the poles of relation to its "medium" or betweenness, which remains obviously more open to chance, to flexible, contingent participation. Not surprisingly in the age of the Internet, the "inter" becomes the new "center," since the link takes precedence over what it connects. The work of art comes to be disclosed as a cooperative venture of mediation, links, and intermediaries, extended in time and virtual space, intrinsically open to intervention and redefinition. The changes that this shift in emphasis brings to our understanding of the work of art remain to be fleshed out more fully and rigorously as time goes by.

In many respects, the work of art in the age of Web interactivity promises much more than film did when Benjamin wrote about it in his famous essay on reproducibility: there is no easily enforced censorship, there is transcendence of geographical boundaries and distances, there is virtually global accessibility, and so on. The twenty-first-century artwork is no longer just a matter of intrinsic reproducibility; rather, it is also a matter of interactivity and open-ended spatial-temporal e-volution. Both change and intermediality, therefore, so critical to the avant-garde conception of the artwork, come to be constitutive of the very technological mode of existence of the electronic Web. The two channels opening the work of art to the potential of revolt and change—participation of the audience, and temporal fluidity and open-endedness—have come to be instantiated into the very operations of information technology. As a result, the artist no longer has to resort to innovative efforts to elicit participation and extend the mantle of activity and creativity to the audience. Audience participation, so much desired and provoked by radical twentieth-century art, has become inscribed, even prescribed, into the very matrix of the Internet, into the very principle of interactivity.

Furthermore, Web interactivity also renders Web-based art intrinsically exposed to alteration and evolution over its temporal span of existence. The e-work of art is essentially e-volutionary; that is, its very virtual/electronic modality of existence is multiply open to participation, change, and turning, which means that such a work is spatially-temporally interactive, flexible, changeable, and multilinked. All these aspects of current and future e-art undercut the notions of the stable, uniform, or integrated identity of the creator and the creative process. With the advent of Internet art, artworks appear to have incorporated into their existence the ontological possibilities and virtualities that characterize contemporary social life in its unprecedented fluidity. It has therefore become possible to say that Web-based artworks, like the temporality of being, are metamorphic in their character, enacting in their mode of being the interactive, hybrid, and omnilinked operations of modern reality.

By the same token, the work of art has also come to be determined by technology, to an unprecedented degree, and thus it has come to reflect the intensifying technicity of being, the technologic of relations constitutive of modern global capital. On closer examination, works like those placed on the World Wide Web by Mikami or Kac illustrate the degree to which today's technicity of relations has extended its power to manipulation of the interlinked processes spanning the entire globe. In the domain of interactivity, works like the interactive, molecularly e-volutionary *Molecular Clinic* and *Genesis* make evident how manipulative power has incorporated by now even the element of chance. Chance compositions, happenstance, and coincidence constitute the fabric of John Cage's musical and poetic works. The structure of Cage's musical and poetic texts, often intrinsically open to the accidents of happening, is unpredictable and, in a way, welcoming to what art previously had held to be external to it, and therefore threatening to contaminate the integrity of artistic work. Cage's music is not only left open to musicians' interpretations and interventions but also inclusive of noise and accidental sounds. In this respect, Cage can be seen as opening up musical composition beyond the scope of Schoenbergian revolutionary dissonance, and, by incorporating the chancelike operations of the *I Ching*, as clearly freeing music from the compositional restrictiveness of the tonal and dodecaphonic systems. After Cage, the work of art became more than ever before "in tune" with the chancelike character of the event.

Internet art, with interactivity as its fundamental principle, also appears to incorporate the aleatory temporality of existence with unprecedented openness and scrupulousness, and yet in the same gesture it also subordinates chance to manipulation and programming. If chance, in Cage, disrupts both the author's control over the work and the work's apparent structural unity, then in Internet art, even though the frequency of chancelike operations increases geometrically, all such operations become part of an extended program matrix. In virtual reality and in interactive Web-based art, chance becomes incorporated and activated, so to speak, to an unprecedented degree, but such inscription comes at a price: the infinitely more subtle operations of programming and reprogramming. For instance, even though anyone can affect the molecular composition of *The Spider,* one can do so only within the parameters prescribed by the program. In a way, all possible interactions, alterations, and e-volutions—at least their manner or modality—though not necessarily predicted explicitly, are contained within and determined by the nature of the programming. Interactivity appears to be free, from the perspective of those who participate in its development over time, but from the point of view of the program regulating such interactivity, the parameters have already been determined within which cocreators' or users' participation can take place. What is clear is that chance no longer instantiates the rupture of manipulative power, which for Cage extended to the very persona of the artist and to the constitution of the artwork. Rather, chance, alteration, and evolution have all become matters of programming and thus part of the technicist organization of being, since even the province of participation, the idea of multiple creative agency, and the aleatory character of existence, when it comes to interactivity and Web art, come to be inscribed into the structural operations of informational technology. No doubt this technology facilitates the integration of all these elements, much desired by the early-twentieth-century avant-garde as a critical response to the bourgeois aesthetics and institutionalization of art; the effect, however, is that these elements have now become not the goal but the basis of the interactive Web artwork. But the artwork, in the same gesture, can become, as I showed in chapter 2, a telematic total work of art, a *Gesamtelewerk*, that is, a truly unprecedented total integration of all aesthetic and experiential aspects that incorporates the very principle of mediation, interactive openness, and transformation into the paradigm of

Internet artwork. The incorporation of interactivity, which a hundred years ago was critical to the survival and development of modern art, has now become "virtually" guaranteed by advances in contemporary technology. Thus, as Adorno would have been keen to point out, with the change in the historical situation the valence of the previously disruptive aesthetic elements has also undergone irreversible change. What helped art, in the context of the modernist avant-garde, unlock its transformative potential cannot be embraced and celebrated uncritically by twenty-first-century art, even though just such uncritical celebration seems predominantly to be the case.

With electronically based work comes the unprecedented reach and flexibility of power, which the avant-garde had already tried to contest while celebrating the technological advances of the early twentieth century. The technoinformational, telematic character of Internet art must itself be examined critically. The incorporation of temporal e-volution and cyberinteractivity into the very constitution of future art has also exposed mediation, interactivity, and transformation to an unprecedented degree of control and programmability. As we know from computer games, interactive shows, and Web browsing, the very principle of interactivity was commodified even before it was extended into the realm of art. Just as virtual reality is itself programmed, so too do the interactivity and patterns of transformation underlying interactive Web art expand the principle of programmability and manipulation into the very "core" of art. Thus the aesthetic of Internet art comes to reflect, with unprecedented accuracy, the power momentum of contemporary global reality. While this unprecedented correlation between technical manipulability and aesthetic construction gives art historically unequaled powers of disclosure—the ability, in fact, to participate in and interact with the technoinformational flow of power—at the same time this disclosive force comes at the price of possibly circumscribing the very transformative potential of art, for the kind of change opened up by the new aesthetics of Internet art is already preprogrammed, prescribed by the very kind of "manipulative writing" at the basis of the technicity manifest in digital/informational forms of power. Thus, Internet art, if we follow Adorno's and Horkheimer's analyses, can become an instantiation of novelty as the principle of the technoinformational operational basis of the twenty-first-century electronic culture industry. Therefore, since interactivity is the manifestation of novelty in

the age of telematics, it may be more repetition than rupture, more of the same rather than of the new within the event.

Adorno understood mediation to be the force of negativity, and thus the radical breaker in the endless repetition of the same under the guise of the novelty of products and commodities. Mediation in the negative was the answer to art's critical role in the capitalist economy of novelty, for it gave art a radical critical impetus, which allowed artworks to undo domination in the process of creation. By the beginning of the twenty-first century, however, interaction and mediation, whether dialectical or multiphasic and hyperlinked, have become the very arena of the most far-reaching and agile transactions of manipulative power. In other words, the negative force of mediation no longer functions as a preserve of critique, for the kind of transformativity encoded into the "medium" of interactivity remains highly programmed and thus intrinsically subject to manipulation and reprogramming. The negativity of mediation therefore no longer appears radical enough, for its has become part of the manipulative operations of modern power; in fact, it has become instrumental in allowing this power both unprecedented scope and participatory force. *It is the "genius" of information technology that action, critique, and change may have become "virtually" indistinguishable from the operations of manipulative power.* The unequaled scope of the information technologies, and of the potential they make available for interactive and hybrid forms of art, extends the indistinguishability of critique/complicity into new globally interlinked realms. The transformativity made possible by interactivity as the basis of new Internet art comes at the price of power, because inscribed into its very matrix is the operation of modern power at its current stage of telematic technicity. The interactive work of art discloses contemporary operations of power with unprecedented accuracy, by making the audience simultaneously into conduit and partial agent in the global flows of infopower. Thus everyone can be, in the same gesture, both critic and conduit for the ostensibly criticized power, a possibility made available to Internet "subscribers" through the "interactive" cooperation of information technology and telematic artist/engineers.

The issues briefly outlined here, from the perspective of power and artistic forcework, will have to be carefully scrutinized and rethought as new directions appear in the continuing parallel developments of artistic possibilities and different channels of technopower. But I would like to close this reflection on the contemporary directions of art by recalling the possibility, encoded in the notion of artistic forcework, of a more radical and critical transformation. While the interactivity and e-volution programmed into the "structure" of Web-based art seem to remain co-optable by and pre-scribed within the expanding realms of manipulative power, the redisposition of force relations figured in art's forcework can, by contrast, exceed and revise the parameters of power. As I have tried to show in my discussion of twentieth-century art and aesthetic conceptions, the radical "poietics" of the avant-garde, from its very inception, entertained and strove for the possibility of a novel sense of transformation, a transformation that would not simply change or amend social practices but reform the very idea of praxis. But this transformation has to be understood beyond the parameters of change and novelty, for these categories have already been co-opted by capital and no longer mark anything essentially new except further extensions and added flexibility in the operations of power. Art's forcework, both more and less than praxis, exposes and transforms the intensifying power momentum of relations in the epoch of digital technology, and the radical character of this transformation explains itself in terms of a specific disinvestment from power. What is at stake in contemporary art—and in this sense, the avant-garde of the twentieth century continues to be contemporary—is the possibility of reassigning the momentum of relations, of releasing forces from the formative sway of power. Kac's *Genesis* project emerges here as the most recent instance in which art telescopes the issues of complicity and revolt into a transgenic work that literally dramatizes the boundary between manipulative power and its "otherwise." The transformation evidenced in such artworks reaches beyond the notions of resistance and opposition, as well as beyond power and powerlessness, as it instantiates an alternative, power-free disposition of relations. To the extent that art, beyond ideology, politics, or moralism, remains a question of power, it continues to be socially significant; and it concerns power precisely to the extent that the artwork can become a matter of a power-free, nonmanipulative relationality. Here, "nonmanipulative" relationality pertains to an artwork that is still capable of letting go of power, of unfolding an event in which relations can have a power-free, enabling momentum. In the age of Web interactivity, of informational inundation and overflow of data, of global networks and telematic transmissibility, art's silent transformation retains/inaugurates—

the line here remains as untraceable as the never-present "present" moment—the possibility of an "otherwise" to power. In the context of the Internet revolution, this "otherwise" to power gives a new meaning to revolt—the possibility of a turn in the increasingly technic organization of relations in contemporary society. This turn or *volta* in the momentum of power, art's revolt within technicity, determines art's relevance in contemporary culture. This nonpower, giving artworks critical significance, constitutes the radical force of art.

REFERENCE MATTER

Notes

INTRODUCTION

1. Shusterman, *Performing Live.*

2. What comes to mind here is obviously Heidegger's critique of aesthetics and his attempt to understand the work of art beyond aesthetic categories in "The Origin of the Work of Art." More recent examples of this approach can be found in Carroll's *Paraesthetics* or in Agamben's *The Man Without Content.* With clear echoes of Heidegger, Agamben writes of the need "to exit the swamp of aesthetics and technics and restore to the poetic status of man on earth its original dimension" (67).

3. The limitations of Heidegger's approach to art are often pointed out: insufficient attention to modernist and avant-garde art or to the complex implications of modern art in consumerist mass society. Adorno, on the other hand, presents a "merely" negative conception of the artwork and, unlike Heidegger, does not really push the conceptual approach to art beyond the boundaries of aesthetics.

4. Adorno speaks about art as a force field in *Aesthetic Theory,* without, however, drawing out the implications of such an approach to the artwork.

5. In the context of his discussion of cultural revolution, Jameson (*The Political Unconscious,* 98) defines the artwork "as a field of force in which the dynamics of sign systems of several distinct modes of production can be registered and apprehended." In my reading, the artwork's event not only inscribes modes of production but also calls into question and transforms the very mechanics—or, better, technics—that underlies the constitution of reality *in terms of* production.

6. My approach here builds on Heidegger's elaboration of the "thingly" and the "workly" aspects of the artwork in "The Origin of the Work of Art."

7. This line of thinking is signaled in Heidegger's distinction between

the artwork and equipment in "The Origin of the Work of Art," 155: "The matter-form structure, by which the Being of a piece of equipment is first determined, readily presents itself as the immediately intelligible constitution of every being [including the artwork], because here man himself as maker participates in the way in which the piece of equipment comes into being." The critical variance between making and art is also the pivot of Adorno's elaboration of the "negative" force of art in relation to the social determinations of power and production (*Aesthetic Theory*, 241): "The critique exercised a priori by art is that of action as a cryptogram of domination. According to its sheer form, praxis tends toward that which, in terms of its own logic, it should abolish; violence is immanent to it and is maintained in its sublimations, whereas artworks, even the most aggressive, stand for nonviolence."

8. Deleuze, *Foucault*, 94–95.

9. For such an articulation of democratic politics, see Laclau, *New Reflections on the Revolution of Our Time.*

10. "Every work is a force field. . . "; see Adorno, *Aesthetic Theory*, 206.

11. Photographs and descriptions of these installations can be found in Ross et al., *Bill Viola.*

12. Ziarek, *The Historicity of Experience.*

CHAPTER 1

1. Heidegger, "The Origin of the Work of Art," 191.

2. This approach to writing and English grammar is most in evidence in Stein's *How to Write.*

3. Dabrowski, *Liubov Popova,* 25.

4. Heidegger, "The Origin of the Work of Art," 191.

5. I discuss Wodiczko's work in chapter 3. For his theoretical statements and description of his projections, interrogative designs, and performative instruments, see Krzysztof Wodiczko, *Critical Vehicles.*

6. Adorno, *Aesthetic Theory*, 31.

7. Deleuze, *Foucault*, 77.

8. See ibid., 70–75, for Deleuze's discussion of force relations.

9. Adorno, *Aesthetic Theory*, 16–17.

10. Ibid., 17 (modified).

11. Deleuze, *Foucault,* 87.

12. Heidegger, "The Question Concerning Technology," 321.

13. Ibid.

14. Ibid., 340.

15. Adorno, *Aesthetic Theory*, 225–26.

16. Heidegger, *The Will to Power as Art*, 100. In German, these remarks can be found in vol. 1 of the Neske edition of *Nietzsche,* 120.

17. Foucault, *Discipline and Punish,* 138.

18. It is certainly not a matter of violence. Enhancement refers to such a relation between forces that does not form a technology of power, because the enhanced bearing reciprocally enhances all the elements of relation: it lets them unfold as "more in being" rather then disciplining them to (re)produce an arrangement, a technology of power. Force here, as Deleuze makes clear, cannot be violence, since violence is not inherent in force. Rather, violence becomes possible only within a power-relation of forces: only when power forms itself does force become "prone" to violence. See Deleuze, *Foucault*, 28.

19. Heidegger, *What Is Philosophy?*, 70–74.

20. Stein, "Poetry and Grammar," 242.

21. Heidegger, *Die Geschichte des Seyns*, 71.

22. "Das Wesende dieser Mache ist die *Machenschaft*: das Sicheinrichten auf die Ermächtigung der Macht und die von dieser vorgerichtete weil aus der Übermächtigung vorgefordete Machsamkeit alles Seienden" (Heidegger, *Die Geschichte des Seins,* 186). In colloquial use, *Mache* signifies make-believe or show, which suggests that power produces itself as a spectacle and a make-believe, which tends to obscure the manipulative bent of power.

23. The terms Heidegger uses to distinguish "letting" from passivity or indifference are *Gleichgültigkeit* and *Nichtsdazutun*; see Heidegger, *Besinnung,* 103.

24. Blanchot, *The Infinite Conversation*, 23.

25. Ibid., 44; emphasis in original.

26. Ibid., 23.

27. Bruns, *Maurice Blanchot,* 46.

28. Heidegger, *Besinnung*, 67.

29. Ibid., 83.

30. Heidegger employs the term in several sections in *Besinnung*; see pp. 187–88.

31. *Machtlos* becomes equivalent to *machtfrei* (power-free), but Heidegger prefers to use the former term because of the connotations of release and letting be contained in the suffix *-los.*

32. Heidegger, *Besinnung*, 188.

33. As Gerald Bruns explains, Blanchot espouses a certain anarchism,

in the sense of the absence of principle, which marks an interruption of the dialectics of domination and resistance. His idea of revolution points beyond both active and passive resistance; it is an affirmation outside negation. See Bruns, *Maurice Blanchot*, 31–32.

34. This discussion appears in Heidegger, *Besinnung*, 188.

35. Blanchot, *The Infinite Conversation*, 208–9; emphasis in original.

36. Bruns, *Maurice Blanchot*, 22–23.

37. And poetics, as Bruns suggests (*Maurice Blanchot*, 3–6), is always a (philosophical) effort to conceptualize, grasp, and control poetry.

38. Heidegger, *Hegel*, 49.

39. "*Das Nichts* der Ab-grund: Versagung des Grundes, jeder Stütze und jedes Schutzes im Seienden; doch diese Versagung ist die höchste Gewährung der Not der Entscheidung und Unterscheidung" (Heidegger, *Hegel*, 47).

40. The charges, which Adorno levels with repeated insistence, that Heidegger's being stands for immediacy and indeterminacy are based on a misreading of Heidegger's notion of *Sein*. Adorno still operates with the Hegelian and Nietzschean notion of being as the emptiest of all concepts, as pure immediacy and lack of determination, and thus as devoid of any "negating" and critical force. It is on the basis of such a misreading that Adorno and, later, Habermas claim that Heidegger's questioning of being means inaction and complicity with what is. In *Hegel*, Heidegger makes clear that *Sein* is neither immediate nor indeterminate but constitutes the very "force" that makes difference and determination possible; as such, *Sein* is the originary force of nihilation, the "activation" of the event prior to activity, negation, critique.

41. Stein, *Tender Buttons*, 9.

CHAPTER 2

1. Marinetti's nationalism made him a fervent supporter of Italy's participation in World War I and, later, of Mussolini's political program. His fascination with war, however, seems to have less to do with admiration for violence than with the idea that war releases culture from the hold that the past and the traditions have on it. As his frequent references to war suggest, Marinetti considers war a purifying factor. It is as though Marinetti thought of World War I as Italy's chance to shake off the garb of Europe's museum and set free the truly "Italian," ultramodern spirit, so completely misrepresented by those Europeans and Italians alike who remain fascinated with the remnants of Italy's past. The terrifying dynamism of

war, "the swirling poetic and geometric mechanics of a bombardment," becomes a reflection of the changing dynamic of modern life. See Marinetti, "From the Café Bulgaria in Sofia," 253.

2. For a more sustained discussion of Gastev's work in the context of the Russian avant-garde and the proletarian revolution, see Todorov, *Red Square, Black Square,* in particular pp. 68–71.

3. Lacoue-Labarthe and Nancy, *Le mythe nazi.*

4. *The History of Sexuality,* 149.

5. See Foucault's discussion of bio-power in the last chapter of vol. 1 of *The History of Sexuality,* in particular pp. 139–50.

6. Lista, *Le Futurisme.* Lista's explanations of Marinetti's ideas about war and nationalism, as well as his relation to Mussolini and Fascism, are spread throughout the book, in particular in parts II and III, dealing respectively with Futurism in the 1920's and 1930's; see pp. 239–352. Here are some particularly important and interesting moments in Lista's discussion: Marinetti on war (49); Marinetti on war and nationalism, in distinction from other Futurists (217–23); Marinetti's radical political program after World War I (242); Futurism and its relation to Fascism (247–48, 258, 341, 350); Marinetti's critique of Hitler's attack on the avant-garde, and his own defense of radical art (348–49).

7. Marinetti, "Technical Manifesto of Futurist Literature," 95.

8. Ibid.

9. This and other polarities typical of fascist aesthetics are discussed by Kaplan in *Reproductions of Banality,* 25–35.

10. "Carrà, Boccioni et Russolo veulent évoquer l'intensité vitale du phénomène, voire sa dimension émotionnelle et lyrique, et non se livrer à une simple reconstitution optique du mouvement" (Lista, *Le Futurisme,* 64).

11. Lista writes about the "champ de l'énergie qui transcende la matière" and negates "l'opacité, la fixité, la matérialité et les limites des objets au nom du flux continu qui intègre toute chose au sein du dynamisme universel." Dematerializing the visual givens, Futurist painters lean toward an abstract vision of the phenomena; see Lista, *Le Futurisme,* 59–60.

12. Ibid., 64.

13. Marinetti, "Geometric and Mechanical Splendor and the Numerical Sensibility," 106.

14. Marinetti, "Technical Manifesto of Futurist Literature," 93.

15. Ibid., 95.

16. Ibid., 95.
17. Lista, *Le Futurisme*, 201.
18. Khlebnikov, *The King of Time*, 205.
19. Khlebnikov, "To the Artists of the World," in ibid., 146.
20. See Butler's discussion of the polemics between Futurism and Cubism in *Early Modernism*, 152.
21. See Lista's discussion of Severini in *Le Futurisme*, 124.
22. Butler, *Early Modernism*, 150.
23. Quoted in ibid., 151.
24. Goldberg's *Telegarden* can be found at http://telegarden.aec.at, accessed Mar. 2004; Kac's projects are available at http://www.ekac.org, accessed Mar. 2004.
25. This description was previously available at http://www.cast.canon.co.jp/cast/al5/spidere.html (accessed in 2001). The spider can currently be found at *Molecular Clinic 1.0*, available at http://web.canon.jp/cast/artlab/artlab5/index.html (accessed Apr. 2004).
26. Eduardo Kac, *Teleporting an Unknown State*, 9.
27. Examples of such poetry can be found at UBUWEB, http://www.ubu.com, accessed Mar. 2004, or at one of the Web directories for interactive poetry: http://dmoz.org/Arts/Literature/Poetry/Interactive.
28. This is an excerpt from "Net Art in the Age of Digital Reproduction," in *The Telematic Manifesto: A Hypertextual Collectively-Generated Net Document Organized by Randall Packer*; see http://www.zakros.com/manifesto/index1.html, accessed Mar. 2004.
29. See Tony Pinkney's introduction to Williams, *The Politics of Modernism*, 19.
30. Williams, *The Politics of Modernism*, 131.
31. Ibid., 139.
32. Orlan, "L'avant-garde n'est plus dans l'art."
33. Kac, *The Eighth Day, a Transgenic Net Installation*; see http://www.ekac.org/8thday.html, accessed Mar. 2004.
34. Adorno, *Aesthetic Theory*, 241.
35. Ibid., 54.
36. Kac, *GFP Bunny*, 112.
37. Ibid., 105: "As a transgenic artist, I am not interested in the creation of genetic objects, but [in] the invention of transgenic social subjects. In other words, what is important is the completely integrated process of creating the bunny, bringing her to society at large, and providing her with a loving, caring, and nurturing environment in which she can grow safe and healthy. This integrated process is important because it places genetic

engineering in a social context in which the relationship between the private and the public spheres [is] negotiated. In other words, biotechnology, the private realm of family life, and the social domain of public opinion are discussed in relation to one another. Transgenic art is not about the crafting of genetic objets d'art, either inert or imbued with vitality. Such an approach would suggest a conflation of the operational sphere of life sciences with a traditional aesthetics that privileges formal concerns, material stability, and hermeneutical isolation. Integrating the lessons of dialogical philosophy . . . and cognitive ethology . . . , transgenic art must promote awareness of and respect for the spiritual (mental) life of the transgenic animal. The word 'aesthetics' in the context of transgenic art must be understood to mean that creation, socialization, and domestic integration are a single process."

38. Gessert, "Art Is Nature": "Kac's best-known transgenic work is Genesis. . . . For this work he translated into the four-letter alphabet of DNA a passage from the Bible, 'Let man have dominion over the fish of the sea, and the birds of the air, and all creatures that crawl upon the land.' He then ordered a strand of DNA that contained the sequence—there are now mail order places that do this sort of thing. The order took about two weeks to complete, and cost a mere $8,000. I say 'mere' without irony. Just a few years ago the sequencing would have cost many times as much. . . . With the help of yet another technician Kac had the DNA inserted into an E. coli bacterium.

At the O.K. Centrum in Linz, Austria, where Genesis was first displayed in 1999, it occupied a room in which the Biblical passage was on one wall, the DNA sequence on another, and a projection of a petri dish of genetically altered bacteria on a third. They looked like glowing rain. The effect was visually stunning—but also shocking, especially in the context of Linz, which is near where Hitler was born, and one of his favorite cities. Genetic engineering lends itself to the megalomanias that thrive on collective hubris. Genesis brought this point home."(This citation is from http://www.ekac.org/gessertap.html.)

39. For an illuminating and detailed discussion of the questions of writing, translation, and artistic/scientific creation in *Genesis,* see Tomasula, "(Gene)sis."

40. Heidegger, "The Question Concerning Technology," 339.

41. Adorno, *Aesthetic Theory*, 138.

42. The description and photographs of *The Crossing* can be found in Ross et al., *Bill Viola.*

43. Perloff, *Poetry On and Off the Page,* 319.

CHAPTER 3

1. See Heidegger, "Der Ursprung des Kunstwerkes," 12–24; translated into English as "The Origin of the Work of Art," 153–65.

2. Heidegger, "The Origin of the Work of Art," 153; emphasis in original.

3. Ibid., 155.

4. Adorno, *Aesthetic Theory*, 259.

5. Heidegger, "The Origin of the Work of Art," 202.

6. I provide a more detailed explanation of Heidegger's understanding of grounding and of his notion of art as "grounding history" in *The Historicity of Experience,* 72–85.

7. Marx, *Capital*, 164–65.

8. Ibid., 165.

9. Adorno, *Aesthetic Theory*, 227.

10. Marx, *Capital*, 163–64.

11. A concise account of this divide can be found in Narmore and Brantlinger, *Modernity and Mass Culture*; see "Introduction: Six Artistic Cultures," 1–23.

12. Shusterman, *Performing Live.*

13. Ibid., 6–7.

14. Ibid., 7.

15. See in particular pp. 44–54 and 108–15.

16. Huyssen, *After the Great Divide,* 21.

17. Ziarek, *The Historicity of Experience*, 109–11.

18. Tzara, *Seven Dada Manifestos and Lampisteries.*

19. Adorno, *Aesthetic Theory*, 138.

20. Heidegger, *Die Geschichte des Seyns*, 180–82.

21. Adorno, *Aesthetic Theory*, 255.

22. Hardt and Negri, *Empire,* 290–95.

23. *The Crossing* is a sound/video installation (see Ross et al., *Bill Viola,* 126): "A large double-sided projection screen stands in the middle of the room, its bottom edge resting on the floor. Two video projectors mounted at opposite ends of the room project images onto the front and back sides of the screen simultaneously, showing a single action involving a human figure culminating in a violent annihilation by the opposing natural forces of fire and water." See also p. 122: "Inspired by Pontormo's Mannerist painting *Visitation* (1528–29), *The Greeting* is a video image sequence projected onto a screen mounted to the wall of a dark room. . . . Presented as a single take from a fixed camera position and projected in a

vertical aspect ratio more common to painting, the actions of the figures are seen in extreme slow motion. An original event of forty-five seconds now unfolds as an elaborate choreography over the course of ten minutes."

24. "Artistic expression, expanded beyond recognition from the grudging gifts offered by the masters as a token substitute for freedom from bondage, therefore becomes the means toward both individual self-fashioning and communal liberation. Poiesis and poetics begin to coexist in novel forms—autobiographical writing, special and uniquely creative ways of manipulating spoken language, and, above all, the music" (Gilroy, *The Black Atlantic,* 40).

25. Baraka, *Funk Lore*, 9.

26. Ibid.

27. Ibid., 55.

28. Ibid., 10.

29. Ibid., 109.

30. Ibid., 61.

31. Ibid., 60.

32. See Heidegger's discussion of measure in ". . . Poetically Man Dwells . . . ," 221–25.

33. In a brief note, "Rimbaud Vivant," Heidegger reads the Greek *rhythmos* as a mode of relatedness, a disposition and gathering of bearings, relations, and references, which composes the "rhythm" of being; see Heidegger, *Aus der Erfahrung des Denkens*, 225–27.

34. The projection on the facade of the Hirshhorn Museum took place over three consecutive nights during the week preceding the 1998 United States presidential elections. For Wodiczko (*Public Address,* 151), the projection "is what I think of politics in this election, resembling more and more a crime story. For example, George Bush on the one hand is for the death penalty and on another is anti-abortion, on one hand he goes on about 'a thousand points of light' and on another defends guns and a strong militaristic policy. Media and microphones are also used as weapons."

35. Here, taken from the World Wide Web, is a description of the projection: "Held on the bank of the river in Hiroshima, the video was initially projected beneath the A-bomb Dome, the building which was directly under the bomb, which exploded on August 6, 1945. During two nights, on August 7 and August 8, 1999, over 4,000 people gathered to watch and hear Krzysztof Wodiczko's emotional evocation of stories of various survivors, the 'hibakusha' and their children, the 'radiated nisei.' These testimonies, without giving [in to] sentimentality, skillfully pene-

trated some of the myths and biases which still exist in Japan against survivors. The projection intended to expose the hidden psychological, ethical, and political fallout of the atomic bomb, its physical and cultural hypocenter. Examples of people who chose [to] have their hands and voices animate the monuments are:—Survivors who had to face the official justification of the American attack;—Second generation victims, who suffer from the psychological abuse rendered by traumatized war veterans;—Slave laborers brought from Korea, who constituted a large but invisible population among the hundred thousand A-bomb survivors;—People born in Hiroshima who feel stigmatized by the common prejudice that they may represent a potential genetic threat to society"; see http://www.artincontext.org/listings/pages/exhib/d/c7j2v3dd/press.html, accessed Mar. 2004.

36. Wodiczko, *Critical Vehicles,* 46.

37. Ibid., 4.

38. Ibid., 51–52.

39. Ibid., 52.

40. Ibid., 104.

41. Ibid., 12.

42. Ibid.

43. Ibid., 17.

44. "A critical vehicle is, therefore, a medium; a person or a thing acting as a carrier for displaying or transporting vital ingredients and agents. It is set to operate as a turning point in collective or singular consciousness" (Ibid., xvi).

45. Ibid., xvii.

46. Ibid., xv.

47. Adorno, *Aesthetic Theory*, 243.

48. Ibid., 31.

49. In *The Historicity of Experience,* where the artwork is understood in terms of a poietic event, I propose an alternative to thinking of the work of art in terms of the object and aesthetic experience; see in particular chaps. 1 and 2.

50. Heidegger, "Letter on Humanism," 220.

51. Ibid.

52. Ibid., 252.

53. Ibid., 261.

54. Ibid.

55. Adorno, *Aesthetic Theory*, 228.

56. Heidegger, "The Question Concerning Technology," 340–41.

57. Heidegger, "Letter on Humanism," 262.

58. See Heidegger's remark ("The Origin of the Work of Art," 191) about the displacement from the habitual modes of knowing, perceiving, acting, and evaluating.

59. Adorno, *Aesthetic Theory*, 79.

60. Ibid., 241.

61. Ibid., 12.

62. Hejinian, *My Life*, 55.

63. Ibid., 7.

64. Adorno, *Aesthetic Theory*, 34.

65. Ziarek, *The Historicity of Experience*, 151–85, 263–93.

66. I discuss the importance of Irigaray's rethinking of difference in "Proximities: Irigaray and Heidegger on Difference."

67. Irigaray, *This Sex Which Is Not One*, 207.

68. See Irigaray, "Plato's *Hystera*," 241–364.

69. See her discussion of the negative in *I Love to You*.

70. This conception of "être deux" forms the backbone of Irigaray's argument in *Être Deux*.

71. In his reflections on the contribution of African Americans to American culture, Du Bois underscores in particular the importance of music and religion, introduced by Africans into what he calls "a dusty desert of dollars and smartness" (that is, the American culture; see Du Bois, *The Souls of Black Folk*, 52). At the end of the book, Du Bois returns to this problematic by enumerating the three gifts brought by African American culture: "a gift of story and song," "the gift of sweat and brawn," and "a gift of the Spirit" (275). This idea of supplementing the "arid" culture of the intellect and enterprise with the gifts of music and spirit is reformulated by Gilroy into a more explicit critique of the production paradigm in *The Black Atlantic*.

72. Gilroy, *The Black Atlantic*, 40.

73. Fanon, *Peau noire, masques blancs*, 6.

74. Fanon, *Black Skin, White Masks*, 231.

75. Fanon, *Peau noire, masques blancs*, 112, and *Black Skin, White Masks*, 138.

76. Fanon, *Black Skin, White Masks*, 232.

77. Ibid., 231.

78. Ibid., 223.

79. Ibid., 229; emphasis in original.

80. Fanon, *The Wretched of the Earth*, 35–106. Fanon ends his chapter "Concerning Violence" by underscoring the need of "reintroducing

mankind into the world, the whole of mankind" (106). This idea of reintroducing mankind into the world would need to be developed in the context of the concept of the actional human being from Fanon's *Black Skin, White Masks.*

81. Fanon, *Black Skin, White Masks*, 131.
82. Senghor, "Negritude and Modernity," 161.
83. Ibid., 146.
84. Ibid., 157.
85. Ibid., 150.
86. Ibid., 153; emphasis in original.
87. See Fanon, *Black Skin, White Masks,* 231.

CONCLUSION

1. Kristeva, *Sens et Non-sens de la Révolte*, 21.
2. Hardt and Negri, *Empire*, 218.
3. Ibid., 357; emphasis in original.
4. Ibid., 358; emphasis in original.
5. Ibid., 408.
6. Ibid., 413.
7. Ibid., 52.
8. Tzara, "Lecture on Dada," 251.
9. Ibid., 251.
10. Khlebnikov, *The King of Time,* 126.
11. Ibid., 128.
12. Ibid., 130–32.
13. Ibid., 34.
14. Ibid., 35–36.
15. For a longer discussion of *Zangezi*, see my *The Historicity of Experience,* 203–10.
16. Elsewhere I have discussed the complicated notion of revolution in Khlebnikov; see ibid., 211–21.
17. Lyotard engages in this polemic in *The Postmodern Condition;* see especially pp. 73–76.
18. "Othello Jr." is a bitingly ironic "recasting" of the O. J. Simpson trial as a modern version of Othello: "(One Moor Time) / $ / = / " / A Ne(gr)o Classical / Tragedy / of / 'Amusement / & Contempt'. . . "; see *Funk Lore*, 90. In the first of "Incriminating Negrographs" entitled "Perceiving Miss," Baraka launches a direct attack on Spike Lee's version of Malcolm X's life: "What do you think / of the movie / 'X'? // Spike / Lie!" (65), reinforced in negrograph #4, "'The Wages of Sin' Explained":

"Invoke the Nation / to secure your fortune // Betray the Nation / to receive your fortune" (66). "Who Killed Malcolm X" (69) accuses "the same murderer / cracker imperialism" for a whole series of political assassinations, pointing toward confluences in the operations of power, beyond any notions of political plots and conspiracies, that tend toward the perpetuation of existing forms of domination and social injustice; thus Malcolm X is mentioned together with John F. Kennedy, Martin Luther King Jr., Patrice Lumumba, Medgar Evers, and others. Among the most openly outspoken political poems in the collection is "Sin Soars!" which begins with "The American Peoples' Voice / is never heard well / is seldom heard / ABC CBS NBC Rocky Dupont Mellon Rich / Thieves & Murderers is / Pretend human real animals . . ." (27). Raging against multinational capital and its power over national governments, Baraka alternates the angry invocation about American "peoples'" voices not being heard with ironic portrayal of American politics under Ronald Reagan: "Our savior rolls across the clouds / in Air Force One / Is our voice / riding w/ him? / Heading for Panama, Nicaragua, Grenada. . ." (35).

19. Baraka, *Funk Lore*, 60.

20. Baraka, *Transbluesency*, 33.

21. Wodiczko, *Critical Vehicles*, 83.

22. See Wodiczko's discussion of public art in "Avant-Garde as Public Art: The Future of a Tradition," in ibid., 27–31.

23. Ibid., 27.

24. Ibid., xvii.

Bibliography

Adorno, Theodor W. *Aesthetic Theory*. Trans. Robert Hullot-Kentor. Minneapolis: University of Minnesota Press, 1997.

———. *Ästhetische Theorie. Gesammelte Schriften*, vol. 7. Ed. Rolf Tiedemann. Frankfurt am Main: Suhrkamp, 1970.

———. *Hegel: Three Studies*. Trans. Shierry Weber Nicholsen, intro. Shierry Weber Nicholsen and Jeremy J. Shapiro. Cambridge, Mass.: MIT Press, 1993.

———. *The Jargon of Authenticity*. Trans. Knut Tarnowski and Frederic Will. London: Routledge & Kegan Paul, 1973.

———. *Negative Dialectics*. Trans. E. B. Ashton. New York: Seabury Press, 1973.

Agamben, Giorgio. *The Man Without Content*. Trans. Georgia Albert. Stanford: Stanford University Press, 1999.

Armstrong, Isobel. *Radical Aesthetic*. Oxford: Blackwell, 2000.

Baraka, Amiri. *Funk Lore*. Ed. Paul Vangelisti. Los Angeles: Littoral Books, 1996.

———. *Transbluesency: The Selected Poems of Amiri Baraka/LeRoi Jones (1961–1995)*. Ed. Paul Vangelisti. New York: Marsilio Publishers, 1995.

Benjamin, Walter. *Illuminations*. Ed. Hannah Arendt. New York: Schocken, 1969.

Blanchot, Maurice. *The Infinite Conversation*. Trans. Susan Hanson. Minneapolis: University of Minnesota Press, 1993.

Breitwieser, Sabine, ed. *Designs für die wirkliche Welt/Designs for the Real World*. Köln: Walter König/Generali Foundation, 2002.

Bruns, Gerald L. *Maurice Blanchot: The Refusal of Philosophy*. Baltimore: Johns Hopkins University Press, 1997.

Butler, Christopher. *Early Modernism: Literature, Music, and Painting in Europe, 1900–1916*. Oxford: Clarendon Press, 1994.

Carroll, David. *Paraesthetics: Foucault, Lyotard, Derrida*. New York: Methuen, 1987.

Dabrowski, Magdalena. *Liubov Popova*. New York: Museum of Modern Art, 1991.

Danto, Arthur C. *The Wake of Art: Criticism, Philosophy, and the Ends of Taste*. Ed. Gregg Horowitz and Tom Huhn. Amsterdam: G+B Arts International, 1998.

Deleuze, Gilles. *Foucault*. Trans. Séan Hand. Minneapolis: University of Minnesota Press, 1988.

Du Bois, W. E. B. *The Souls of Black Folk*. New York: Penguin Putnam, 1995.

Fanon, Frantz. *Black Skin, White Masks*. Trans. Charles Lam Markmann. New York: Grove Press, 1967.

———. *Peau noire, masques blancs*. Paris: Éditions du Seuil, 1952.

———. *The Wretched of the Earth*. Trans. Constance Farrington. New York: Grove Press, 1963.

Foucault, Michel. *Discipline and Punish: The Birth of the Prison*, 2d ed. Trans. Alan Sheridan. New York: Vintage, 1995.

———. *The History of Sexuality*, vol. 1. Trans. Robert Hurley. New York: Random House, 1978.

Gessert, George. "Art Is Nature: An Artist's Perspective on a New Paradigm." *Art Papers* (March/April 2001): 16–19. Available at http://www.ekac.org/gessertap.html, accessed Apr. 2004.

Gilroy, Paul. *The Black Atlantic: Modernity and Double Consciousness*. Cambridge, Mass.: Harvard University Press, 1993.

Goldberg, Ken, ed. *The Robot in the Garden: Telerobotics and Telepistemology in the Age of the Internet*. Cambridge, Mass.: MIT Press, 2000.

Goldsmith, Marcella Tarozzi. *The Future of Art: An Aesthetics of the New and the Sublime*. Albany: State University of New York Press, 1999.

Hardt, Michael, and Negri, Antonio. *Empire*. Cambridge, Mass.: Harvard University Press, 2000.

Hegel, G. W. F. *Aesthetics*, vols. 1 and 2. Trans. T. M. Knox. Oxford: Clarendon Press, 1975.

Heidegger, Martin. *Aus der Erfahrung des Denkens. Gesamtausgabe*, vol. 15. Frankfurt am Main: Vittorio Klostermann, 1983.

———. *Basic Writings*, 2d ed. Ed. and intro. David Farrell Krell. New York: HarperCollins, 1993.

———. *Besinnung. Gesamtausgabe*, vol. 66. Frankfurt am Main: Vittorio Klostermann, 1997.

———. *Gelassenheit*. Pfullingen: Neske, 1959.

———. *Die Geschichte des Seyns. Gesamtausgabe*, vol. 69. Frankfurt am Main: Vittorio Klostermann, 1998.

———. *Hegel. Gesamtausgabe*, vol. 68. Frankfurt am Main: Vittorio Klostermann, 1993.

———. "Letter on Humanism." In *Basic Writings*, 2d ed. Ed. and intro. David Farrell Krell. New York: HarperCollins, 1993.

———. *Metaphysik und Nihilismus. Gesamtausgabe*, vol. 67. Frankfurt am Main: Vittorio Klostermann, 1999.

———. *Nietzsche*, vol. 1. Pfullingen: Neske, 1961.

———. *Nietzsche. The Will to Power as Art*, vol. 1. Trans. David Farrell Krell. San Francisco: Harper and Row, 1979.

———. *On the Way to Language*. Trans. Peter D. Hertz. San Francisco: Harper and Row, 1971.
———. "The Origin of the Work of Art." In *Basic Writings*, 2d ed. Ed. and intro. David Farrell Krell. New York: HarperCollins, 1993.
———. ". . . Poetically Man Dwells . . . ." In *Poetry, Language, Thought*. Trans. Albert Hofstadter. San Francisco: Harper and Row, 1971.
———. "The Question Concerning Technology." In *Basic Writings*, 2d ed. Ed. and intro. David Farrell Krell. New York: HarperCollins, 1993.
———. *Unterwegs zur Sprache*. Pfullingen: Neske, 1959.
———. "Der Ursprung des Kunstwerkes." In *Holzwege*. Frankfurt am Main: Vittorio Klostermann, 1950.
———. *Vorträge und Aufsätze*. Pfullingen: Neske, 1954.
———. *What Is Philosophy?* Trans. William Kluback and Jean T. Wilde. New York: Twayne, 1958.
Hejinian, Lyn. *The Language of Inquiry*. Berkeley: University of California Press, 2000.
———. *My Life*. Los Angeles: Sun & Moon, 1987.
Horkheimer, Max, and Adorno, Theodor W. *Dialectic of Enlightenment*. Trans. John Cumming. New York: Continuum, 1993.
Howe, Susan. *The Europe of Trusts*. Los Angeles: Sun & Moon, 1990.
———. *The Non-Conformist's Memorial*. New York: New Directions, 1993.
———. *Singularities*. Middletown, Conn.: Wesleyan University Press, 1993.
Huhn, Tom, and Zuidervaart, Lambert, eds. *The Semblance of Subjectivity: Essays in Adorno's Aesthetic Theory*. Cambridge, Mass.: MIT Press, 1997.
Huyssen, Andreas. *After the Great Divide: Modernism, Mass Culture, Postmodernism*. Bloomington: Indiana University Press, 1986.
Irigaray, Luce. *An Ethics of Sexual Difference*. Trans. Carolyn Burke and Gillian C. Gill. Ithaca: Cornell University Press, 1993.
———. *Être deux*. Paris: Grasset, 1997.
———. *I Love to You*. Trans. Alison Martin. New York and London: Routledge, 1996.
———. *The Irigaray Reader*. Ed. Margaret Whitford. Oxford: Basil Blackwell, 1991.
———. *Marine Lover of Friedrich Nietzsche*. Trans. Gillian C. Gill. New York: Columbia University Press, 1991.
———. "Plato's *Hystera*." In *Speculum of the Other Woman*. Trans. Gillian C. Gill. Ithaca: Cornell University Press, 1985.
———. *Sexes and Genealogies*. Trans. Gillian C. Gill. New York: Columbia University Press, 1993.
———. *Speculum of the Other Woman*. Trans. Gillian C. Gill. Ithaca: Cornell University Press, 1985.

———. *This Sex Which Is Not One.* Trans. Catherine Porter. Ithaca: Cornell University Press, 1985.

Jameson, Fredric. *The Political Unconscious: Narrative as a Socially Symbolic Act.* Ithaca: Cornell University Press, 1981.

Kac, Eduardo. *GFP Bunny.* In *Eduardo Kac: Telepresence, Biotelematics, Transgenic Art.* Maribor, Slovenia: KIBLA, 2000.

———. *Teleporting an Unknown State.* In *Eduardo Kac: Teleporting an Unknown State.* Maribor, Slovenia: KIBLA, 1998.

Kant, Immanuel. *Critique of Judgment.* Trans. Werner S. Pluhar. Indianapolis: Hackett, 1987.

Kaplan, Alice Yeager. *Reproductions of Banality: Fascism, Literature, and French Intellectual Life.* Minneapolis: University of Minnesota Press, 1986.

Khlebnikov, Velimir. *The King of Time: Selected Writings of the Russian Futurian.* Trans. Paul Schmidt. Cambridge, Mass: Harvard University Press, 1985.

———. *Letters and Theoretical Writings. Collected Works,* vol. 1. Ed. Charlotte Douglas, trans. Paul Schmidt. Cambridge, Mass.: Harvard University Press, 1987.

———. *Sobranie sochinenii.* 5 vols. Reprint of the Moscow Edition, 1928–33. Munich: W. Fink, 1968–73.

———. "To the Artists of the World." In *The King of Time: Selected Writings of the Russian Futurian.* Trans. Paul Schmidt. Cambridge, Mass: Harvard University Press, 1985.

Kristeva, Julia. *La Révolte Intime.* Paris: Fayard, 1997 .

———. *Sens et Non-sens de la Révolte.* Paris: Fayard, 1996.

Laclau, Ernesto. *New Reflections on the Revolution of Our Time.* London: Verso, 1990.

Lacoue-Labarthe, Phillipe, and Nancy, Jean-Luc. *Le mythe nazi.* La Tour d'Aigues: Editions de l'Aube, 1991.

Levinas, Emmanuel. *Otherwise than Being or Beyond Essence.* Trans. Alphonso Lingis. The Hague: Martinus Nijhoff, 1981.

Lista, Giovanni. *Le Futurisme: création et avant-garde.* Paris: Les Éditions de l'Amateur, 2001.

Lyotard, Jean-François. *The Postmodern Condition: A Report on Knowledge.* Trans. Geoff Bennington and Brian Massumi. Minneapolis: University of Minnesota Press, 1984.

Marinetti, F. T. "From the Café Sofia in Bulgaria to the Courage of the Italians in the Balkans and the Military Spirit of Désarrois." In *Let's Murder the Moonshine: Selected Writings.* Trans. W. R. Flint and Arthur A. Coppotelli. Los Angeles: Sun & Moon, 1991.

———. "Geometric and Mechanical Splendor and the Numerical Sensibility." In

Let's Murder the Moonshine: Selected Writings. Trans. W. R. Flint and Arthur A. Coppotelli. Los Angeles: Sun & Moon, 1991.

———. "Technical Manifesto of Futurist Literature." In *Let's Murder the Moonshine: Selected Writings*. Trans. W. R. Flint and Arthur A. Coppotelli. Los Angeles: Sun & Moon, 1991.

Marx, Karl. *Capital,* vol. 1. Trans. Ben Fowkes. London: Penguin, 1990.

Menke, Christoph. *The Sovereignty of Art: Aesthetic Negativity in Adorno and Derrida*. Trans. Neil Solomon. Cambridge, Mass.: MIT Press, 1999.

Motherwell, Robert, ed. *Dada Painters and Poets*. Cambridge, Mass.: Harvard University Press, 1951.

Mörchen, Hermann. *Adorno und Heidegger: Untersuchung einer philosophischen Kommunikationsverweigerung*. Stuttgart: Klett-Cota, 1981.

———. *Macht und Herrschaft im Denken von Heidgger und Adorno*. Stuttgart: Klett-Cota, 1980.

Narmore, James, and Brantlinger, Patrick, eds. *Modernity and Mass Culture*. Bloomington: Indiana University Press, 1991.

Nietzsche, Friedrich. *The Birth of Tragedy*. Trans. Shaun Whiteside. London: Penguin, 1993.

———. *The Will to Power*. Trans. Walter Kaufmann and R. J. Hollingdale. New York: Random House, 1967.

Orlan. "L'avant-garde n'est plus dans l'art, elle est dans la génétique." *Le Monde,* June 7, 2001.

Osborne, Peter, ed. *From an Aesthetic Point of View: Philosophy, Art, and the Senses*. London: Serpent's Tail, 2000.

Perloff, Marjorie. *The Futurist Moment: Avant-Garde, Avant-Guerre, and the Language of Rupture*. Chicago: University of Chicago Press, 1996.

———. *Poetry On and Off the Page: Essays for Emergent Occasions*. Evanston: Northwestern University Press, 1998.

———. *21st Century Modernism: The "New" Poetics*. Oxford: Blackwell, 2002.

Rabaté, Jean-Michel. *The Future of Theory*. Oxford: Blackwell, 2002.

Ross, David A., et al. *Bill Viola*. Published on the occasion of the exhibition "Bill Viola" organized by the Whitney Museum of American Art. Paris: Flammarion, 1997.

Senghor, Léopold. "Negritude and Modernity." In *Race*. Ed. Robert Bernasconi. Malden, Mass.: Blackwell Publishers, 2001.

Shusterman, Richard. *Performing Live: Aesthetic Alternatives for the Ends of Art*. Ithaca: Cornell University Press, 2000.

Stein, Gertrude. *How to Write*. Los Angeles: Sun and Moon, 1995.

———. "Patriarchal Poetry." In *The Yale Gertrude Stein*. New Haven: Yale University Press, 1980.

———. "Poetry and Grammar." In *Lectures in America*. New York: Random House, 1935.

———. *Stanzas in Meditation*. Los Angeles: Sun & Moon, 1994.

———. *Tender Buttons*. Los Angeles: Sun & Moon, 1991.

———. *The Yale Gertrude Stein*. New Haven: Yale University Press, 1980.

Stockhausen, Karlheinz. *Helikopter-Streichquartett*. Arditti String Quartet. Montaigne Auvidis. MO 782097.

Todorov, Vladislav. *Red Square, Black Square: Organon for Revolutionary Imagination*. Albany: SUNY Press, 1995.

Tomasula, Steve. "(Gene)sis." In *Eduardo Kac: Telepresence, Biotelematics, Transgenic Art*. Maribor, Slovenia: KIBLA, 2000.

Tzara, Tristan. "Lecture on Dada." In *Dada Painters and Poets*, ed. Robert Motherwell. Cambridge, Mass.: Harvard University Press, 1951.

———. *Seven Dada Manifestos and Lampisteries*. Trans. Barbara Wright. New York: Riverrun Press, 1992.

Vertov, Dziga. "Between How and Why." In *Reasons for Knocking at an Empty House: Writings 1973–1994*. Ed. Robert Violette in collaboration with the author, intro. Jean-Christophe Ammann. Cambridge, Mass./London: MIT Press/Anthony d'Offay Gallery, 1995.

———. *Man with the Movie Camera*. DVD. Chatsworth, Calif.: Image Entertainment, 1997.

———. *A Survey of A Decade*. Ed. Marilyn Zeitlin. Houston: Contemporary Arts Museum, 1988.

Williams, Raymond. *The Politics of Modernism: Against the New Conformists*. London and New York: Verso, 1989.

Wilson, Stephen. http://userwww.sfsu.edu/~infoarts/links/wilson.artlinks2.html, accessed Mar. 2004.

———. *Information Arts: Intersections of Art, Science, and Technology*. Cambridge, Mass.: MIT Press, 2002.

Wodiczko, Krzysztof. *Critical Vehicles: Writings, Projects, Interviews*. Cambridge, Mass.: MIT Press, 1999.

———. *Public Address*. Minneapolis: Walker Art Center, 1992.

Ziarek, Krzysztof. *The Historicity of Experience: Modernity, the Avant-Garde, and the Event*. Evanston: Northwestern University Press, 2001.

———. "Proximities: Irigaray and Heidegger on Difference." *Continental Philosophy Review* 33.2 (2000): 133–58.

Zuidervaart, Lambert. *Adorno's Aesthetic Theory: The Redemption of Illusion*. Cambridge, Mass.: MIT Press, 1991.

Index

Cultural Memory in the Present

Krzysztof Ziarek, *The Force of Art*

István Rév, *Prehistory of Post-Communism: The Afterlife of the 1956 Revolution in Hungary*

Paola Marrati, *Genesis and Trace: Derrida Reading Husserl and Heidegger*

Ban Wang, *Illuminations from the Past: Trauma, Memory, and History in Modern China*

Martin Seel, *Aesthetics of Appearing*

Marie-José Mondzain, *Image, Icon, Economy: The Byzantine Origins of the Contemporary Imaginary*

Cecilia Sjoholm, *The Antigone Complex: Ethics and the Invention of Feminine Desire*

Jacques Derrida, *For What Tomorrow . . . : A Dialogue*

Elisabeth Weber, *Questioning Judaism: Interviews by Elisabeth Weber*

Jacques Derrida and Catherine Malabou, *Counterpath: Traveling with Jacques Derrida*

Jacques Derrida, *Eyes of the University: Right to Philosophy 2*

Nanette Salomon, *Shifting Priorities: Gender and Genre in Seventeenth-Century Dutch Painting*

Stuart McLean, *The Event and Its Terrors: Ireland, Famine, Modernity*

Eric Michaud, *The Cult of Art in Nazi Germany*

Beate Rössler, ed., *Privacies: Philosophical Evaluations*

Anne Freadman, *The Machinery of Talk: Charles Peirce and the Sign Hypothesis*

Jacob Taubes, *The Political Theology of Paul*

Jean-Luc Marion, *The Crossing of the Visible*

Stanley Cavell, *Emerson's Transcendental Etudes*

Bernard Faure, *Double Exposure: Cutting Across Buddhist and Western Discourses*

Alessia Ricciardi, *The Ends of Mourning: Psychoanalysis, Literature, Film*

Jean-Luc Nancy, *A Finite Thinking*, edited by Simon Sparks

Jonathan Culler and Kevin Lamb, eds., *Just Being Difficult? Academic Writing in the Public Arena*

Patricia Pisters, *The Matrix of Visual Culture: Working with Deleuze in Film Theory*

Gil Anidjar, *The Jew, the Arab: A History of the Enemy*

Alain Badiou, *Saint Paul: The Foundation of Universalism*

Theodor W. Adorno, *Can One Live after Auschwitz? A Philosophical Reader*, edited by Rolf Tiedemann

Andreas Huyssen, *Present Pasts: Urban Palimpsests and the Politics of Memory*

Talal Asad, *Formations of the Secular: Christianity, Islam, Modernity*

Dorothea von Mücke, *The Rise of the Fantastic Tale*

Marc Redfield, *The Politics of Aesthetics: Nationalism, Gender, Romanticism*

Emmanuel Levinas, *On Escape*

Dan Zahavi, *Husserl's Phenomenology*

Rodolphe Gasché, *The Idea of Form: Rethinking Kant's Aesthetics*

Michael Naas, *Taking on the Tradition: Jacques Derrida and the Legacies of Deconstruction*

Herlinde Pauer-Studer, ed., *Constructions of Practical Reason: Interviews on Moral and Political Philosophy*

Jean-Luc Marion, *Being Given That: Toward a Phenomenology of Givenness*

Max Horkheimer and Theodor W. Adorno, *Dialectic of Enlightenment*

Ian Balfour, *The Rhetoric of Romantic Prophecy*

Martin Stokhof, *World and Life as One: Ethics and Ontology in Wittgenstein's Early Thought*

Gianni Vattimo, *Nietzsche: An Introduction*

Jacques Derrida, *Negotiations: Interventions and Interviews, 1971–1998*, ed. Elizabeth Rottenberg

Brett Levinson, *The Ends of Literature: The Latin American "Boom" in the Neoliberal Marketplace*

Timothy J. Reiss, *Against Autonomy: Cultural Instruments, Mutualities, and the Fictive Imagination*

Hent de Vries and Samuel Weber, eds., *Religion and Media*

Niklas Luhmann, *Theories of Distinction: Re-Describing the Descriptions of Modernity*, ed. and introd. William Rasch

Johannes Fabian, *Anthropology with an Attitude: Critical Essays*

Michel Henry, *I am the Truth: Toward a Philosophy of Christianity*

Gil Anidjar, *"Our Place in Al-Andalus": Kabbalah, Philosophy, Literature in Arab-Jewish Letters*

Hélène Cixous and Jacques Derrida, *Veils*

F. R. Ankersmit, *Historical Representation*

F. R. Ankersmit, *Political Representation*

Elissa Marder, *Dead Time: Temporal Disorders in the Wake of Modernity (Baudelaire and Flaubert)*

Reinhart Koselleck, *The Practice of Conceptual History: Timing History, Spacing Concepts*

Niklas Luhmann, *The Reality of the Mass Media*

Hubert Damisch, *A Childhood Memory by Piero della Francesca*

Hubert Damisch, *A Theory of /Cloud/: Toward a History of Painting*

Jean-Luc Nancy, *The Speculative Remark: (One of Hegel's bon mots)*

Jean-François Lyotard, *Soundproof Room: Malraux's Anti-Aesthetics*

Jan Patočka, *Plato and Europe*

Hubert Damisch, *Skyline: The Narcissistic City*

Isabel Hoving, *In Praise of New Travelers: Reading Caribbean Migrant Women Writers*

Richard Rand, ed., *Futures: Of Jacques Derrida*

William Rasch, *Niklas Luhmann's Modernity: The Paradoxes of Differentiation*

Jacques Derrida and Anne Dufourmantelle, *Of Hospitality*

Jean-François Lyotard, *The Confession of Augustine*

Kaja Silverman, *World Spectators*

Samuel Weber, *Institution and Interpretation: Expanded Edition*

Jeffrey S. Librett, *The Rhetoric of Cultural Dialogue: Jews and Germans in the Epoch of Emancipation*

Ulrich Baer, *Remnants of Song: Trauma and the Experience of Modernity in Charles Baudelaire and Paul Celan*

Samuel C. Wheeler III, *Deconstruction as Analytic Philosophy*

David S. Ferris, *Silent Urns: Romanticism, Hellenism, Modernity*

Rodolphe Gasché, *Of Minimal Things: Studies on the Notion of Relation*

Sarah Winter, *Freud and the Institution of Psychoanalytic Knowledge*

Samuel Weber, *The Legend of Freud: Expanded Edition*

Aris Fioretos, ed., *The Solid Letter: Readings of Friedrich Hölderlin*

J. Hillis Miller / Manuel Asensi, *Black Holes / J. Hillis Miller; or, Boustrophedonic Reading*

Miryam Sas, *Fault Lines: Cultural Memory and Japanese Surrealism*

Peter Schwenger, *Fantasm and Fiction: On Textual Envisioning*

Didier Maleuvre, *Museum Memories: History, Technology, Art*

Jacques Derrida, *Monolingualism of the Other; or, The Prosthesis of Origin*

Andrew Baruch Wachtel, *Making a Nation, Breaking a Nation: Literature and Cultural Politics in Yugoslavia*

Niklas Luhmann, *Love as Passion: The Codification of Intimacy*

Mieke Bal, ed., *The Practice of Cultural Analysis: Exposing Interdisciplinary Interpretation*

Jacques Derrida and Gianni Vattimo, eds., *Religion*